Histories of Nations

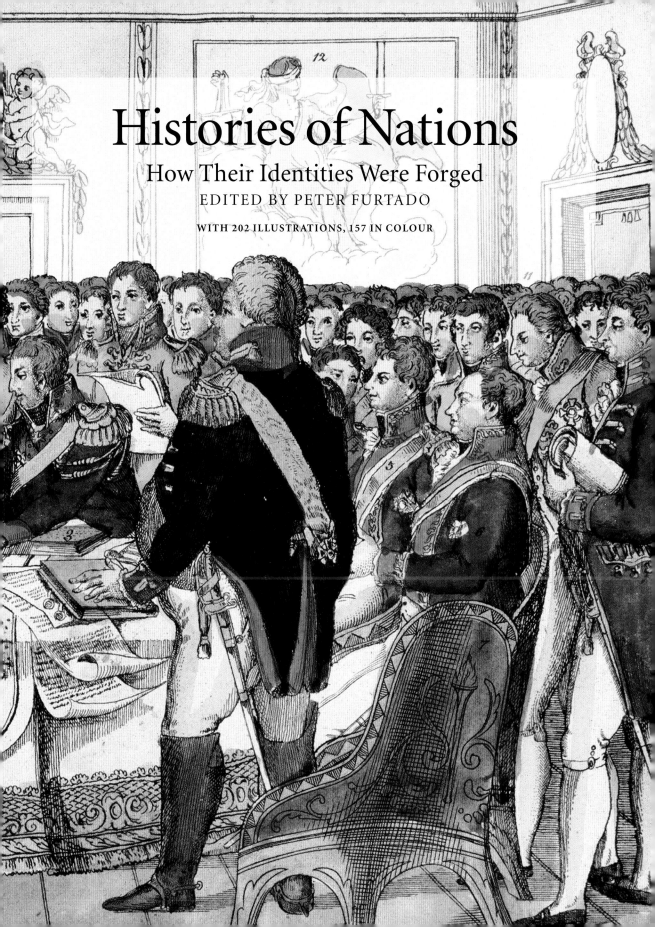

Histories of Nations

How Their Identities Were Forged

EDITED BY PETER FURTADO

WITH 202 ILLUSTRATIONS, 157 IN COLOUR

Page 1: *Gerard van Schagen, World Map, 1689. The European discovery of the world (Terra cognita) and emerging cartographic techniques in the 17th century made it possible to contextualize each country within the known world for the first time, as seen in this rare set of world maps produced in Amsterdam.*

Pages 2–3: *A 19th-century print showing the leaders of Europe in debate during the Congress of Vienna (1814–15). By restoring the 'status quo ante bellum' in the wake of the Napoleonic wars, the Congress of Vienna left the national aspirations of many European peoples unsatisfied, resulting in a surge of nationalism across the continent over the subsequent century.*

First published in the United Kingdom in 2012 by Thames & Hudson Ltd, 181A High Holborn, London WC1V 7QX

Copyright © 2012 Thames & Hudson Ltd, London

British Library Cataloguing-in-Publication Data
A catalogue record for this book is available from the British Library

ISBN 978-0-500-25181-2

Printed and bound in China by
Toppan Leefung Printing Limited

To find out about all our publications, please visit **www.thamesandhudson.com**.
There you can subscribe to our e-newsletter, browse or download our current catalogue, and buy any titles that are in print.

Contents

PETER FURTADO

Introduction

The histories of nations and the history of the world

The world's largest-ever history lesson, the opening ceremony of the Beijing Summer Olympics in 2008, was seen by more than a hundred heads of state and an estimated television audience of two billion people. A giant flexible LED screen was unrolled across the stadium floor, on which were projected aspects of China's cultural history, including the first of what it claims as its great inventions: paper. Three more of these inventions – the compass, gunpowder and printing – were then celebrated in spectacular fireworks and enacted in vast moving tableaux that drew on images of the Chinese past, the Terracotta Army, the Great Wall and the voyages of Zheng He. Awed by the colour, scale, discipline and lavishness of the show, the world saw how China wants its past, and its present, to be viewed: as a majestic civilization that owes little to outsiders and has bestowed great gifts on the rest of the world.

Four years earlier Athens had done much the same, albeit on a less awe-inspiring scale. Greece presented itself both in terms of the indisputable gifts of its own civilization to the world – classical sculpture and, of course, the Games themselves – and its 'national' history, from the Bronze Age Minoans and Mycenaeans to the reign of Alexander the Great, the creation of the city of Byzantium, the achievement of independence from the Turks and modern ironic popular culture.

The opportunity for a nation to present such a high-profile, massaged image of its history and heritage to the world is a rare and powerful one, and it is hardly surprising that countries compete for the chance to host the Olympics. It is universal, though, for nations to seek ways of manipulating that same self-image internally for their own citizens, particularly through public commemoration and ceremony, as well as through

Previous pages: *The opening ceremony of the 2008 Olympic Games in Beijing, choreographed by film director Zhang Yimou, included a spectacular pageant of Chinese history with a representation of the naval voyages of Zheng He to Africa in the 15th century.*

control of the education syllabus and through the media. A country's history is a vital part of national self-definition, and as such it is often highly controversial. In recent decades 'history wars' over the content of school textbooks have broken out in countries as diverse as Australia, Canada, Russia and Japan, while in Britain successive governments have sought to propagate the elusive (and perhaps vanishing) concept of 'Britishness' through a particular reading of the island's history.

Such national histories have been the backbone of the entire historical profession since the 19th century, when many state historical institutions were set up. Although today the field of history has broadened to include many topics unimaginable to those earlier historians, all countries make their own past the centrepiece of their education and their historical research, sometimes to the virtual exclusion of all else. In addition, most countries make history a compulsory subject in school, recognizing how vital a component it is in shaping national identity and in moulding society's energies.

But history is not just the creation of academies and governments: it is ubiquitous. It is in the air we breathe, in the cities we inhabit and in the landscapes we roam. People learn their own history at home, in stories told by family members and by the media, in folk tales and on television, from public statues and war memorials, and from prominent architecture, museums and galleries. The history imbibed from such sources is rarely questioned, and sometimes barely even recognized. This can make it very different from the history practised in Western colleges, where the liberal instinct is to be sceptical of received wisdom, to question the authority of the source, to frame knowledge in a broad context and to seek a novel interpretation. As a result, in many countries – perhaps especially those with the most firmly established traditions of academic life – there is a deep disjunction between the history of the academy and that of the people.

The 'academic' history of the world has been written many times, especially in the last fifty years when the emergence of a world economy and ideological conflicts have made a search for a unified world history a realistic endeavour. Sometimes it has been done by hugely energetic and polymathic individuals with a line to argue, such as, for example, the 'triumph of the West' of which John Roberts spoke in the 1980s, the 'clash of civilizations' of Sam Huntington from the 1990s, or the environmental history of John McNeill in the 2000s. Sometimes it has been the product of teams of scholars or educators working to an agenda in an attempt, so far as is possible, to remove subjectivity, perhaps by ensuring that each part of the world is given equal weight. Either way,

every completed account of the history of the world is a work of synthesis that contextualizes the more detailed research of others, and as such is a reflection of the wider preoccupations of the years in which it was produced.

This volume inevitably reflects the preoccupations of the present. It is less a history of the world than a selection of histories, planned in the belief that a single point of view, a single overarching agenda, is neither possible to realize successfully, nor desirable in our polycentric, postmodern age. It also aims to explore popular understandings of history around the world, and asks professional historians and other established writers to step outside their usual frames of reference and write about how history is understood in the culture of their homelands at large.

It has become a cliché that the past is a 'foreign country', in the phrase of novelist L. P. Hartley, a place where 'they do things differently'; but less often we remember that this feeling of 'foreignness' we sense when we visit another country comes, more than anything, from its past, and particularly from its conception of its own special past.

So the premise of this volume is simple: if we fail to understand how others think and feel about their past, we will fail to understand them. If we want to get to grips with the national and cultural differences that both enliven and endanger our world, we do not need travel guides or even historical companions written by our own compatriots; we need to listen to people describing their own past in their own words. The passions, the emphases in what they choose to say – perhaps even the omissions – will speak volumes. Should any readers doubt that the sense of history can differ dramatically from country to country, I urge them to look at just two essays in this collection: Peter Onuf's exploration of the origins and implications of what he calls the myth of 'historylessness' that the United States received from its Founding Fathers; and Zhitian Luo's explanation of the crucial role of history in legitimizing imperial authority in China for 3,000 years.

In this volume twenty-eight historians of twenty-eight countries, each of them a native of the state concerned and most of them still resident and active there, describe the history of their countries as they understand them. They have not written encyclopaedic histories – such things are readily available at the click of a mouse – but personal essays, in which the tone of voice and the selected themes convey as much as the familiar facts. Like the organizers of the Olympic opening ceremonies, but on a vastly

Previous pages: Berlin's Holocaust memorial, designed by Peter Eisenman, opened in 1999. The history of many nations includes the perpetration of appalling crimes and the suffering of massive trauma – how these are dealt with within the national memory says as much about a nation as the original events themselves.

different scale, they have set out to present their national histories to the world, warts and all.

The questions that can be addressed using this approach include the existence and nature of the general narrative of a country's past, or what might be called its 'deep history'. In this narrative, every country celebrates what it thinks of as its great achievements – the fight for independence, the struggle for liberty, the cultural glories – but there will be other elements in its past that it regrets and how it deals with those can be very revealing. It may choose to adopt a policy of aggressive self-justification. Or it may resort to silence – it was noticeable that in the first drafts of the essays in this volume, several contributors avoided all mention of some of the most prominent skeletons in their national cupboards. Alternatively a country might have constructed elaborate processes to enable it to reconcile the pain of the past. Germany's thorough-going self-analysis since the 1960s is a case in point, or the truth and reconciliation commissions set up in South Africa and many other traumatized countries in recent years. Some countries, such as Egypt and Greece, might be blessed – or cursed – with a glorious ancient history that the present can never equal. Others, Israel and Iran being prominent examples, may feel perpetually misunderstood by others and see that misunderstanding itself as a major source of difficulty in the modern world.

Indeed, the chapters make clear the difficulty of writing a coherent history even for a single country. The essay on the Czech Republic demonstrates how hard it is to find any kind of agreement about its own past, while that on Britain stresses the difficulty of building a sense of national history when the nation itself is an artificial political construct – albeit one that has endured for 300 years. The Italian story is not very different.

In the limited space available, it was not expected that any of the contributors would be able to address all of these questions thoroughly, but there is real value to be gleaned from examining the interplay of their topics and comparing the varied ways in which contributors from different countries have approached their essays. Every reader will, I hope, acquire unfamiliar insights into familiar countries: how they see themselves and wish to present themselves today, and how different a contemporary historian's view may be from the rosy picture presented by so many tourist guidebooks.

It is inevitable that this exercise has resulted in interpretations of national history that are often highly coloured by the present. Giovanni Levi, for example, writes of the origins of Italy's current political impasse in the country's deeply Catholic past; Dina Khapaeva traces 21st-century Russia's turning away from the West back to a dichotomy that dates from the very foundation of Muscovy. Even as the book was in production, history continued to unfold. In many countries the economic crisis of the early 2010s meant that existing historic trends continued to evolve. Only a few years after Athens, the 'cradle of democracy', celebrated its new museum for the Acropolis treasures in 2007, the Greek economy collapsed and the continued survival of Greece's democracy was thrown into doubt. The Arab Spring of 2011 brought unexpected and dramatic change to Egypt, a land that had been distinguished by exceptional continuities since the very beginning of its history. Such a revolution brings with it an obligation to revisit the country's past; however, it is clear that this revisiting cannot be done quickly, and must await the resolution of the state of flux that was created by the overthrow of the long-standing Mubarak dictatorship.

The countries selected for inclusion come from every continent and make up two-thirds of the world's population. They range from mature democracies to religious autocracies to one-party states; from countries semi-permanently at war to those that avoid war at all costs; from countries with traditions of liberal scholarship and debate to those where historians can be flung into jail for failing to toe the official line. Many of the world's most troubled regions are those with historic disputes, sometimes going back hundreds of years: the failure of each side to appreciate the historic passions of the other can be fatal to efforts to build peace. Readers who encounter their opponents' voices in this volume are invited to contemplate what is said and how it is said, but are by no means compelled to agree with it.

As well as the problem of selecting the countries to be included, there was the issue of choosing a suitable contributor for each. None of those who have written here would wish to be seen as some kind of official spokesman for their nation, nor, indeed, as anything other than themselves. All of them are practising historians, some very distinguished and approaching the ends of their careers, others much younger. Most live and work in the country about which they are writing; those who do not return frequently or remain in close touch. Many have made a special study of their national past. Even so, some of the results may be truly surprising; all of them are genuinely interesting and instructive.

An Iraqi stands triumphantly in the bronze boots of ousted President Saddam Hussein, whose statue was pulled down in April 2003 following the American-British invasion. The success of the initial invasion was wasted as the Allied forces failed to take into account sufficiently the attitudes of the Iraqi people towards occupation by Western powers.

Egypt

Pharaohs, kings and presidents

Wherever you go in the world it is likely that you will come across some element of Egypt's history or influence, and so it could be said that Egypt and history are synonymous. Civilization itself began in Egypt's Nile valley and delta: indeed, the Greek historian Herodotus described Egyptian civilization as 'the gift of the Nile', though it might perhaps have been better described as 'the gift of the Nile *and* the Egyptian people'. The Nile passes through many African countries, but none has achieved the progress, continuity and prosperity of Egypt. Egyptians, the builders of this unique civilization, have always been distinguished by their skill, perseverance, patience, silence, calmness, forbearance, faith and tolerance.

Egypt lies in the northeastern corner of the African continent and extends into southwest Asia through the Sinai peninsula, Egypt's eastern gateway and access route for invaders throughout history. Egypt is considered an important and influential country in both the Middle East and Africa: it is at the heart of the Arab world, and a defender and preserver of Islam. The country is also close to southern Europe and southwest Asia, overlooking the Mediterranean and the Red Sea. Its location has thus made Egypt a meeting place for civilizations, a crucible for cultural exchange and an object of desire for invaders throughout its long history.

The names given to the land are numerous. The name 'Egypt' comes from the ancient term *Hutkaptah*, meaning 'temple of the soul of Ptah', who was the god of the ancient capital Memphis. Misr, the modern name for the country in Arabic, is derived from the ancient Egyptian word *mejer* ('the edge'), from which comes the current term *al-Misriyun* ('the Egyptians'). Egyptians also refer to the capital city of Cairo as 'Misr', using the name of the country as shorthand for their capital. Modern Egyptians belong to both the Semitic and Hamitic peoples, and include, among others, Fellahin (people of

The Great Sphinx was built c. 2500 BCE by King Khafre to the east of his pyramid complex on the Giza plateau. The largest statue in the ancient world, it represents the king as a human-headed lion couchant and proclaims the divine kingship of ancient Egyptian rulers.

the Nile delta and the Mediterranean coast), Sa'eedis (the people of Upper Egypt), Bedouins (inhabitants of Sinai and the Eastern and Western Deserts) and Nubians (the people of Aswan and the surrounding area).

The written story of Egypt begins around 3000 BCE, when writing itself was first invented. Inherited human experience could now accumulate and memory could be preserved. This was an age of centralization, a trend that was to become a feature of Egyptian government throughout its long history, so much so that it eventually represented an obstacle to progress for those who wished to decentralize decision-making. When the legendary king Menes unified Upper Egypt (the south) and Lower Egypt (the Delta) and established a centralized state around 3000 BCE, values and standards were introduced that still govern the state of Egypt and colour the Egyptian personality to the present day. Egypt then entered the period of the Old Kingdom, the age of the pyramids, which lasted from 2686 to 2160 BCE. During this time the Egyptians built the pyramids at Giza and Saqqara, and carved the statue of the Great Sphinx by the pyramids on the Giza plateau as a representation of King Khafre, builder of the second pyramid at Giza. These magnificent monuments bear witness to the architectural, engineering, astronomical and administrative skills of the ancient Egyptians.

After that golden age Egypt entered a period of decline before re-emerging as a powerful force during the Middle Kingdom (2055–1650 BCE), the age of Egyptian classical literature. Following this second golden age, Egypt embarked on the most difficult period in its early history, namely the occupation by Asian tribes known as the Hyksos, meaning 'rulers of foreign lands'. They crept peacefully over the country's eastern borders and took control of large parts of the land when the Egyptian state was weakened. After a long and bitter struggle the southern Egyptian king, Ahmose I (1550–1525 BCE), managed to expel them from Egypt, driving them to Palestine. The New Kingdom, the third and final golden age of ancient Egypt, was now established. Egypt adopted a new foreign policy based on

TIMELINE

c. **3000** BCE Egypt is united as the first nation in history

c. **2** BCE The Great Pyramid of Giza is built

1550–1069 BCE Egyptian power is extended during the New Kingdom period

332 BCE Egypt is conquered by Alexander the Great

30 BCE Egypt becomes a Roman province

641 CE Arab conquest of Egypt

1250 Formation of the Mamluk dynasty

1517 Egypt is conquered by the Ottomans

1798 Egypt is conquered by the French under Napoleon Bonaparte

1882 Egypt is controlled by British troops

1918 Egypt becomes a British protectorate

1922 Egypt gains independence under King Fuad I

1952 Overthrow of the monarchy by a military coup led by the Free Officers Movement

1967 Egypt is defeated by Israel

1973 Egypt defeats Israel in the battle of 6 October

1981 Assassination of President Muhammad Anwar al-Sadat

2011 President Hosni Mubarak steps down following a revolution supported by the military

expansion and foreign conquests, and brought numerous powers under its control. This period, which lasted until 1069 BCE, is known as Pharaonic Egypt's age of empire. Thutmose III (1479–1425 BCE) is considered the founder of the Egyptian Empire in Asia and Africa; other famous pharaohs of this age include Hatshepsut, Akhenaten, Tutankhamun, Seti I, Ramesses II and Ramesses III.

After this age of empire Egypt entered the Third Intermediate Period (1069–664 BCE), in which tension and a lack of centralization prevailed. The Late Period (664–332 BCE) followed, during which various Egyptian dynasties ruled, with some periods of Persian occupation, until the arrival of Alexander the Great in 332 BCE. At his hands and those of his successors, the Ptolemaic kings (332–30 BCE), Egypt was transformed into a Graeco-Ptolemaic kingdom. With the defeat of the Ptolemaic queen Cleopatra VII by the Romans in 30 BCE Egypt became an important part of the Roman Empire (30 BCE–395 CE) and then the Byzantine Empire (395–641 CE). In 641 CE the Muslim Arabs took control and Egypt became one of the states of the Islamic Caliphate, until the early 19th century when the Albanian soldier Muhammad Ali Pasha (1769–1849) founded the modern state of Egypt along European lines. His family's rule came to an end with the revolution of 23 July 1952, which established the republic of Egypt under President

A portrait of Muhammad Ali Pasha, the founder of modern Egypt. He transformed the country from an inactive province of the Ottoman Empire to a superpower of its time. Through his various military campaigns he created a large state and threatened many European powers.

Muhammad Naguib (1952–54), and his successors Gamal Abdel Nasser (1954–70), Muhammad Anwar al-Sadat (1970–81) and Muhammad Hosni Mubarak (1981–2011). An unavoidable characteristic of Egyptian cultural experience throughout this long history is its stability; it is distinguished by continuity and accumulation, not interruption.

The 1952 revolution, carried out by a group in the army known as the 'Free Officers Movement' during the reign of Farouq I, king of Egypt and the Sudan (1920–65; r. 1936–52), represented the end of the monarchy that had prevailed since the beginning of

Pharaonic Egypt. It introduced a military republican regime and established a police state that denied the freedom of the individual and made him a doormat for the authoritarian regime. The revolution destroyed the democracy that had prevailed under the monarchy, even though one of its principles had been to establish free democratic life; political parties were dissolved and human rights ignored. Throughout the sixteen years of his solitary rule President Nasser constantly feared a new revolution by enemies lying in wait – or so he claimed in order to tighten the clench of his fist. He removed the Egyptian people from the political sphere: why should they concern themselves with politics while the inspired leader was thinking and working for them? As the republican slogans endlessly repeated, 'no voice rises over the sound of the battle', so no voice rose over that of Nasser.

It was within Nasser's grasp to lead Egypt towards justice and democracy, but he forsook the opportunity and instead planted in the Egyptian soil the seeds of tyranny, which then spread to the rest of the Arab world. One result of his poor management of the regime was that Egypt suffered a crushing defeat at the hands of Israel on 5 June 1967. That defeat caused a deep fissure in the Egyptian, and Arab, personality, and its effect endures in the souls of the Egyptians today. The people were shocked that Nasser and the pillars of his regime, particularly the military, had failed to fulfil their responsibility to defend their nation. Severe depression engulfed a country that, until the 1952 July Revolution, had considered itself great. This was the beginning of the end for Nasser, who nevertheless still tried, in the years before his death in 1970, to reform the army and purge it of the corrupt factions who bore the shame of the defeat.

An image of King Farouq I, ruler of Egypt and the Sudan, the last reigning monarch from the Muhammad Ali Pasha dynasty. He was overthrown in 1952 by a military coup led by the Free Officers Movement which forced him to abdicate and left his infant son, crown prince Ahmed Fuad, to succeed him briefly as king.

While the defeat of 1967 was a shock, the glorious victory against Israel on 6 October 1973, in the opening stages of the October War, was unprecedented. The hero of this conflict, President Sadat, described it as 'one of the greatest days in history'. On this day Egyptian armed forces washed away the shame that the 1967 defeat had attached to Egypt and the entire Arab race, and eventually restored the territory that had been lost. Yet Sadat's visit to Israel in 1977, and his subsequent signing of a peace agreement, was a cause of anger for many people within Egypt, the Arab states and beyond. His readiness to deal with Israel was a major factor in his assassination on 6 October 1981, carried out while he was celebrating the eighth anniversary of his major victory. This was one of the blackest days in Egypt's history: how could anyone kill the Pharaoh, surrounded by his army, while he was celebrating his unprecedented victory?

The establishment of the Islamist movement known as the Muslim Brotherhood by Sheikh Hassan al-Banna in 1928 in the coastal city of Ismailia has had a great influence on Egyptian politics in the 20th and early 21st centuries. A number of contentious issues began to emerge, such as Islam and modernity, Islam and democracy, the religious state, the system of rule and counsel, religious power, the position of the Coptic Christians in an Islamic state, the Islamic economy, and the role of women and hijab. Most of these problems were concerned with form rather than substance. Political Islam disturbed the rule of law in both the monarchic and republican eras. It also gave the rulers, particularly during the republican era, an excuse for not implementing true democracy: they argued that the Islamists would achieve power through the ballot box and then discard their democratic pretensions. One republican regime after another scared the West, in particular the United States, about the Islamists' possible arrival to power. The West, taking a 'devil you know' approach, therefore tended to support the ruling party, which helped to keep dictatorial regimes in power for decades without real legitimacy; this in turn provoked Islamist hatred of the West. Many observers considered the long absence of

President Gamal Abdel Nasser was the true leader of the Free Officers Movement which overthrew the monarchy and ended the rule of Muhammad Ali Pasha's family. He is pictured here with the first prime minister of the Sudan, Ismail al-Azhari, on an official drive during Azhari's visit to Egypt in July 1954.

democracy in Egypt to be a consequence of the presence of the Islamists, who publicly threatened the stability of the ruling regime while being secretly allied to it in killing off any free movement promoting a civil society, political pluralism, human rights and other fundamentals of Western democracy.

King Farouq, a television series broadcast in 2007, related the story of Farouq I, the last king of Egypt and the Sudan, who reigned from 1936 to 1952. It presented him as a humane ruler who loved his people and yielded to the expression of their power through

Soldiers holding up an image of President Muhammad Anwar al-Sadat during the war against Israel in 1973. Sadat was the most controversial president in Egyptian history: he achieved an unprecedented victory during the conflict, but later signed a peace agreement with Israel. He was assassinated by Islamists in 1981 while celebrating the eighth anniversary of his victory.

the ballot box and did what the president and government ministers asked of him; who consulted his officials and did not enforce his own opinions. The series was unprecedently popular, particularly among the younger generations born after Farouq's reign. This nostalgia for the past, and for the monarchic era in particular, suggested the Egyptian people's interest in revival and keen awareness of their history. Even so, an Egyptian state official, while on a visit to the United States, described his country as not yet ready to enter into the age of democracy. His implication that Egyptians could not bring about political change proved utterly mistaken.

In fact, Egypt, though apparently quiet on the surface, was going through a process of contemplation and adjustment, searching for the right way to achieve this renaissance.

There were many shades of opinion. Some were proud of the monarchic era, citing the effectiveness of its authorities, the power and vitality of its economy, and the progress and cultural openness it had achieved. Others fervently supported the July Revolution, calling it the beginning of history. They tended to worship Nasser – some even considered him the last of the prophets. Yet there was much disagreement between the followers of Nasser and supporters of Sadat, who had discarded the model of the single-party socialist state and its solitary leader. Sadat's supporters were proud of his great strides towards political openness and liberalization of the economy, particularly with respect to social responsibility and care for the poor. A third group rejected both eras, and lamented that Egypt was stagnating. They took a largely negative stance, claiming that many Egyptians had sold their souls for personal gain, while keeping silent about what the revolutionaries were doing to the land and people. Yet the vast majority of Egyptians felt nostalgia for monarchy, which the men of 1952 had tried to obliterate from history .

But history cannot be erased. On 25 January 2011, thousands of young Egyptians protested across the country against the military regime of President Hosni Mubarak. Millions joined in and the demonstrations went on for eighteen days until Mubarak

The Muslim Brotherhood, established by Sheikh Hassan al-Banna in 1928, has a great influence on politics in Egypt and embraces many Islamist movements and leaders. The Brotherhood was the only party to have any organization before the revolution of 2011, and built on this in the elections of 2012.

stepped down on 11 February 2011, ending almost thirty years of corrupt dictatorship and its police state. The regime of the 1952 July Revolution had finally come to an end.

Yet it was democracy, and not monarchy, that Egyptians now wanted for the future. A wide range of opinions was heard, from the Islamism of the Muslim Brotherhood to the Western-style liberalism of many in the cities. Political parties – previously banned – were urgently established, and any attempts by outside powers to influence events were rejected as the search continued for an Egyptian solution to the situation. Until a democratic system and government could be installed, the army remained the only authority in the land – yet it continued to be viewed by many with skepticism, even hostility. Parliamentary elections in 2012 brought success for the Muslim Brotherhood, which attempted to allay fears of a new religious dictatorship by asserting its commitment to democractic pluralism. The shape of the new country would still take time to emerge.

Throughout this period of transformation, the spirit of ancient Egypt – a spirit of persistence, renewal and continuity – may yet continue to motivate modern Egyptians to restore the country to its former glory.

India

The civilization with no home-grown history

The past in India is not a foreign country. It casts a long shadow on the present and makes Indian history literally lethal. This was gruesomely illustrated in December 1992, when a Hindu mob pulled down the Babri Mosque in Ayodhya, claiming that it was built by medieval Muslim rulers who had first destroyed a more ancient temple dedicated to the Hindu god Ram. Hindus believe Ayodhya to be the birthplace of Ram. The politics of the Ram Temple, a historical legacy of India's Hindu–Muslim problems, have shaped Indian politics: there is no agreement on whether the Hindu claim is justified, only continuing tension and violence, much of it directed against the Muslim minority.

In 2003 a biography of the 16th-century Maratha king Shivaji by American scholar James W. Laine apparently questioned the memory of a Hindu hero regarding the struggle against the Muslim Mughals. The book generated such rage that the Bhandarkar Institute in Pune, where the research was done, was vandalized and Oxford University Press was forced to withdraw the book from India.

Indians cannot agree on their history because it has very few straight lines. To make matters worse, its history has largely been written by foreigners. India, like China, has one of the oldest continuous cultural traditions in the world, but India has nothing like China's ancient historical records.

In 1960 historian R. C. Majumdar introduced *The Classical Accounts of India,* a collection of writings about India by foreigners such as Herodotus, Megasthenes, Arrian, Plutarch, Pliny and Ptolemy: 'There was no history of pre-Muslim India written by the ancient Indians themselves and consequently very little was known of its political history.' This meant, as D. P. Singhal noted in *A History of the Indian People,* that 'from the earliest times to the advent of the Muslims…a period of about 4,000 years, there is no historical text except Kalhana's *Rajatarangini,* much less a detailed narrative like those of Greece, Rome and China'.

Hindu activists commemorate the 1992 destruction of a mosque in Ayodhya in December 2008. Alleging that Muslim invaders had destroyed a Ram temple in order to build a mosque, they wanted to turn back the pages of history to correct what they saw as a historic injustice.

For a country claiming a history of 5,000 years, there exist no known histories left to us by Indians for three-quarters of this period. Myths and fables, yes, but nothing that would be considered historically authentic.

Majumdar's statement that Muslims brought history to India is a reference to one of the classics of world history, written by Abu Raihan, popularly known as Alberuni, called *Alberuni's India*. A scholar who came to India with Mahmud of Ghazni's forces in the 11th century, he wrote his classic while his master was killing Hindus or making them slaves and looting their wonderfully rich temples to create a wealthy kingdom in Ghazni, now in modern Afghanistan. Every winter for sixteen years Mahmud raided India, gathering vast wealth. Amid this carnage Alberuni calmly observed the world of the Hindus, so different from his own. Alberuni's later status as a scientific celebrity in the Muslim world owed much to the Indian scientific and mathematical discoveries he had learned from the Hindus and his mastery of Sanskrit: a story of India giving and taking at the same time.

Even the name India was invented by foreign invaders. The Persians and the Greeks, trying to define the people who lived along the River Sindhu, wrestled with this Sanskrit name. They corrupted it to 'Indus' – the name of the great river of the Punjab – and then, in trying to define the inhabitants of the region around the River Indus, the Persian and Greek tongues diverged. The Persian word was aspirated and came out as 'Hindu', the Greek one was softly breathed and came out as 'India'. So 'India' is a convoluted way of denoting the subcontinent beyond the Indus bounded by the Himalayas, while 'Hindu' is the word that defines the religion of the people who inhabit the region.

Many centuries later the European orientalists, realizing that Hindus had no name for their religion (the Hindus themselves call it Sanatan Dharma, 'The Eternal Way'), invented the term 'Hinduism' to describe the religious beliefs. As Nirad Chaudhuri has pointed out, this is like calling the Greek religion 'Hellenism' or even 'Graecism'. This invention added

TIMELINE

c. 2500 BCE Harappan civilization flourishes in the Indus Valley

1500 BCE Aryan culture spreads southwards from north India

c. 563–483 BCE Traditional dates of the Buddha, Siddartha Gautama

321 BCE Emperor Chandragupta Maurya destroys Magadha and creates a new empire in northern India

273–232 BCE The Mauryan king Ashoka extends the empire across most of India and makes Buddhism his state religion

320 CE Chandragupta I founds the Gupta Empire (to 720)

1206 The Delhi Sultanate is set up by the Turkic ruler Qutb-ud-Din Aibak

1526 Emperor Babur establishes the Mughal Empire by his victory at Panipat over the Delhi Sultanate

1757 The British under Robert Clive win control of Bengal in a victory over the French and the Nawab of Bengal at Plassey

1857 The Indian Mutiny (First War of Independence) breaks out across northern India in a protest against British rule

1885 The Indian National Congress Party is established

1947 India gains independence from Britain but is partitioned, with Muhammad Jinnah as prime minister of Pakistan and Jawaharlal Nehru as prime minister of India

For many Hindus mythological stories function as historical reference points and provide cultural consciousness. The Ramayana *epic tells of the classic fight between good and evil. This 17th-century miniature painting depicts the battle in which Ram and his brother Laksman destroy the Lankan demon Ravana and rescue Ram's kidnapped wife Sita.*

the most curious twist. In modern India, the word 'Indian' represents all Indians of whatever religion. The country is secular, but Muslims happily call themselves Indians without realizing that they might as well be calling themselves Hindus.

Even modern Indians are content to let foreigners tell their story. The one truly popular history, *Freedom at Midnight* (1975), describing how India gained its independence, was written by two foreign journalists, the Frenchman Dominique Lapierre and the American Larry Collins; the famous 1982 film about Mahatma Gandhi was made by an Englishman, Richard Attenborough.

On gaining independence in 1947 India did not change its foreign-acquired name but decided to use two names, one for internal and the other for external purposes. In Indian languages the country is called Bharat and the Indian government is called the Bharat Sarkar, the Bharat government. Bharatvarsha, the land of Bharat, was the ancient name by which the subcontinental land mass was known. The highest honour in independent India is called the Bharat Ratna, the Jewel of Bharat. Yet in all official correspondence the name India is used.

D. D. Kosambi (1907–66), the most innovative Indian historian, responded to this lack of written knowledge by walking to Indian sites around his base at Pune to research their

Robert Clive and Mir Jafar after the Battle of Plassey (1757) by Francis Hayman illustrates a turning point in Indian history: Robert Clive has won the Battle of Plassey, defeating Nawab Siraj-ud-daulah. He owes his victory to bribing the Nawab's general Mir Jafar, to whom he now gifts the throne of Bengal. Both know the British are the real rulers.

history from an archaeological perspective, starting a new trend in Indian historical research. Since then others have followed the Kosambi trail, with fieldwork being done around ruins, rocks, bricks and other physical evidence at the sites.

For Indians today the most difficult task is to come to terms with the British legacy – a historical minefield. No group of foreigners had a more loaded agenda. The British were unlike any previous foreign rulers of India, all of whom, starting with Alexander in 326 BCE (the first for whom we have reliable historical records), came with the sword; the Mughals arrived in 1526 with the cannon, and the Koran as well. But in the end these foreigners stayed in India and became part of the land; even Alexander left behind Greeks who eventually became Indians. The first British, on the other hand, arrived looking for trade with a begging letter from Queen Elizabeth I to the Mughal Emperor Akbar (in which she mis-spelled his name), emphasizing that they were mere sojourners in India.

Recent historians have focused on the fact that, before the British acquired the country, India was a world economic power. In 1750, seven years before Robert Clive's victory over the Nawab of Bengal and the French at Plassey launched the British Empire in India, China had a one-third share of the world manufacturing output, India a quarter and Great Britain less than 2 per cent. By 1860, after just a century of British rule, Britain had 20 per cent and India 8.6 per cent. In 1900 the United Kingdom had 18.5 per cent and India was down to 1.7 per cent. In effect, Britain denuded India of its pre-industrial manufacturing dominance, converting it into a primary producing country that provided raw materials to industrial Britain.

Yet even as the British of the late 18th century made money from India there were men such as William Jones (1746–94) and Warren Hastings (1732–1818), one a scholar who pioneered the study of Sanskrit, the other Governor-General of India, who together did much to unearth ancient Indian learning. They brought what they learned to an astonished generation of Indians who had forgotten what their forefathers had achieved. Jones, known as 'Oriental Jones', set up the Asiatic Society of India with Hastings's support and started a whole British tradition of scholarship on India that benefited Indians, although for many years no Indian was allowed to become a member of the Asiatic Society or attend its meetings.

The British, starting with Hastings and Jones, were also catalysts for change. They brought new ideas and ways of looking that reconnected India to the world. The effect on the Indian mind, and particularly the Hindu mind, was immense. The most significant reforms of Hinduism – removing some of its barbaric customs, for instance – were not carried out by the British but by Indians who looked at their own society with the help of British ideas and, finding it wanting, sought to change it.

Having helped to open the Indian mind the British also chained it, putting a ceiling on what Indians could aspire to. A classic illustration of this is the naming of Mount Everest in 1865. It was named after George Everest, a British colonel who helped to map India. His work resulted in the first accurate measurements of the Himalayas, including the world's highest peak. But who actually calculated that Mount Everest was the highest in the world? Not Everest himself. In the early stages of the mapping it was denoted as Peak XV while efforts were made to measure it. Andrew Waugh, Everest's successor as Surveyor-General of India, asked their 'Chief Computor' to provide the mathematical formula. This was a young mathematical genius named Radhanath Sikdar, a Bengali whose skills had been admired by Everest. He worked out that Peak XV was 8,840 metres (29,002 feet) above sea level. But the world's highest peak could not be named after an Indian subordinate, and Waugh made sure it was called Everest – as he put it, a 'household word among civilized nations'.

If Alberuni had brought historical writing to India then the British relied on British experts on India who had never visited the country themselves. James Mill wrote his *History of British India* (1818) – a standard work for generations of British students – without ever setting foot in India. John Maynard Keynes worked in the India Office, wrote books on how Indian finance should be organized and helped to create the Reserve Bank of India. But he, too, never visited India. Indeed, he said that he never needed to. His closest contact with an Indian was a student called Bimla Sarkar, who may have been his lover. If so, Keynes, one of the greatest minds of Britain, clearly felt that taking one Indian to bed was one thing, actually meeting millions of them quite another.

The other great feature of the British connection was that from the very beginning the British behaved as if they always occupied the moral high ground. This is best summed up

For the British, with their love of charts and maps, India was a wonderful virgin territory to be discovered. George Everest, a British colonel, helped to map the country. The world's highest peak was named for him even though it was a Bengali, Radhanath Sikdar, who actually calculated its height.

The British at play during the height of the Raj. This scene shows a luncheon party hosted by the commander-in-chief, with elephants managed by Indian mahouts in the background, designed to emphasize both the ease of the British and the absolute control they exercised over their dominion.

in the annual reports presented to the British Parliament by the secretary of state for India. The red bound books are full of the sort of dry government facts and figures you would expect, but what is remarkable is the title: *Moral and Material Progress in India*. The message was clear: the British were not only improving the economic condition of the Indians – a claim still maintained by some British historians – they were also improving the morals of a barbaric, decadent people.

Indians have always found it difficult to cope with such British moral superiority. The Indian answer has been consistently to play down their own dark side and pretend that the crimes they committed were mistakes, or simply did not happen. Indian atrocities against the British, such as the 'Black Hole of Calcutta' of 1756, when the Nawab of Bengal reportedly locked 146 prisoners of war in an airless room where many suffocated, or the massacre of men, women and children in Bibighar, Kanpur, during the 1857 revolt, are ignored or glossed over.

The Indians have a problem even more acute than the post-Vichy French with their history of occupation: without the active collaboration of the Indians, the British could never have conquered India, let alone ruled it. At the height of the empire there were never more than 900 British civil servants and about 70,000 white troops in a country of over 250 million Indians. Even at Plassey more Indians died fighting for Robert Clive than British soldiers (four English soldiers died, nine were wounded and two went missing, while sixteen Indian sepoys were killed and thirty-six were wounded). In 1857 (the violence that the British called the Mutiny, but which is now often known as the First Indian War of Independence) the British would never have survived but for the help they received from the locals – in particular the Sikhs and the Gurkhas.

Drummers of Britain's Sikh troops. The defeat of the Sikhs in 1849 eliminated the last possible challenge to the British. The Sikhs turned into collaborators, fighting to extend the power of the British in various parts of the world and preserving their rule in India by crushing the 1857 revolt.

That the British could recruit Indians to fight for them and even wage war against other Indians was the most remarkable achievement of the Raj. Indeed, across the whole empire the fighting was done by Indian soldiers commanded by a British officer corps. The financing of the army came from Indian revenues. In all except the Anglo-Boer War, a war between white tribes in which it was considered inadvisable to have brown soldiers, Indians fought for the British, extending their dominions and preserving their rule. During the half century before 1914 Indian troops served in more than a dozen imperial campaigns from China to Uganda.

The modern Indian response is to play down the collaboration and try to prove that, contrary to British assertions, India was a nation under British rule. Churchill famously said that calling India a nation was like calling the Equator a nation. Indians stress the cultural unity that long pre-dated British rule, but pre-British India never had political unity. Neither the Mauryan king Ashoka (304–232 BCE), nor the Mughal Akbar (1542–1605), the two great rulers of pre-British India, ever ruled the entire land mass of the Indian subcontinent. Even when it comes to cultural unity there are limitations. Indians, for instance, do not have an agreed day for the New Year. In much of India it is celebrated in autumn at the time of the Diwali festival; in the east and north it falls in spring, around April.

The most elaborate Indian spin-doctoring relates to how India won independence in 1947. In the Indian version it was all due to Mahatma Gandhi (1869–1948) working his magic of non-violent resistance, winning freedom without the shedding of blood. Gandhi

Mahatma Gandhi pictured with his granddaughter Ava (left) and his personal physician Dr Sushila Nayar
(right), dressed in the classic garb of the Indian peasant. Gandhi saw this costume, dismissed as a pose in the West,
as a way of identifying with India's poor, whom he believed could only be rescued through rediscovering India's past.

On 15 August 1947 the British Indian Empire was dissolved and partitioned. Gandhi refused to celebrate, but vast crowds thronged Delhi as Jawaharlal Nehru, India's first prime minister, hoisted the Indian flag. India became a republic on 26 January 1950.

is thought of as the 'father of the nation' in the same way that George Washington is the father of the United States. A visit to Delhi's Rajghat, where Gandhi was cremated, is obligatory for all official visitors. Yet, unlike Washington's defeat of the British at Yorktown, historians cannot point to one decisive moment when Gandhi seized power. He led four non-violent campaigns, the last of them five years before the British left. His campaigns transformed India and Indians, making Indians walk tall and believe they had nothing to fear from their colonial masters. On 15 August 1947 (Independence Day), however, Gandhi refused to celebrate freedom, preferring to spend the day with Muslims in Calcutta trying to calm tensions between Hindus and Muslims, and mourning the division of India that was the result of the independence negotiations and the violence that it had brought.

The independence of India in fact came about through a whole host of circumstances, not least Japan's initial victories in the Far East in 1941–42, which destroyed the myth of white supremacy.

Indians have often underplayed the nation-building they had to undertake since winning independence. There is no more widely held myth than that the British ruled the whole of India, but in 1947 more than a third of the Indian subcontinent was actually ruled by native Indian princes who were not part of British India. They had treaties with the Raj governing external relations. The Raj appointed a resident in each state but, a prince could do what he liked within his boundaries as long as he did not do anything to threaten overall British control. Often their most important engagement as far as the British were concerned was to make sure the viceroy bagged a tiger when he visited. The princes even had their own armies, some of which fought as part of the Allied effort in both World Wars. Neither the British courts nor the railways built by the British extended into these princely dominions. In 1947 each of the 565 princely states on the subcontinent had the option of joining either India or Pakistan, or going independent. The integration of these states into the modern republic of India was the work of Sardar Vallabhbhai Patel (1875–1950), the tough, no-nonsense Gujarati politician who ran Gandhi's political machine and became deputy prime minister in Jawaharlal Nehru's first Indian post-independence cabinet.

The other amazing feature of British India was that, while it had the appearance of a state, it lacked one essential requirement of a state: a commonly accepted legal system. There was a common criminal law and English-style high courts were established, but there was never a common civil law. Throughout their rule the British never made any moves to change, let alone modernize, the personal law of Hindus and Muslims or other Indian communities. They remained as they had for centuries – indeed, the British went out of their way to reinforce the indigenous ancient customs.

Since independence India has struggled to impose a common civil law, leading to many problems with its Muslim minority. When India gained independence there were neither war crimes trials for Indians who had collaborated with the British nor a truth and reconciliation commission such as that held by the South Africans after apartheid. On 15 August 1947, with a shrug, the collaborator joined the freedom fighter.

India is a land that has had no problems creating history but great problems finding good native historians. Indeed, in ancient India poetry was considered of higher value than history. Indians are constantly trying to reclaim their history from the various accounts left to them by foreigners. The result is continuing controversy and turmoil.

آتش است این بانگ نای و نیست باد
هر که این آتش ندارد نیست باد

آتش عشق است کاندر نی فتاد
جوشش عشق است کاندر می فتاد

نی حریف هر که از یاری برید
پرده‌هایش پرده‌های ما درید

همچو نی زهری و تریاقی که دید
همچو نی دمساز و مشتاقی که دید

نی حدیث راه پر خون می‌کند
قصه‌های عشق مجنون می‌کند

محرم این هوش جز بی‌هوش نیست
مر زبان را مشتری جز گوش نیست

در غم ما روزها بیگاه شد
روزها با سوزها همراه شد

روزها گر رفت گو رو باک نیست
تو بمان ای آنک جز تو پاک نیست

HOMA KATOUZIAN

Iran

A long history and short-term society

The history of Iran is a long and complex one. The subject of bitter power struggles for centuries, the land has absorbed a diverse range of cultures and opinions, which have in turn given rise to some of the world's most admired literature, art and architecture.

From the time of the ancient Greeks Iran was known to the Europeans as Persia; in 1935 the Iranian government, prompted by Nazi contacts in Germany, demanded that the rest of the world officially call it Iran, largely to highlight its Aryan origins. After the change of name the country was often confused with Iraq, and many in the West mistakenly thought that it too was an Arab country.

'Farsi' is the Persian term for the language of Iran, but its use in contemporary English is confusing. Unlike the word 'Persian', which many Europeans would understand to be a language of culture and literature, 'Farsi' has no cultural or historical connotations: few English-speakers would have heard of Farsi literature, or be able to locate it geographically. Persian literature is indeed the most glittering jewel in the crown of Iranian history and culture, the collective product of countless poets and writers, both native and non-native Persian speakers. Persian poetry, famous the world over through the works of Rumi, Hafiz, Khayyam, Ferdowsi and Sa'di, is one of the greatest literary legacies of humankind.

Iranians have had far more success in the arenas of poetry, arts and crafts, religion and mythology than in those of science and social institutions. Ancient and medieval Iranian architecture, represented by such historic monuments as the pre-Islamic Persepolis and the post-Islamic congregational mosque of Isfahan, is one of the world's major architectural legacies. Persian miniature paintings, mosaic designs and modern Iranian art – together spanning more than a thousand years – are unique in their artistic identity. Persian carpets are the most advanced and exquisite in the world.

Frontispiece of a manuscript of poems by the 13th-century poet Rumi dating from 1453. Rumi was the most renowned Persian mystical poet. His voluminous verses and many of the tales of his narrative poem Mathnavi *have been translated into all major languages.*

Archaeological evidence of early civilizations goes back several thousand years, but the country's written history dates to over 2,500 years ago, when the Persian king Cyrus the Great founded the first world empire, stretching from Central Asia to Cyprus, Egypt and Libya. This was the culmination of almost two millennia of the movement of Aryan tribes to the Iranian plateau, most likely from the steppes of northern Central Asia. There were many tribes, including Scythians, Parthians, Alans, Medes and Persians, the last of which established an empire that came to embrace all the others.

The Persian Empire was often in conflict with the ancient Greeks, but, unlike Greece, it managed to run a large imperial state that concentrated all power in its own hands. It was a legacy that essentially lasted up to the 20th century and beyond. This concentration of power was a source of strength for the state as well as its weakness. The state could exercise arbitrary power over society, but society therefore often saw it almost as an alien force and perennially revolted against it – most notably in the 18th century – or failed to defend it against foreign invaders, such as the Muslim Arabs in the 7th century. Thus there has been a fundamental antagonism between state and society throughout Iranian history, in spite of the country's vast imperial and cultural achievements. The state tended towards absolute and arbitrary rule; the society tended towards rebellion and chaos. One of four situations normally prevailed in Iranian history: absolute and arbitrary rule, weak arbitrary rule, revolution or chaos – which was normally followed by a return to absolute and arbitrary rule.

Traditional Iranian revolutions were intended to overthrow the existing ruler and state rather than to abolish the system of arbitrary rule, which until the 19th century was believed to be natural. The general cycle of arbitrary rule–chaos–arbitrary rule meant that change was more frequent in Iranian than in European history. What persisted was the arbitrary nature of state power, which both justified and was justified by the rebellious nature of society.

TIMELINE

c. 550 BCE Foundation of the Achaemenid Empire

330 BCE Conquest of the Achaemenids by Alexander the Great

248 BCE Foundation of the Parthian Empire

224 CE Foundation of the Sasanian Empire

651 Overthrow of the Sasanians by the Abbasid Arabs

1040 Conquest of Persia by the Seljuk Turks

1220 Mongol conquest of Persia

1501 Foundation of the Shia Safavid Empire

1722 Collapse of the Safavid Empire

1796 Foundation of the Qajar dynasty

1906 Constitutional reform is introduced by the Shah

1921 A military coup brings Reza Khan Pahlavi to power, founding the Pahlavi dynasty in 1926

1953 Overthrow of Prime Minister Mohammad Mosaddeq in a coup

1979 Overthrow of the Pahlavi dynasty by an Islamic revolution led by Ayatollah Khomeini

1980–88 Iran–Iraq War

Zoroaster (c. 1200 BCE) founded the Zoroastrian religion, although it did not become the state religion of Persia until the foundation of the Sasanian Empire in the 3rd century CE. The Behistun inscription in western Iran attributes the glories of the Achaemenid king Darius I (522–486 BCE) to Ahura Mazda, the Zoroastrian god.

The state's independence from all social classes accounted for its extraordinary power, but this independence was also its main vulnerability, as there was no particular social class which, if the state were in trouble, could be depended upon to support it. Since the right of succession was not guaranteed in law or entrenched in custom, any rebel could overthrow and replace the reigning ruler. This gave rise to a 'short-term society', which was both cause and effect of the absence of an established aristocratic class and social institutions. A man could be a humble person one year, a minister the next, and lose his life and possessions not long after that.

The empire founded by the Achaemenid dynasty in about 550 BCE lasted for over two centuries until it was conquered by Alexander the Great in 330 BCE. A period of Greek rule and settlement was followed by the rise of another Iranian empire, that of the Parthians in 248 BCE, who were to become first neighbours and then rivals to the Romans. The Irano-Roman conflict continued even when the Persian Sasanian Empire replaced that of the Parthians in 224 CE. They made Zoroastrianism, an ancient Iranian cult, their state religion. Zoroastrians identified three 'states' of existence: the first was a state of harmony and bliss; this was followed by the 'mixed state', containing both good and evil, in the present world; it would eventually be brought to an end by a saviour, ushering in the third state of permanent bliss. These concepts of heaven, hell, reward and punishment in the next world are quite similar to those of the Abrahamic religions of the

Middle East. The Zoroastrian orthodoxy was challenged in the 3rd century by Mani, the prophet of Manichaeism, a hybrid form of Zoroastrianism, Christianity and Buddhism. This was suppressed but later had a considerable impact on post-Islamic Persian Sufism. The Mazdakites also challenged Zoroastrian orthodoxy in the 6th century but they too were suppressed after attempting to launch an egalitarian social movement.

In 651 the Sasanian Empire was overthrown by Muslim Arabs. This fresh force, combining an egalitarian and Abrahamic faith with the spiritual force of a revolutionary movement, faced a vast but archaic, exhausted and conflict-ridden empire that was not energetically defended by its own people. It took two centuries for all Iranians to convert to Islam, by which time the first autonomous Persian states had come into being. During this period Iranians made considerable contributions to Islamic culture and civilization as administrators, writers, scientists and physicians. Various Persian states emerged in the former Sasanian territories until the 11th century when they all began to be conquered by hordes of incoming nomads, mainly Turkic, from Central Asia, who formed

Evening prayers at the shrine of Imam Reza, Mashhad. Twelver Shias venerate their twelve founding Imams as the rightful successors to the Prophet Mohammad and legitimate rulers of the Islamic community. Imam Reza's shrine is visited by large numbers of people every year, many of whom pray for his intervention in solving their problems.

the vast Seljuk Empire. This was followed by the Mongol devastation of Iranian lands in 1220, then by the foundation of various Turkic states in the 14th century. Throughout this period of turmoil, however, Persian remained the language of culture and administration, as well as the lingua franca in many non-Iranian lands such as Anatolia, Turkistan, western China and western India, later stretching to the whole of the Indian subcontinent and at times beyond it to the Indochinese peninsula.

In 1501 Persia was again reunited under one banner as 'the protected realm of Iran' and the Shia branch of Islam was made the state religion. This was the Safavid Empire, which peaked in the early 17th century but fell to Afghan rebels in 1722. Decades of civil and foreign wars followed.

Towards the end of the 18th century the Qajars founded a dynasty and brought relative peace to the country. But Iran then became subject to an acute Anglo-Russian rivalry for imperialist domination, subsequently dubbed 'the Great Game', which robbed the country of full sovereignty. This was the origin of modern Iranian conspiracy theories, which are still strongly held by those of virtually all shades of political opinion. Iranians developed the habit of attributing even the slightest political event in their country to the machinations of foreign powers, and saw themselves as helpless pawns in the chess games of outside players.

The intellectuals found the remedy in law, pointing out that, unlike in Europe, the state still exercised arbitrary power over society. The Constitutional Revolution of the early 20th century was intended to establish a government based on law as well as to modernize the country along European lines. But the fall of the arbitrary state resulted in chaos rather than democracy, as it had done throughout Iranian history.

In 1921 a coup led by Reza Khan Pahlavi (1878–1944) brought the chaos to an end and by 1926 he had founded

Reza Khan Pahlavi pictured on his 'peacock throne' in 1931. He had gained power in 1921, outmanoeuvred his rivals and founded the Pahlavi dynasty. Having established an authoritarian government he ruled as a dictator for many years. He abdicated in 1941 following the Allied invasion.

the Pahlavi dynasty, which lasted until 1979. The coup was aided by British diplomats and military officers, but the British government did not have a direct hand in it. It resulted in a dictatorship that within a decade led to the restoration of the ancient arbitrary rule. Steps were taken during this period to modernize administration, transport, industry and education. While it benefited only a small minority of the population at the time, the modernization drive did lay the foundation for later developments in the 20th century.

A revolutionary propaganda poster publicizing the role of Islamist women in the revolution and the ensuing intra-revolutionary conflicts. Secular women also took part in large numbers, although many of them were disappointed when the Islamists gained complete power.

Modern Iranian elites, deeply influenced by European nationalist ideologies, redis-covered and romanticized ancient Persia's glorious Aryan past and blamed the contemporary country's backwardness on Arabs and Islam: without the Muslim con-quest, they believed, Iran would now have been on a par with Western Europe. This became the state ideology under the Pahlavi dynasty. But true to the tradition of state–society antagonism, not only traditionalists but even secularists and modernists later turned towards Shia Islam as a faith and an instrument with which to confront the secularist and arbitrary rule of the second Pahlavi, Mohammad Reza Shah (1919–80). The revolution of February 1979 became fully Islamic only through the power struggles that followed its triumph. Since then, Aryanist romantic nationalism has again become popular among modern and secular Iranians.

Modern nationalism also had important implications for the vexed question of Iranian identity. Pan-Persian Aryanism inevitably led to the downgrading, sometimes even denial, of the multi-ethnic and multi-linguistic nature of Iranian society since its very foundation, leading to deep resentments and sometimes animosity towards the state as well as towards Persian speakers. Yet not only did describing Iranians in terms of a single pure race fly in the face of the facts, it also more importantly ignored the Iranians' remarkable capacity to receive, absorb and adapt foreign cultures, from the Babylonian culture of the 6th century BCE to the American culture of the 20th century. Indeed, this is the secret of the richness and continuity of Iranian culture and civilization, in spite of historic interruptions and perennial revolutions.

Although ancient and medieval Iranian empires sometimes included even more diverse peoples than does modern Iran, a quality and characteristic of Iranianism (Iranian-ness or *Iraniyat*) always distinguished the country from its neighbours. It was not nationalism in any modern sense, but consciousness of a social and cultural collectivity that made its people distinct from the Greeks, Romans, Arabs, Chinese and Indians. The factors that bound Iranians together and determined their identity were not necessarily the same throughout the ages, although three have played an important

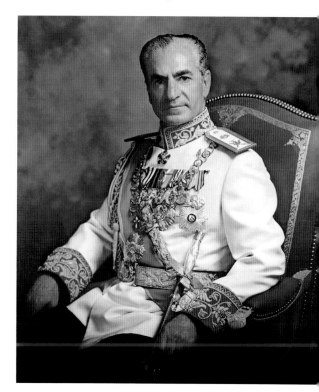

Under Mohammad Reza Shah, pictured here in 1973, Iran went from a constitutional monarchy (1941–53), through a dictatorship (1953–63), to an absolute and arbitrary rule (1963–79). He had wholly unrealistic ambitions for both himself and his country, resulting in policies which led to his own ruin and the foundation of the Islamic Republic.

role since medieval times. One is the Persian language, the medium of literature and high culture that even became the official and spoken language other countries, including Mughal India. Another is Shia Islam, which is unique to Iran as a state religion and is followed by the majority of Iranians; aspects of it have also been ingrained in Iranian culture since pre-Islamic times. The third is territoriality: the fact that despite territorial expansion and contraction through the ages, there has usually been a recognizable Iranian territory – at least as a cultural region.

The 1941 Allied invasion of Iran led to the abdication of Reza Shah and accession of his son Mohammad Reza Shah. Once again chaotic politics returned, the Tudeh (later Communist) Party being the most organized political movement in the 1940s. The end of that decade saw the rise of Mohammad Mosaddeq (1882–1967) as leader of the National Front. He was elected prime minister and nationalized the oil industry, but could not reach a settlement with Britain and was overthrown in 1953 by a coup organized and financed by the American and British governments, and manned by his own domestic opposition.

The coup established a pro-Western dictatorship that lasted until the mid-1960s, when Mohammad Reza Shah eliminated the loyal political establishment as well as the National Front, and renewed absolute and arbitrary rule in what is known as the White Revolution. The most important principle of the revolution was land reform, although in reality it excluded many of the peasants, resulted in the relative decline of agriculture and filled the cities with rural migrants. The quadrupling of oil prices in the early 1970s damaged the economy by encouraging state expenditure beyond its capacity, and intensified the Shah's inflated sense of self-confidence, which in turn exacerbated the lack of freedom of expression felt by the population.

A portrait of the Shah carried atop an army tank. The 1953 coup against Mosaddeq was organized and financed by the American and British governments and carried out by the rightist and Islamist opposition. The Shah was particularly angry about Mosaddeq's motto that 'the Shah must reign, not rule'.

This state of affairs brought together all strands of the opposition, including liberals, leftists and Islamists. When the Shah tried to loosen his grip slightly in response to the American president Jimmy Carter's call for the extension of human rights throughout the world, the revolutionary movement, led by the charismatic and uncompromising Ayatollah Khomeini (1900–89), overthrew his rule in February 1979.

The ensuing Islamic Republic was ridden with conflict, but the power struggles eventually resulted in the triumph of the Islamist forces led by Ayatollah Khomeini. When in November 1979 American diplomats were taken hostage in Tehran, relations with the United States continued to deteriorate, and the West subsequently supported Saddam Hussein in his long war with Iran which ended in 1988.

In 2009 a clash between reformist and pragmatist forces within the Islamic Republic and their fundamentalist and conservative counterparts led to demonstrations and riots triggered by the belief that the presidential election had been fraudulent.

Since Khomeini's death in 1989, Ayatollah Khamenei (b. 1939) has been supreme leader, overseeing three presidencies: Ali Akbar Rafsanjani's pragmatist-conservative presidency (1989–97); Mohammad Khatami's reformist-pragmatist presidency (1997–2005); and Mahmud Ahmadinejad's fundamentalist-conservative presidency (2005–). Ahmadinejad's re-election in June 2009 was widely disputed, and led to massive demonstrations and a serious rift within the Islamist regime itself. This was not just a crisis of authority, but also of legitimacy.

Once the reformists were chased out of politics, cracks began to appear in the ranks. The conservative faction went its own way and the fundamentalists split into two: the hardline Steadfast Front and the group, described as 'deviationist' by their opponents, who supported Ahmadinejad. Meanwhile the conflict over Iran's nuclear programme hardened and the United States and European Union imposed tough new economic sanctions. The question now was whether the situation would eventually lead to military confrontation with Israel and the United States.

PICTURE POST

A GREEK COMMANDO

HULTON'S NATIONAL WEEKLY THE WAR FOR GREECE 4ᴰ

ANTONIS LIAKOS

Greece

A land caught between ancient glories and the modern world

What is it to be Greek? Two poems might provide an answer. The first, by Kostis Palamas, the poet responsible for the lyrics of the first Olympic Games anthem in 1896, wonders 'What is my motherland'? Is it her landscape and the monuments left behind by all previous inhabitants – the ancient Greeks, the Romans, Byzantines, Venetians, Ottomans and others? The second, 'Mythistorema', written in 1935 by the Nobel prize-winner George Seferis, likens the poet's feelings about Greece to those of someone waking up from a deep sleep, holding in his hands an ancient marble head, having dreamed his entire life that he was inseparable from it; he does not know what to do with the head and he is tired of holding it. In Palamas's poem contemporary Greece is nothing less than an amalgam of 2,000 years of history, including the deeds of her conquerors, all of which left traces on the physiognomy of the land. In the second poem contemporary Greece is unable to decide her identity; instead, she swings between the present and antiquity, as the latter is unbearable for a country trying to obtain a contemporary consciousness.

Greece originated as a modern nation state in a revolt against the Ottoman Empire in the 1820s. Before this it was not evident that the new state would be called 'Greece' ('Hellas' in Greek) or its inhabitants 'Greeks' ('Hellenes'). 'Greek' in the vernacular denoted a pagan, a meaning given to the word by the Church Fathers. When Christianity rose to supremacy in the Eastern Mediterranean in the 4th century, it replaced the old religions and the culture of the Greek city – its public worship, debates on public issues at the agora, theatre performances, wrestling arena and Olympic Games. This was undeniably a dramatic change. The question has often been asked: did the Hellenic world survive after the end of antiquity?

The civil wars of the late 1940s originated in the partisan opposition to the Italian and Nazi occupying forces and were stoked by Cold War tensions. The victory of the Western-supported government produced a powerful military and a polarized political environment in which the legacy of the ancient world contributed relatively little but tourist income.

49

Thucydides, whose History of the Peloponnesian War *recounted the events of the war between Athens and Sparta in the 5th century* BCE *and provided a model for future historians, placed great importance on 'being Greek', a way of life ruled by law.*

But what was the Hellenic world? Plato described the Greeks as frogs sitting around a pond, a reference to the Greek settlements around the Mediterranean and the Black Sea. But did the term 'Greek' refer to an ethnicity or a civilization? For the historian Herodotus in the 5th century BCE, the Greeks had a common language and religion, and shared the same ancestors: therefore they were one race, even if they lacked political unity and national consciousness. A few decades later the historian Thucydides put forth a more sceptical view. He wrote, for example, of barbarians who became Greeks, by which he meant that previously they solved their problems with arms, as barbarians did, but later turned to the law, as Greeks did. In these terms, anyone could be identified as Greek so long as he shared Greek values. In the 4th century BCE Isocrates observed that Greeks were those with Greek education, suggesting that Hellenism was a cultural rather than ethnic category. In the 'Hellenistic' era inaugurated by Alexander the Great and the Macedonians, Hellenism was largely a cultural force, as cities with a Greek way of life extended deep into Central Asia. Many Greek writers of that time were not writing in their first language. Under the Roman Empire, Hellenism, through poetry, philosophy, theatre, sculpture and architecture, became the culture of the Roman – or rather the Graeco-Roman – aristocracy.

The Christians adopted the Greek language and safeguarded a selection of Greek philosophical and poetic texts, as well as writings on medicine, mathematics and

TIMELINE

776 BCE Traditional date for the first Olympic Games

480 BCE The Greeks defeat a Persian invasion after battles at Thermopylae, Artemisium and Salamis

432–404 BCE The Peloponnesian War ends with the defeat of Athens by Sparta

323 BCE The death of Alexander of Macedon, whose conquests spread Hellenistic culture across the Middle East and Western Asia

146 BCE Rome completes its conquest of Greece

330 CE The foundation of Constantinople as the eastern capital of the Roman Empire

1453 The Ottoman Turkish conquest of Constantinople ends Byzantine civilization

1821–30 The Greek War of Independence from the Turks results in the establishment of the Kingdom of Greece

1896 The first modern Olympic Games are held in Athens

1912–13 The Balkan Wars and expansion of Greek territory

1919–22 War with Turkey, leading to an exchange of populations between Greece and Turkey

1941–44 Greece is occupied by Germany, Italy and Bulgaria

1947–49 Civil wars between left and right

1967–74 Military rule by 'the Colonels' ends with the restoration of parliamentary democracy

2004 Athens Olympic Games

2010–12 Financial crisis leads to the imposition of widespread austerity measures

astronomy. However, they destroyed 'visible Hellenism' – its schools of philosophy, statues, temples, theatres and wrestling arenas – along with everything that involved the agora and public debate. In other words, the Christians wrought the destruction of the Greek way of life – which is why the words 'Greek' and 'pagan' became synonymous for Christians. Nevertheless, Christianity might not have acquired the form by which it is known today, had its precepts not been expressed in a Greek conceptual language. So the question remains: was Hellenism destroyed or did it survive?

If we consider Hellenism as the civilization of a particular era, then it began with the Hellenic settlements in the Mediterranean in the 8th century BCE and ended with the complete Christianization of the Roman Empire in the 6th century CE. The prohibition of the ancient forms of worship and the Olympic Games by the Byzantine emperor Justinian in 528, and the con- version of the Parthenon to a Christian church, signalled its end. This is a civilization that had lasted for twelve centuries. Certainly many of its cultural features were passed on to the modern era: they survive in aspects of the linguistic and conceptual background of European lan- guages, as well as in languages of the Eastern Mediterranean (including Coptic, Arabic, Syrian, Armenian, Slavonic and Turkish). Modern European culture has reassessed, reused and competed with Greek and Roman concepts and forms. From this perspective, especially from the time of the 18th-century Enlighten- ment, cultural Hellenism has emerged as a reference point in philosophy, political theory,

Classical Greek culture flowered across the Mediterranean, albeit in a distinctly Christian guise, under the emperor Justinian (r. 527–65), based in Constantinople. He turned the Parthenon into a Christian church and suspended the Olympic Games. Christians adopted the Greek language but destroyed 'visible Hellenism' in statues, temples and theatres.

visual arts and architecture, and has become the core of the canon of Western civilization.

However, Greeks today do not see Hellenism in this manner, as essentially a level of civilization. Needless to say, they do attribute primacy to it, regarding it as a supreme civilization and the mother of modern civilization. Moreover, they consider Hellenism to be a manifestation of the Greek nation's brilliance and ingenuity. But modern Greeks believe that Hellenism corresponds to a nation, one that lived on after the end of antiquity in the Eastern Roman Empire. This nation in its second life was shaped in conjunction with the Hellenized Eastern Orthodox Church (rather than the Latinized Church of the West). Greeks believe that, despite the Ottoman occupation of Asia Minor and the Balkans from the 12th century CE, their nation managed to survive until its assertion of independence in the early 19th century.

Greek scholars of the 19th century nurtured the notion of an uninterrupted history of their nation from Greek antiquity to the Greek kingdom in 1830. Firstly, they archaized the spoken language and developed a written one as close as possible to the Hellenistic vernacular. Secondly, they changed the names of towns, villages, mountains and islands back to their ancient forms; for them archaeological sites constituted a geographical network of historical reference points, underlining their Greek identity. Thirdly, they adopted neoclassicism as their architectural style for public and private buildings. The same style was used for national symbols and monuments. But above all, Greek scholars created a powerful narrative of a nation with a continuous history from antiquity to the present, using supporting evidence from historiography, folklore and art history. The Greeks convinced not only themselves with this notion of Hellenism but also non-Greeks – both tourists and scholars of Greek culture and civilization. Those foreigners who were mesmerized by ancient Greek civilization assisted in the 'rebirth' of the Greeks. But the Greeks have paid a heavy price for persuading themselves and others of an uninterrupted Hellenic history: they are often perceived to fall short when compared to their invented, but distant, ancestors.

A painting of the blessing of the flag of revolution, by Theodoros Vryzakis, 1865. The Greek War of Independence against the Ottoman Turks (1821–30) was supported across Western Europe as a national liberation struggle, attracting Romantics such as Lord Byron, not least with its echoes of the Trojan Wars. The Orthodox Church first opposed the uprising but later claimed rights to the victory.

There has always been a disjunction in how Greeks regard themselves and how others do. Prior to mass tourism, only a few learned visitors knew about Greece from their books. These were the people who admired ancient Greece, but looked down on any of her other historical periods. In the 19th century the newly independent Greeks themselves manifested a similar contempt: for example, by 'purifying' the Acropolis and Athens of any Roman or Byzantine structures. Then there was a change of course in which they strove to display elements from all earlier periods in order to demonstrate the uninterrupted

Greece has become one of the world's most popular tourist destinations, both for its historic attractions and for its traditional rural and island culture. Pictured here is the Parthenon of the Acropolis: built in the 5th century BCE and dedicated to Athena, it is now the most venerated of the ancient sites and an emblem for modern Greece.

history of Hellenism. In doing so they stumbled on a great obstacle: Byzantium was missing not only from the Greek historical canon, but also from the European. This meant that the history of Eastern Orthodoxy was also absent. Many Western scholars of Byzantium viewed Orthodoxy and Eastern Europe as a civilization separate from that of Western Europe. The Greeks now tried to appropriate the history of Byzantium for themselves and promote it as a link in their own national history, portraying Byzantium as the conduit through which ancient Greek literature passed to modern Europe. It is interesting, though, that just as Western Europeans had turned their backs on the Greeks, the Greeks themselves had turned their backs on Balkan and Middle Eastern peoples. Greek historical encounters with Venetians, Serbs, Albanians, Bulgarians, Arabs and Turks were not ignored, but they were interpreted within a framework of national antagonisms.

A reference to the Balkans often brings to mind issues such as ethnic conflict, war and even ethnic cleansing: this is considered to be a region where everyone fights against everyone else. However, there is hardly anything exceptional about the Balkans; no more

Turkish prisoners during the Balkan War of 1912, when the weakness of the Ottoman Empire allowed Greece, in alliance with Bulgaria, Montenegro and Serbia, to drive the Turks from most of their territory in the Balkans. The following year Greece confirmed its hold over much of Macedonia.

blood has been shed in this region than in any other part of the world. The problems there stemmed from the coexistence of different ethnic populations in the same territory. So when individual nations began to gain political will following the decline of the Ottoman Empire, they claimed areas that other nations were also claiming. For example, Greece and Bulgaria both claimed Macedonia. The former also disputed Constantinople (Istanbul) and Asia Minor with the Turks. The years leading up to the First World War brought an explosion of nationalistic fervour, leading to a decade of constant wars and bloody conflicts (1912–22). In the process Greece quadrupled in size by acquiring the largest part of Macedonia, which was Hellenized, mainly by the transportation of refugees from Asia Minor. These wars were followed by violent and unwilling mass expulsions or population exchanges, and in some cases massacres. In 1922 1.5 million Christian refugees were forced to leave Turkey for Greece. Six hundred thousand of their Muslim counterparts left Greece to settle in Turkey. Greek populations from around the Balkans converged within the borders of the Greek state. In the following years the state made a huge effort to assist the refugees, who comprised 20 per cent of the population, assimilating them into Greek life.

War changed the political scene of Greece; the army became stronger, often resulting in coups d'état that brought crises to the country's parliamentary system. The 1929–32 depression resulted in social unrest. The spectre of social revolution hovered over the country until 1936 when a dictatorship was established, under General Ioannis Metaxas (1871–1941), as in other European countries of this period. In fact, Greece entered the Second World War under a dictatorship imitating fascism, but allied with Britain.

For Nikos Svoronos, a leading 20th-century Greek historian, a key element throughout Greek history has been the spirit of 'resistance'. Greeks, he claimed, were always resisting foreign invaders and internal tyranny. This widespread attitude is the result of the fact that the modern Greek state was a product of a revolution, which in turn created a strong subject: 'We, the people!' It gave rise to a tradition of popular patriotism and nationalism, of intense politicization and strong political parties, as well as a relatively stable parliamentary tradition. Yet Greece won its independence through the intervention of the major powers of that period, in particular Britain and Russia. For most of her modern history Greece has been dependent, first on Britain, then on the United States. Consequently both powers have often had a say in domestic policy. Greece, in other words, was something between an independent state and a colony, without having ever actually turned into a colony. At the same time, Greece maintained an ambivalent stance towards Europe and the West, although Western powers were needed when it was lined up against Turkey or any other Balkan neighbour. Interestingly, though, Greece held on to an anti-imperialist spirit, risking being regarded as the naughty child of the West. This ambivalence was reinforced after the Second World War, and has had a profound impact on contemporary Greece.

In 1940–42 the Greeks repelled the Italian invasion, but were then themselves defeated by the Germans. From April 1941 to October 1944 Greece endured a tripartite German, Italian and Bulgarian occupation. During this period the entire state mechanism collapsed. Famine hit the urban population and the currency was devalued in uncontrolled inflation. The people had to organize their own survival, and this, together with a resistance movement against the occupiers, resulted in the merging of patriotic spirit and social revolt. Liberal and conservative political parties were inactive, so the National Liberation Front, a coalition of leftist parties, took up leadership of city and village resistance groups. Its military branch was a guerrilla army known as ELAS (the Greek Resistance Army). Despite the leadership's cautious declarations that Greek resistance was on the side of the Allies and against the Axis, the movement acquired the characteristics of an undeclared social revolution. Furthermore, ELAS attempted, sometimes bloodily, to dominate other political or armed groups. As a revolution often brings a counter-revolution, so this was the case in occupied Greece. With the cooperation of the occupying forces, rival armed groups evolved and were to lead the country into a bloody civil war. This did not come to an end after Greece's liberation from the Germans in October 1944, but escalated in December 1944 and then again in 1947–49, when it turned into a full-blown war.

The Greek Civil War was one of the first episodes of the Cold War: the British and the Americans responded with immediate interference. It ended with a crushing defeat for the Communists; a large number were either executed or exiled to barren islands of the Aegean, or fled to Eastern Bloc countries. Until 1967 the country was governed by a very weak democracy. Greece had now ceased to be an agricultural society, most of its population having moved into the cities. The economy was not strong enough to support its people and a large wave of emigrants left for Western Europe. However, Europe's post-war prosperity also impacted on Greece. Steadily the country's living standards began to move closer to those of other European countries, even though, together with Spain, Portugal and southern Italy, it belonged to a slower-paced Europe. This direction was interrupted by the military junta that ruled for seven years from 1967, bringing significant disaster to Greece as well as to Cyprus, where it dismantled the legitimate government and triggered a Turkish invasion that has become permanent. The military junta was the final stage in a period of wars and fierce political unrest that had begun in the early 20th century. Yet the last quarter of the 20th century saw a period in which the country's democratic institutions were consolidated. Moreover, thanks to tourism, the standard of living improved, and in 1981 Greece became the tenth member of the

The 2004 Olympic Games were held in Athens – where the modern Olympics were first celebrated in 1896 – in conscious commemoration of the ancient tradition. Games had been held in Olympia every four years for over a thousand years, between 776 BCE and 528 CE.

European Union. The accession into the European club proved highly beneficial, especially for the country's economy and institutions, both of which were modernized.

During the second half of the 20th century the vast majority of tourists who visited Greece had not read any of the ancient Greek writers, but they might have seen the films *Zorba the Greek* (1964), starring Anthony Quinn, and *Never on Sunday* (1960), starring Melina Mercouri. Post-war cinema manifested a fresh, unconventional and jovial Greek identity. Although many Greeks, especially males, adopted this identity, the truth is that Greeks today have both an optimistic and pessimistic view of their history and identity.

Immigrants at a Labour Day rally in Athens in 2009, demonstrating for their children's right to education. Since the 1990s there has been a wave of immigrants coming to Greece, with people from Eastern Europe, the Middle East, Central Asia and Africa now making up about 10 per cent of the Greek population.

Furthermore, the collapse of the socialist regimes in Eastern Europe in 1989 and consequent globalization have had tremendous consequences for Greece: a constant influx of new migrants from Albania, Eastern Europe, Asia and Africa has reached the most remote parts, and they now make up 10 per cent of the population. There are neighbourhoods and schools in Athens and Thessaloniki where migrants outnumber locals. Xenophobic outbursts that the Hellenic identity is in danger from immigration are frequent – ironic in a land in which people regard hospitality as an ancestral trait. Meanwhile, the 21st century found Greece celebrating her entry into the euro and hosting the 2004 Olympic Games in Athens. Yet there was a huge bill to pay that was exacerbated by a world-wide economic crisis and the unexpectedly high cost of having joined the euro. Enormous government debt and loss of confidence by the international financial markets forced a series of severe austerity measures from 2010, resulting in widespread public anger towards the government. Newspaper headlines proclaimed that the very fabric of the Eurozone was under threat, should Greece default. Even as the crisis was impoverishing Greek society, it was making European economic integration obligatory.

China

History writing: linking the past and the future

History has always held an extremely important place in Chinese society, quite unlike that which it has occupied in most other countries. Indeed, China probably has the longest continuous tradition of formal history writing in the world, stretching from at least 1600 BCE, with precise records from 841 BCE, to the present. In the ancient period official history was written by the court astronomers, who also performed ritual duties and were tasked with observing and recording heavenly phenomena, and even communicating with Heaven (*tian*) itself. Their chief duty as historians was to record the great events of the dynasty, and the words and deeds of sovereigns. Some scholars probably just recorded rulers' speeches, while others focused on wider events. The records they produced were free from political interference: until the Tang dynasty (618–907 CE) an emperor had no authority even to read the record of his own deeds.

Ancient Chinese people had an enormous respect for Heaven, but it was never worshipped as an omnipotent spirit or god. Instead, there was a constant interaction between the human world and Heaven. Emperors were considered to be the sons of Heaven, whose purpose was to implement Heaven's will in the human world. However, the evidence of whether or not this had been properly realized was in the attitude of the common people, hence the saying 'The views of Heaven are as the views of the people'. The emperor's method of finding out what the common people thought was known as *caifeng* ('gathering from the wind'); that is, collecting popular songs and stories in order to understand what sentiments were prevalent. So another duty of historians was to collate and organize the information from *caifeng*, to let the sovereign know whether or not his rule was indeed a manifestation of the mandate of Heaven.

It is said that in ancient times the major concerns of states were religious sacrifice and war. Sacrifice was directed towards both the imagined heavenly spirit and ancestors. In

Confucius (551–479 BCE) is often considered the father of Chinese history writing. It is believed that China's earliest historical works, the Book of History *and* Spring and Autumn Annals, *were compiled and edited by him. Both texts were later accorded the status of classics and Confucius himself became known as 'the great sage'.*

ancient China ancestors were not only the source of all knowledge, but also the foundation of people's identity, and as such were highly respected. Maintaining historical memory of ancestors was also the state historians' fundamental duty, a function that originated before the development of writing. After the invention of writing, the difficulties inherent in the ancient methods (the carving of seal-form characters in the early period) and the limited supply of writing materials meant that only extremely important matters could be written down and records were extremely short. More detailed stories had to be passed on through the songs and oral narratives of the blind poets, about 300 of whom resided in the ruling court. There was a clear distinction between the two kinds of history. As one ancient text put it: 'Books are to the historian what chants are to the blind.'

Thus the role of state historians was to provide linkages both spatially, from the lowest ranks of society all the way up to Heaven, and temporally, from the past to the present. The directive of the great Han historian Sima Qian (c. 145–87 BCE) to historians that they should 'investigate the connections between Heaven and the human world, and be versed in the transition from ancient times to the present' graphically illustrated this. From the central government to the fiefdoms, all courts employed this kind of state historian. Functionaries created records and collections of *caifeng* even for local affairs. It is because of this great respect for historical memory that the Chinese historical record is so long and unbroken. In later times, when the status of the state historian declined, the transmission of records was still treated with great respect. During the Tang dynasty the government established a records office charged with producing written histories. From the Song dynasty (960–1279 CE) onwards each new dynasty wrote the history of the preceding one, both to summarize the lessons that could be learned from history and to prove the legitimacy of the new dynasty.

TIMELINE

c. **2800** BCE Legendary first emperor of China – the Yellow Emperor

c. **2070–1600** BCE Xia dynasty

c. **1600–1046** BCE Shang dynasty begins recorded Chinese history

c. **1046–771** BCE Western Zhou dynasty

770–221 BCE Spring and Autumn and Warring States periods

551–479 BCE Life of Confucius

221 BCE Unification of China under the first emperor of the Qin dynasty

202 BCE Beginning of the Han dynasty

c. **145–87** BCE Life of Sima Qian, historian

618–907 CE The Tang dynasty rules from Chang'an

960–1279 Song dynasty

1644 Overthrow of the native Ming dynasty by the Manchu Qing dynasty

1842 Defeat of China in the First Opium War

1911 Overthrow of imperial China

1919 May Fourth Movement

1949 Overthrow of the Republic by the Communists led by Mao Zedong

1966–76 Cultural Revolution

2008 Beijing Olympic Games

China entered the Bronze Age in c. 2000 BCE, a period that lasted about 1,600 years. This Shang vessel is distinguished not only by its exquisite form, but also by its symbolic significance. Such vessels were usually presented at the royal court where they were used in religious and political ceremonies.

The earliest works of history known today are the *Book of History* and the *Spring and Autumn Annals*. The former is a collection of political documents from the Shang (*c.* 1600–1046 BCE) and Western Zhou (*c.* 1046–771 BCE) periods, and the latter the historical records of the Kingdom of Lu (722–481 BCE). It is believed both were compiled and edited by Confucius (551–479 BCE). Another compilation believed to have been edited by Confucius is the *Book of Songs*, which is primarily a collection of poetry from the

Zhou court and various local courts, and is possibly related to the practice of *caifeng*. If all these documents were indeed compiled and edited by Confucius, then the sage certainly could be described as the father of Chinese history writing.

Confucius was deeply dissatisfied with the political and cultural chaos of his time. It is believed that his aim in compiling the *Spring and Autumn Annals* was to instil a sense of remorse in those who violated what he saw as the natural order, by passing judgment on them in his work. His opinions were expressed through descriptions of concrete 'deeds' (*xingshi*). Praise and criticism were delivered by his selection of events and persons: the manner in which they were recorded presented a judgment as to whether their actions were a manifestation of the mandate of Heaven or not. Thus, the act of creating records was also an act of interpretation. History writing bore the heavy responsibilities of evaluating select events and accrediting governments, exercising a direct influence over the legitimacy of a particular sovereign's rule as well as his historical status.

The historian therefore had two tasks: to create a record that was as accurate as possible, and also to show appropriate praise and criticism through the selection of content. There was clearly a tension between these responsibilities. However, after the custom of producing a history of the previous dynasty became established, this internal conflict was externalized through a fixed division of labour. The task of recording the present dynasty's actions (which would be the subject of future histories) was separated from that of writing of a judgmental history of the previous dynasty. The former could produce an approximate 'true record' (which is how many later dynasties referred to these official records), and the production of the latter history could therefore proceed with relatively few restrictions.

The result was that linking the past and the future became an ever more important aspect of the function of records. Newly established dynasties felt obliged to grant their predecessors their rightful place in history. Thus the creation of an archive of records was a duty that those in the present owed to their successors, and the writing of history was a responsibility that later generations owed their forebears. This process was gradually systematized as states, localities and individuals all strove to leave appropriate records of their deeds.

Although Confucius aimed to appraise the past and the present, he established the principle of 'seeing truth in deeds and events'. From this foundation, the tradition that theory must be presented via accounts of events became entrenched in Chinese history writing. At the centre of events were individuals. Until the 20th century biographies of important people dominated the content of all Chinese history books. However,

A scene from a ceremony celebrating the ancient philosopher and educator Confucius' 2,557th birthday, taking place inside a Confucian temple in Qufu, Shandong province, on 28 September 2006. For the first time in history, women were officially recognized in the line of descendants of the great sage.

Guan Yu (c. 160–220 CE) was a famous general in the Eastern Han dynasty (25–220), known for his extraordinary military talent as well as his familiarity with Confucian classics. Although his career actually ended in failure, he was deified in Chinese popular culture and later accorded the status of a military sage.

achievements were not necessarily the best criteria for judging the importance of an individual: historians also paid attention to those who displayed moral strength. Apart from the lives of emperors, the first biography in *Records of the Grand Historian* by Sima Qian is that of Bo Yi, which narrates the opposition of Bo Yi and his brother Shu Qi to King Wu of Zhou who, before becoming king, had led an army to attack his own sovereign, King Zhou of Shang. After King Wu defeated the Shang and became the new monarch, Bo Yi and his brother starved themselves to death, refusing to eat the grain of the new state of Zhou.

The importance of this kind of historical memory in China is indicated in a line from the ancient *Book of Changes*: 'A wise man studies the words and deeds of his forebears in order to improve himself.' Bo Yi and Shu Qi entered the historical record because of the strength of their moral character in not attaching themselves to King Wu's conquest. Naturally, official histories were written from the point of view of the victors in political contests, but there is also a long tradition of not viewing greatness in terms of success or failure. Even if a dynasty repudiated the previous dynasty, it was still bound to produce faithful representations of the people involved. Historians always had to seek a balance between these two imperatives. The notion that moral character was of greater importance than success was even more pronounced in popular culture. In history, two revered heroes of the Chinese, Guan Yu and Yue Fei, both saw their ambitions go unfulfilled – the former a general involved in the collapse of the Han dynasty in the early 3rd century CE, the latter a patriot fighting for the Southern Song in the 12th century – and indeed both could be said to have been failures. However, they became objects of worship within popular culture.

So history and historiography played a much more central position in China than they did in the West. History elucidated and justified the basic assumptions of the heavenly order (*tian dao*) and the human world, as well as cultural and political identities. To a large extent it was the arbiter of whether or not emperors were manifestations of the mandate of Heaven, and thus determined their legitimacy.

In the Spring and Autumn and Warring States periods (770–221 BCE) the chaotic political order and growing independence of the feudal lords contrasted with an increasing centralization within culture. At that time there was intense competition between different schools of thought, in which scholars sought to change the world according to their own prescriptions. This is usually taken as an expression of a great liberation of ideas. However, they were concerned with the whole world, not just the affairs of a single kingdom. The concept of 'all under heaven' (*tianxia*) was very flexible, and could refer to the entire physical world, or the totality of human society, or the land ruled by a monarch. Frequently all three meanings were present.

By the time of the Han emperor Wu (r. *c.* 140–87 BCE), Confucian texts were accorded the status of classics, and the scholars who studied and interpreted them were the most important of the 'four social classes' (the other three were farmers, artisans and merchants). For the following 2,000 years a major difference between China and the West was that in China 'truth' did not necessarily come from a supernatural power or god. The Xia, Shang and Zhou dynasties (known collectively as the Three Dynasties), as interpreted by Confucius, were a golden age in which an apparently ideal society existed. Throughout later history, educated men aimed to facilitate the re-emergence of the Three Dynasties' social order within the present, and usher in a transformation of an unjust world into a just one.

With the sanctification of the Confucian classics, the status of history writing declined somewhat. However, because the classics were relatively stable and their content confined to remote antiquity, history writing still performed a key legitimizing function for individuals and events. It was considered a path to the truth, especially because the views and attitudes of Heaven were expressed in those held by the common people, and because an ideal society was seen to have existed during the remote Three Dynasties period. Accordingly, a large proportion of the content of both elementary education and advanced scholarship was devoted to historiography.

This changed with the flood of Western influence into every aspect of Chinese society in the 19th century. In light of China's vast size and massive population, the aim of the invaders was not to occupy its territory, but to adopt a less costly strategy of control: to achieve a cultural infiltration that would pave the way for economic profit. Although China's buying power turned out to be limited, the West was extremely successful in the struggle for cultural control, and this gradually changed the thinking of many educated Chinese. Because Confucianism was not in itself able to make China prosperous and strong, it retreated step by step from its paramount position in society.

With the foundations of their own culture thus undermined, Chinese attitudes towards it underwent a dramatic transformation. Chinese people now came to view their culture as barbarous, occupying a marginal position in the world. By the early 20th century China had lost its centre of gravity.

A clear shift in power relations between different fields of scholarship now took place. The Confucian classics could not meet the demands of the new quest for national power and wealth, and subsequently faded from prominence. Instead, a broad understanding of history became seen as essential for the very survival of the nation and its culture, and historical study subsequently gained an unprecedented status. However, the intellectuals now had such a lack of confidence in Chinese traditions of scholarship that, just when historical study had been bestowed with the great task of revitalizing the Chinese nation, it plunged into the embrace of Western intellectual traditions.

From the beginning of the 20th century many progressive intellectuals believed that traditional culture must be relegated to museums in order to clear the way for modernization. Even some conservative scholars accepted the view that traditional culture was an antique. Most people agreed that tradition could not solve the problems of the age, and saw it as a threat to the development of the new society. Thus there was a strong emphasis on distinguishing 'the old' from 'the modern' in order to eliminate it.

After the May Fourth Movement of 1919, truth was increasingly seen as epitomized by science. Historical study was re-conceptualized as a scientific methodology with a mission to 'reorganize the nation's past'. Nationalism and science thus now came together. Without the scientific method, national studies meant little, while without the

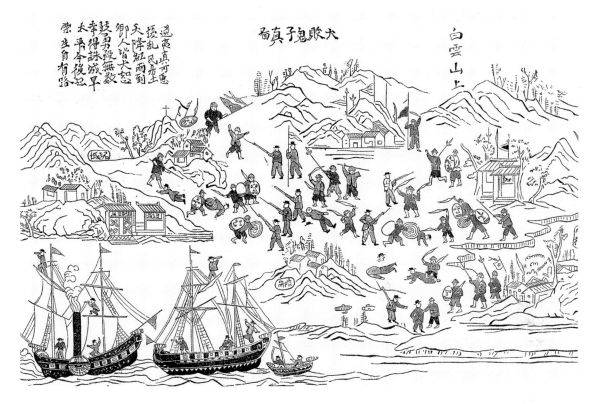

A wood engraving of the Second Opium War (1856–60). The period of the Opium Wars, when Britain's Royal Navy defeated the Chinese army to prevent restrictions on the opium trade, is often regarded as the beginning of modern China. The Qing court did not pay much attention to this military failure, yet it remains a symbolic turning point.

'national past' that Chinese intellectuals were accustomed to studying, the scientific method would have had no subject matter. The Marxist theory of historical materialism, a manifestation of the scientific approach, gained in popularity, and after 1949 became the guiding paradigm of historical study.

Thus in the 20th century almost all Chinese scholars adopted Western theories and practices. History had to become a kind of science itself and compete for space among a multitude of disciplines. History, like classical studies, was unable to serve the quest for national strength and power, and it gradually gave up its weighty duty of sparking a national renaissance. However, this left it freer to grow as a regular academic discipline. From the mid-1990s, alternative approaches to history appeared, bringing new perspectives on historical problems, using new materials and adopting alternative forms of expression.

In modern China the kind of history that is taught in schools and to which the public pays attention has changed dramatically. The opening ceremony of the Beijing Olympics in 2008 was a dramatic sign of this transformation of the role of history in China. In what has been regarded as a kind of historical poem, or tableau, the ceremony emphasized paper-making and the other technologies that make up the historical 'four great inventions' (the others are the compass, gunpowder and printing). These inventions, which are now seen as representative of Chinese culture, were seldom the object of any attention a century ago, and have only in recent times been rediscovered and granted their new significance. They are undoubtedly a part of Chinese history, but science never occupied the central position in China that it did in the West. Thus what was on display in the opening ceremony can be described as Chinese history from a Western perspective.

The transformation of history's function and content in the last hundred years has created a certain confusion. Its former significance has gradually withered and many

The Cultural Revolution in China (1966–76) was a significant historical event. Culture, which had always occupied a central position in Chinese society throughout history, suddenly became a subject of revolution. Radical revolutionary ideology affected every aspect of society – including the teaching of history in Chinese schools.

Fireworks above the National Stadium, known as the Bird's Nest, during the opening ceremony of the Beijing Olympics on 8 August 2008. Gunpowder is one of the 'four great inventions' in Chinese history that are now seen as representative of Chinese culture. These inventions were seldom the object of historical attention a hundred years ago.

people – scholars and ordinary people alike – have wondered what the use of history is. Around fifty years ago, history was still a very important discipline, and among the Chinese science academies there were at least three research institutes devoted to history (other disciplines typically only had one each). But in the last twenty years, a sense of crisis has emerged in university history departments and, in these times of rapid change, the significance of cultural identity has dramatically increased. Society at large has started to take a keen interest in the history of China and its people. As for the question of whether this new attention will be a boon or a disaster for the study of history, we can only wait for history itself to answer.

Ireland

In the shadow of the fond abuser

For good or for ill, the single most important fact of Irish history from the 12th century on has been the intense and troubled relationship with Britain, inaugurated through the 'conquest' of the country by a group of Anglo-Norman feudal adventurers. Other influences partially countervailed this fateful connection, notably Ireland's deep and enduring links with Continental Europe. Following the 5th-century mission of St Patrick, the Christianizing of Ireland progressed rapidly, and between the 8th and 11th centuries Irish monks made a major contribution to the (re-)Christianization and cultural development of Western and Central Europe. Complex trading connections and associations existed long after the 12th century, though they were disrupted and reshaped as a direct consequence of that so-called conquest, which began in 1169.

The character of this conquest is not easily defined. Territorially and politically it was not finally secured until the 17th century, while in terms of cultural and ideological hegemony it was arguably never completed at all. It was not, moreover, one long drawn-out process. What the Anglo-Norman barons started was not what the Tudor monarchs attempted to bring to completion 400 years later; and though the Williamite wars and confiscations of 1689–99 succeeded in obtaining almost complete possession of Irish land for the English, the settlement then imposed differed markedly, both in its political and social character and in its ideological foundations, from the powerful but abortive experiments of Oliver Cromwell some forty years before.

Nor was England's engagement with Ireland always one of aggression. Repeated spasms of violence, repression and exploitation alternated with periods of attempted reconciliation, reform and development. Each of these was, moreover, interrupted by longer spells of indifference, irresponsibility and neglect. If the cultural psychology of peoples could be identified with the psychological development of a single individual, it

Chronological tree of Irish history from the first invasion by the English to 1876, when the image was created. On the limbs of the tree important dates and events in Irish history are recorded. Seated to the left is Erin, the female personification of Ireland, with harp and hound; a man, possibly Daniel O'Connell, stands before her.

would be tempting to account for the stereotypical features frequently assigned to the Irish character in terms of the Irish people's suffering at the hands of a dominant, oppressive, exploitative, manipulative, occasionally kind and frequently neglectful close relation – a classic example of the Freudian fond abuser. But rather than stray too far into such untestable speculations, it is better to investigate the concrete economic, political, ideological and cultural spheres in which Ireland's relationship with its neighbour shaped its own history.

Of these impacting forces the most obvious was economic, expressed largely through England's assertion of ownership over Irish land. Though the Anglo-Norman invaders and their successors made substantial inroads into all parts of Ireland, their hold was often tenuous, conditional on their ability to exploit divisions among the native Irish, and on occasional reinforcements from England. By the end of the 13th century most of Ulster, north Connacht and several upland regions in Leinster and Munster had been regained by Gaelic Irish dynasties. A complex pattern began to emerge, of core areas of English government, law and land tenure surrounded by extensive peripheries where hybrid and informal modes of political authority and ownership of wealth prevailed. Misleadingly described as a process by which the colonists had become 'more Irish than the Irish themselves', this was in fact a system of alliance and rivalry, sustained by informal taxation and extortion, which allowed a small group of powerful Anglo-Irish and Gaelic Irish dynasts to share power. It was, however, unstable and prone to local breakdowns. In the long term it was politically decadent and economically wasteful, as the demands of the elite outran the resources of the decreasing number of wealth-producers available to supply them.

After centuries of neglect, the Tudors sought to address this deteriorating situation by transforming the dynastic elites (both Gaelic and Anglo-Irish) into a recognizably English

TIMELINE

432 The Romano-British missionary Patrick arrives to convert Ireland to Christianity

***c.* 800** The Book of Kells is created, representing a high point of Celtic Christian culture

***c.* 850** The Vikings found Dublin and other Irish cities

1167 Invasion of southeastern Ireland by Anglo-Norman knights leads to the establishment of an English state under Henry II

1536 Henry VIII asserts English power and in 1541 recognizes the Irish Crown as distinct in law from the English

1550–1640 The English introduce 'plantations', giving Irish land to English and Scots settlers

1649–53 Oliver Cromwell brutally conquers Ireland

1690 Battle of the Boyne marks the victory of William of Orange and the Protestant ascendancy over the Jacobites

1798 Widespread nationalist revolts against the Protestant ascendancy

1801 The Act of Union of the Irish and British Crowns

1829 The Catholic Emancipation Act is passed at Westminster

1845–47 The Irish Famine brings mass starvation, emigration and depopulation

1916 The Easter Rising – a failed nationalist rising against British rule

1921 Ireland wins its independence, but Ulster remains British; civil war ensues

1998 The Good Friday Agreement ends thirty years of sectarian conflict in Northern Ireland

2011 Queen Elizabeth II visits Dublin, ending a century of continuous conflict and tension between Britain and Ireland

aristocracy, and encouraging them to adopt English modes of law, land tenure and culture. This was a difficult undertaking whose risks were exacerbated by the rudimentary, incompetent and frequently corrupt political and administrative machine through which the Tudors sought to bring about reform. Though most of the nobility were initially attracted to change, few overcame the challenges involved, and by the beginning of the 17th century the many failed initiatives had resulted in a series of noble rebellions and the destruction of many of the largest noble dynasties, Gaelic and Anglo-Irish alike.

In this context colonization – the resettlement of Irish land with new English emigrants – which the Tudors had envisaged as a secondary supplement to the broader campaign of Anglicization, now became the primary means of securing control. A series of further wars occasioned by England's own constitutional upheavals in the mid-17th century completed the ruin of the indigenous Irish nobility. Eventually a new but no more stable structure emerged, under which the large mass of the native peasantry and the dispossessed and impoverished gentry and nobility coexisted in deep hostility with smaller scattered groups of English and Scottish settlers, both ruled over by a tiny elite of English aristocrats, most of whom were rentiers or absentees.

A detail from a plate in The Image of Irelande, *a series of woodcuts by John Derrick, published in London in 1581. Viceroy Henry Sidney, accompanied by an armed force, sets out from Dublin Castle, demonstrating Tudor power in Ireland.*

The weaknesses inherent in this new social structure were aggravated by the deeply divisive factor of religion. Introduced as part of the Tudor programme of Anglicization, the Protestant Reformation posed a serious challenge to the indigenous elite. Ironically, though, while the response of the Gaelic nobility was initially positive, opposition arose among the elite of the old colonial community whose very legitimacy in Ireland – the 12th-century papal bull *Laudabiliter* – was now implicitly repudiated by the English Crown. Counter-Reformation ideology in Ireland was thus initially championed by the ostensibly loyalist Old English (as they now began to describe themselves). But as the Tudor campaign of Anglicization degenerated into violent confrontation, so religious grounds for resistance became central to the Gaelic Irish. In the 17th century, therefore, an uncompromising Roman Catholicism became, for the Old English and native Irish, a medium of common resistance to new Protestant

English settlers, landlords, lawyers and merchants. For some time the ambiguous religious disposition of the Stuart monarchs held back these sectarian divisions. However, the settlement imposed by the triumphant Protestant Williamite regime following its defeat of the Catholic Jacobites at the Battle of the Boyne in 1690 allowed sectarianism to flourish unchecked, in the form of a rigorous penal code designed to sustain the fragile regime through religious intolerance and persecution.

Yet this new English Protestant elite was threatened with deep internal tensions that became more marked as the 18th century advanced. The first of these was religious. The Protestant interest was never homogeneous. In the plantation established in Ulster in the early 17th century, two distinct settler elements – English and Scottish – had markedly different forms of worship and sharply opposing attitudes towards church organization and authority. Such differences widened over the century, and as the Scottish dissent acquired a dominant influence in Ulster, its suppression as an independent force became a priority of the Williamite establishment second only to the repression of Catholicism. Yet the stifling of dissent in Ulster was impeded by the appearance and proliferation of other forms of Protestant nonconformity springing up throughout the island in the mid-18th century in the form of Presbyterians, Quakers, Huguenots and, later on, Methodists.

This religious and cultural threat to the English establishment was accompanied by a further challenge, economic and commercial in nature. Economic exploitation had always been a central element in England's relationship with Ireland. In addition to the acquisition of the richest land and the exploitation of the island's natural resources, medieval monarchs and parliaments had occasionally sought to control trade with Ireland to the advantage of English trading interests, and a fixed rate of exchange was established setting the currency of the Anglo-Irish colony at 33 per cent below sterling. Even more seriously, an attempt was made to support Tudor government in Ireland by raising revenues without the consent of the Irish Parliament. From the mid-17th century such practices became formalized, and Ireland came to be seen in economic and social terms as having an important but subordinate role in the development of a British Empire.

Muted at first by the elite's awareness of its vulnerabilities in Ireland and its dependence on Britain, dissatisfaction mounted throughout the 18th century as leading figures within the Anglo-Irish elite demanded freedom from commercial restraints and greater investment in Ireland's domestic economy, in a manner that paralleled the rising agitation of the colonials in North America. Proximity to Britain, fear of French intervention and anxieties about a revival in the status of the Catholic majority all sapped the momentum of the Irish agitation. Instead, in the later 1790s, Ireland was convulsed by a recrudescence of sectarian violence, an abortive attempt at a republican revolution, a widespread Catholic revolt, a period of bloody repression (in which more people perished than during the entire revolution in France), and finally in the imposition of direct

A painting by Dutch artist Jan van Huchtenburg depicting the Battle of the Boyne. William III's victory over James II at the Boyne on 12 July 1690 represented the triumph of Protestantism and as such remained a flashpoint annually in the sectarian wars of Northern Ireland in the later 20th century.

rule through the suppression of the Irish Parliament and the creation in 1801 of the new United Kingdom.

The Union of Britain and Ireland was presented by its English devisers as a desperate means of preventing the warring communities in Ireland from self-immolation. Undertakings concerning the continuation of reform – including the granting of full civil rights to Catholics – were generously forthcoming. But none of the promises were met. Within this post-Union gloom, two elements of the 18th-century movement for reform retained a vestigial vitality. The first was the demand for full civil rights for Catholics. After more than two decades of agitation under Daniel O'Connell, Catholic emancipation was grudgingly conceded by the Westminster Parliament in 1829. More important than the end was the means by which it had been attained. Through intense popular mobilization O'Connell had himself returned as an MP while refusing the oath of Supremacy, cornerstone of the Protestant establishment. Popular participation now became a central element in Irish politics. In securing this popular movement O'Connell enjoyed the support of what had hitherto been an impeccably conservative force, the Catholic Church, and the emergent democracy in Ireland thus acquired a peculiar characteristic: its pace, purpose and direction would be heavily shaped by one of the least democratic and liberal institutions in Europe.

In this light, a second survival from the reformist 18th century acquired a renewed significance: the determination to maintain an independent constitutional and parliamentary tradition. Though originally an organ of the medieval English colony, as early as

A cartoon by James Gillray (1757–1815), leading political caricaturist of his time, showing the Union Club gathering of Whigs celebrating the political union of England and Ireland. The Union was in part a response to the failed nationalist revolt of 1798. In the 19th century many blamed Ireland's woes on the Union.

1460 the Irish Parliament had declared its independence of the English. In 1541 Ireland had been recognized in English law as a kingdom in its own right, sharing a common sovereign with the separate kingdom of England, though this experiment in dual monarchy never advanced very far in practice. However, the possibility that Ireland might evolve as a separate entity with its own laws, institutions and customs remained an aspiration that attracted Gaelic Irish, Old English and 18th-century reformers until 1801. It was hardly surprising then that, having achieved Catholic emancipation, O'Connell should turn to repeal of the Union. To the irony of an ecclesiastically supported drive toward democracy was added that of a drive toward Ireland's independence that relied on an English tradition of reform through statutory, legal and administrative change.

Underlying such ironies, and sustaining the ambiguous attitudes of Anglo-Irish politics in the early 19th century, was an increasing confidence that England's own constitution had developed to the extent of being capable of addressing and resolving any challenge once the issue had come to fruition. A further, more terrible irony is that it was from this largely unquestioned ideological consensus that the most tragic event of modern Irish history was to issue, in the form of the Famine.

The Famine of 1845–47, caused by blight on the potato crop, constituted the greatest watershed in Anglo-Irish history since the 17th century, its reverberations felt for more than a century. Partly as a consequence of starvation, malnutrition and disease, but more importantly through the constant haemorrhage of emigration, Ireland's population fell from 8.2 million in 1841 to 4.4 million by 1911. Among those who lost most, those who emigrated to the United States and those intellectuals who brooded on the causes of the Famine, radical republicanism surged, in particular a secret organization committed to revolution by violent means and terror: the Irish Republican Brotherhood or 'Fenians'.

Irish emigrants waiting at Ellis Island, outside New York City. Ellis Island served as gateway to the United States for immigrants between 1892 and 1954. Many died during the passage or were refused entry on grounds of poor health.

Next to the very poor and unfortunate, the most prominent victims of the catastrophe were the landlords (both those who tried to alleviate the sufferings of their tenants and those who did not). The collapse of their rental income plunged many of them into debt. Some hurriedly sold out, but any who sought to improve their position by agricultural, administrative and legal initiatives were opposed at every stage by the groups who

A 19th-century map of Ireland depicting the 'Emerald Isle and Fenians' Home'. The Fenians were a radical group dedicated to the establishment of an independent Irish republic; they succeeded in winning support among Irish emigrants in North America.

had suffered least and gained most from the calamity: the middle-level tenants and free-holders. This strong farmer class formed the backbone of the most powerful political movement of the later 19th century, one centred on land reform.

Though O'Connell's movement for repeal of the Union was swamped by the Famine, the aspiration for some form of Home Rule re-emerged in a rather genteel way, led by representatives of the reforming landlord interest. It gained momentum only when, under the shrewd and Machiavellian leadership of Charles Stewart Parnell in the later 1870s, it became tied in with with the movement for a transformation of the ownership of Irish land and with the even more radical republican movement funded by Irish-America represented by the Fenians. Parnell's 'new departure' supplied an energy to constitutional and tenurial agitation in Ireland un- known since the early 1840s. His ceaseless application of pressure to the party system at Westminster forced concessions, in the form of the most radical land legislation ever drafted by an English Parliament, and the commitment by Gladstone's Liberal party to Home Rule.

The responsiveness of the Liberals and the Conservatives to Irish demands, however, was more than a sign of weakness. The leadership of both parties saw Irish policy as a means of differentiating themselves from their rival, and of consolidating control over their own followers. Thus the Liberal Gladstone used the promise of Home Rule as a means of redefining the Liberals, while the Conservative Lord Salisbury committed the Tories to a radical series of land acts as a means – in a phrase epitomizing England's role as Ireland's fond abuser – of 'killing Home Rule with kindness'.

The conditional nature of British support for Irish reform was illustrated when both parties allowed Irish matters to lapse after Parnell was abandoned by the majority of his Catholic supporters, following his citation in divorce proceedings in 1889. But the Liberal commitment to Home Rule again became a central issue in the 1910s as part of Asquith's struggles to reposition his party in English politics, and was finally granted in principle in 1914. Even then it was highly contentious, challenged by the threat of insurrection in

Protestant Ulster, where it was regarded as 'Rome Rule', and by mutiny within the British garrison in Ireland. When the European war broke out later in the year, its implementation was shelved.

In this atmosphere of disillusion, physical-force republicanism recovered its power, the intensity of its appeal enriched by the brutal repression of a small-scale insurrection in Dublin in 1916 known as the Easter Rising. Between 1918 and 1921 Ireland was in the grip of a bloody guerrilla war. Republican anxieties concerning civilian casualties and Britain's embarrassment over the conduct of its paramilitary force, 'the Black and Tans', compelled both sides to seek a truce. The ensuing Anglo-Irish Treaty of 1921 secured Irish independence but at the cost of the Irish Free State remaining within the Commonwealth and, more importantly, of the partitioning of the island, with Northern Ireland remaining a province of the United Kingdom. Though it was the cause of a brief but intense civil war among the political elite, the Treaty was endorsed by the electorate, and in the ensuing two decades the development of a stable democratic system in Free State Ireland was facilitated by another of those long phases of British indifference. The anti-Treaty side re-entered constitutional politics by forming a populist party Fianna Fail under the leadership of Eamon De Valera. In government after 1932, De Valera sought to

A photograph from May 1916 shows Dubliners viewing the ruined buildings that were damaged in the Easter Rising, bewildered by the extent of the shelling. The Easter Rising took place during Easter Week in late April and despite being crushed produced a moral victory that resulted in independence a few years later.

revise the terms of the Treaty unilaterally through drafting a new constitution, and pro-voked an 'economic war' with Britain by his refusal to pay promised land annuities. The 'war' ended largely through the goodwill of the Chamberlain–MacDonald government in 1938 in an agreement that also returned to the Free State the naval ports retained by Britain. The timely return of the ports helped in sustaining Ireland's fragile neutrality during the Second World War. Britain's sustained non-interference between the late 1930s and the early 1950s allowed the experiment in autarchy to be found wanting – its failure registering in persistently high rates of unemployment and emigration. By the later 1950s, the leadership of the Republic of Ireland (declared, without British opposi-tion, in 1949) was prepared for more active engagement with the international world. Ireland and Britain worked closely together seeking favourable terms for inclusion into the growing European Community.

The indifference of Ireland's neighbour between the 1920s and the early 1960s thus contributed to the emergence of a modern democracy where the civil and political rights of citizens were strictly observed – even though the Catholic Church (its position enshrined in De Valera's constitution) enforced a conservative society in which divorce, contraception and abortion were proscribed, and rigorous censorship applied. Within Northern Ireland, however, similar neglect produced less happy consequences. Supported by an inequitable electoral system, an armed police and a sectarian militia, a Unionist one-party-rule state governed in the interests of the Protestant majority and often directly against the interests of the substantial Catholic minority. Untroubled by the nationalist rhetoric in the South and by sporadic efforts of the Irish Republican Army, the province's place in the UK had been consolidated by loyal service during the Second World War. Ironically the grateful determination of post-war British govern-ments to extend the benefits of the Welfare State to the province in the form of investment in education, health, housing and industry served to undermine Unionist rule. Its political and social aspirations at once whetted by the promises of progress and frustrated by persistent Unionist discrimination, the Catholic minority in the later 1960s grew militant in its demands for equality. Crude intimidation and repression provoked sectarian violence, a transformation in the fortunes and power of the (Provisional) IRA and a breakdown of law and order, and led to the suspension of self-government and the imposition of direct rule from Westminster in 1972.

In the quarter century that followed, Northern Ireland represented in microcosm the relation between Ireland and its neighbour. Severe bouts of repression – directed mostly against Republican paramilitaries or suspected associates – alternated with sincere peace initiatives (the 1972 power-sharing agreement, the 1986 Anglo-Irish Agreement). There there were also long periods (especially after the 1981 hunger strikes) when no significant action other than containment was considered; and the situation deteriorated rapidly.

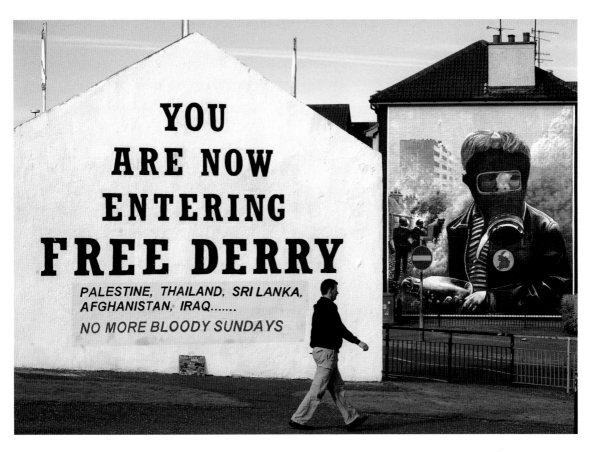

A man walking past a Bloody Sunday mural in Derry in June 2010, on the day families waited for the outcome of the Bloody Sunday Inquiry, which re-examined the deaths of thirteen people killed when British soldiers opened fire on a civil rights march in Londonderry in 1972. The inquiry became the longest-running in British legal history.

Tentative initiatives resumed by the Major government in the 1990s were intensified by New Labour from 1997. This resulted in the most important stage yet achieved in the resolution of the Northern Ireland problem: the Good Friday Agreement of 1998, which led to the establishment of a power-sharing executive headed by representatives of the hitherto irreconcilable Democratic Unionist Party and Sinn Fein. Though not free of difficulties and mistrust, this settlement has survived and progressed. Its success owes much to the sincerity of the British government's sustained commitment to reform, and to the arguably even more constant support of the Irish Republic, whose governments and people steadfastly opposed terrorist tactics over the long period of 'the troubles'. The political and ideological maturity displayed by the Republic in this testing time of its independence is testimony to the claim that, if Ireland's relationship to its powerful neighbour had never been greatly for good, neither had it been entirely for the ill.

Spain

Beyond the Black Legend

Much detail is known about the diverse range of peoples who inhabited the Iberian Peninsula in pre-Roman times, but some of the broad picture is missing. The Iberians traded across the Mediterranean, but their script is undecipherable; the Celts presumably migrated from elsewhere; and just who the Basques were and when they emerged remains hotly disputed. Much of the information that does exist about early Iberia has been twisted by divergent nationalist readings (Spanish, Basque, Catalan, Galician and Portuguese). There were also Phoenician contacts, Punic settlements in the Balearics and on the coast, as well as Hellenic trading posts that became urban colonies.

Hannibal's campaigns on the peninsula in the 3rd century BCE brought Roman conquest in their wake. By about 27 BCE Rome controlled most of what it called Hispania (hence 'Spain'), although the northern Atlantic coast, sheltered behind mountains, was slow to yield. Hispanic Romans provided the empire with many luminaries, including the writers Seneca, his nephew Lucan and Martial in the 1st century CE, and the emperors Trajan and Hadrian in the 2nd century CE. Hispania was eventually integrated into the empire and spoke Vulgar Latin with local variants.

The migrations that broke up the Western Roman Empire in the 5th and 6th centuries imposed 'barbarian' rule: these were mostly Visigoths, with Vandals in the south (hence '[V]Andalusia') and Swabians in the northwest. By the reign of Liuvigild (*c.* 572–86), the Visigoths had cobbled together some form of peninsular unity. The Visigoths largely adopted the language and style of the Hispano-Romans, although there was a long argument about Christian doctrine: Arianism (the denial of the doctrine of the Trinity) was supported until 589 when King Reccared (r. 586–601) converted to orthodox Catholicism. Visigothic Spain also produced one of the great polymaths of the so-called Dark Ages, Isidore of Seville (*c.* 560–636).

A window from the Visigoth church of San Juan Bautista, Baños de Cerrato (in the province of Palencia), c. 661. The effect of Visigothic rule was more symbolic than physical: their buildings are few and generally tiny. 'Godo' or 'Goth', however, became a byword for genealogical purity.

The Islamic invasion from North Africa cut through the Visigoth kingdom with astonishing rapidity: the onslaught began in 711 and was finished about a decade later. The attackers did not bother to occupy the nooks and crannies of the northern Atlantic coast, preferring to continue into Gaul until stopped by the Franks around 732. The new Muslim rulers Islamicized the region and settled North African colonists there, but were not exceedingly harsh with the conquered population, as they were Christian 'people of the book' like the Jews. They called the whole country 'al-Andalus', projecting the Vandal-controlled south northwards. The contest in the Middle East over the Muslim inheritance – the Caliphate or 'successorship' to the Prophet – brought to the far west of Europe a sole survivor of the defeat and murder of the Umayyad caliphs by the new Abbasid dynasty: Abd al-Rahman I. In 756 he proclaimed the rival Emirate of Córdoba against the hegemony of Abbasid Baghdad; in 929 the eighth emir, Abd al-Rahman III, took claim to the Caliphate, as 'successor' and head of all Muslim believers. Córdoba enjoyed a time of cultural splendour, during which scholars such as the Jew Maimonides (1138–1204) and the Muslim Averroes (1126–98) devoted themselves to translating and interpreting the Graeco-Roman classics. In this way the heritage of classical antiquity was passed on to the post-Roman kingdoms in the West, which were fused in a sporadic and symbolic Holy Roman Empire under Charlemagne (c. 742–814) and his heirs.

Charlemagne pushed into the peninsula from the Pyrenees, and established a 'Spanish March' (border territory of his empire) in what became, after about 864, the County of Barcelona, or Catalonia. By then, Carolingian presence had receded and Islamic dominance

TIMELINE

c. 17 BCE Augustus Caesar completes the Roman conquest of Hispania

711 CE Islamic invasion of Visigothic Hispania

756 Abd al-Rahman I proclaims the Caliphate of Córdoba

1492 The Christian 'reconquest' of 'Spain' is completed by the defeat of Muslim Granada; Christopher Columbus sails to the New World

1521 Spanish conquistadors subjugate Mexico

1556 The Spanish 'golden age' begins with the accession of Philip II

1648 The Treaties of Münster and Westphalia mark the end of Spain as a world hegemonic power

1700–14 The accession of the Bourbon King Philip V triggers the War of Spanish Succession

1763 By the Treaty of Paris, British defeat of the French in North America leaves Spain as the main territorial power in the Americas

1808 Joseph Bonaparte is put on the Spanish throne, initiating the Peninsular War against the French

1813 The French are expelled from Spain, but take power again in the 1820s

1824 After the Battle of Ayacucho, Spanish forces are defeated by independentists; Spain only retains Cuba and Puerto Rico

1870 'German candidacy' to the Spanish throne after the Bourbons are expelled in 1868 leads to the Franco-Prussian War

1874 A Bourbon king is re-established on the Spanish throne after a failed republican experiment

1898 The Spanish-American War leads to the loss of Spain's last colonies, Cuba, Puerto Rico and the Philippines

1931 Bourbon dynasty is again overthrown and a republic established

1936 An attempted coup against the Popular Front government by a broad right-wing coalition fails and the Civil War begins; Francisco Franco is chosen as Generalissimo by the Nationalist generals

1939 Franco defeats the Republican forces and begins a period of relatively stable dictatorial rule

1975 The death of Franco; a new Bourbon monarchy under Juan Carlos II facilitates the transition to democracy

1985 Spain joins the European Union

The Alhambra ('Red Fort' in Arabic) was built in the 14th century as a palace citadel for the Nazarí dynasty of Granada. Eventually abandoned, the beautiful buildings have entranced visitors since the American author Washington Irving wrote the romantic Tales of the Alhambra *in 1832.*

was substantially unquestioned except in the mountains of the north, where small powers challenged the Moors, as the Muslim inhabitants of Spain were called in Europe. Asturias became a sovereign entity after 718, expanding slowly until 1065 when it became the kingdom of Castile. Navarre arose as a presence after the mid-8th century and helped to create Aragon, which spun off after about 1035: some hundred years later, the count of Barcelona married the heiress of Aragon and fused both entities. On the Atlantic, the kingdom of Castile recognized the County of Portugal, which soon also claimed its own sovereignty.

The modern languages of the peninsula appeared around the 10th century, spreading downwards from the north. Basque lent its harsh tones to the local late Vulgar Latin dialect, creating Castilian. To its west, Galician evolved into Portuguese and expanded southwards. To the east, Aragonese merged with Castilian, while the Catalan language hugged the coast and was extended by conquest to Mallorca and Valencia in the early 13th century.

A 14th-century manuscript shows Charlemagne's army as it sets off to conquer Spain. Between 795 and c. 988, Carolingian influence on the Iberian peninsula remained strong only in the 'Spanish March', which eventually became the County of Barcelona, out of which evolved Catalonia.

A local crusade against the Muslim occupiers began in the late 11th century, during which Iberian Christians received Crusader support, rather than setting sail for the Holy Land themselves. From before the 12th century, the shrine of St James in Santiago de Compostela in Galicia was one of the great focal points of Christian pilgrimages. In general, what came to be termed the 'Reconquista' brought an ardent, even ugly, religious belligerence to Hispanic cultures, which would be retained for centuries to come. The rise of troubadour culture in the 12th century, however, brought sophistication to courtly Catalan and Galician (which was still the literary language of Castile under Alfonso X the Wise (1221–84)), but a religious revival crushed much of the discourse under a Christian renaissance. Meanwhile, conflict ensued between the new mendicant orders: the

Dominicans, founded in 1216 by the Castilian St Dominic, with their appeal to reason and discipline through the mechanism of the Inquisition; and their bitter rivals the Franciscans, whose theological emotionalism was much esteemed in the Iberian kingdoms.

The Aragonese–Catalan kingdom lost Languedoc to France at the Battle of Muret in 1213, but expanded to Sicily after 1282 and Naples after 1442. Thereafter, Hispanic–Italian interchange, both commercial and cultural, took on an ever-growing intensity.

If Muret signalled the fall of the Aragonese–Catalans in Languedoc and encouraged their thrust towards Mediterranean sea-lanes, the Battle of Las Navas de Tolosa in 1212 marked the beginning of the end for Muslim al-Andalus. The power of the Caliphate had broken up into small entities known as *taifas* or 'party kings' ('party' in the sense of faction). Hegemony was in the hands of Muslim fundamentalists from North Africa, first the Almoravids (*c.* 1062–1147) and then the Almohads (until the defeat at Navas). By the mid-13th century Castile dominated the centre of the peninsula, with a Muslim client state in Granada. Its rivals were an aggressive Portugal, which was pushing by sea towards North Africa and into the Atlantic, and Aragon–Catalonia, which held half of Italy and remained a major player in the Mediterranean.

Just as in the rest of Western Europe, the Iberian Peninsula had evolved forms of loose devolution of power to locals, who could sustain some economic autarchy and generate fighting capacity. This cheap system of delegated governance took varying forms in the Iberian kingdoms. It was to some extent dictated by the frontier between Christian and Muslim areas, which was porous and open to trade but also subject to raids and warfare. The Black Death, which devastated the whole of Europe in the mid-14th century, had considerable impact on the Christian kingdoms. As in Germany, the epidemic set off waves of Christian attacks on Jews; as in France and England, the high mortality rate threw the older rural economy out of kilter and encouraged the new urban artisan and commercial production, oriented towards Castile's wool and Aragon's weaving trade. The end result, however, was to reinforce the authority of preachers, both Dominican and Franciscan, and to exalt the nobility at the expense of the Crowns: Castile, Aragon and Navarre all spent much of the 15th century in ugly civil war. Finally, two branches of the same family of bastard origin, the Trastámara, held the throne in Aragon and Castile. Cousins Ferdinand of Aragon and Isabel of Castile, married in 1469, established their undisputed control of each Crown, and created a peninsular superpower that set Portugal aside (but could not conquer it), annexed Muslim Granada in 1492 and, with Columbus's fateful journey, set up their joint pennant in the Caribbean.

Not possessing any unity beyond dynasty, these new 'Catholic kings' found crusading religion a strong unifying element: in 1492, the same year as the annexation of Granada, they expelled the Sephardic Jews who would not convert. Muslims were initially tolerated if nominally converted, but in 1609, after a series of bitter wars in the Granada

Columbus before Queen Isabella and King Ferdinand in a fanciful 19th-century historical painting. The success of his 1492 expedition helped the dynastic coalition of Castile and Aragon become a dominant world power for a century and a half.

mountains, the last Spanish *Moriscos* were shipped out by force, in a simple act of ethnic cleansing. Castile and Aragon were held by little more than religious exaltation and the thirst for expansion overseas to Africa or the New World. Ferdinand took control of the extended Aragonese holdings in Italy at a time when Valencians held the papacy, thus beginning almost two centuries of continuous war with French kings for hegemony beyond the Alps. Part of this struggle led Ferdinand to annex Navarre in 1515, leaving a rump state on the French side. In the process, modern firepower-based warfare was invented by the Spanish infantry formations known as *tercios*.

Overseas, 'Spain' – as the amalgamation of Castile, Aragon and Navarre was soon known abroad – and Portugal were both lucky at first. The Portuguese invaded the Indian Ocean and the East Indies just after the Ming emperor ordered the Chinese to abandon their own naval patrols: the Portuguese Empire thus expanded in a naval vacuum. Spain, in turn, took over the West Indies with the help of a secret weapon: the native population had no resistance to Old World viral diseases such as smallpox, measles and mumps. The immense number of deaths that this caused gave the Spanish a reputation for fierceness and cruelty that they have never lived down, and an inflated

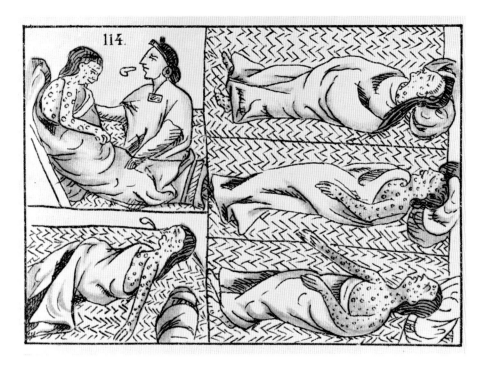

The manuscript of Bernardino de Sahagún's Historia General de las Cosas de Nueva España *(sent to Rome in 1580), includes depictions of Mexicans suffering from smallpox. Native Americans had never been exposed to Old World viruses, which now had a devastating epidemic effect with an immense death toll.*

sense of their own importance and valour, which sadly they have never outgrown. In the short term this capacity for 'biological warfare' was an extraordinary boon to the Spaniards, permitting the conquest of Mexico, Peru and much of the rest of the Americas. The weakness of the Native American population was compensated by the introduction of slaves from Africa, long exposed to Old World viruses. The surviving Amerindian peoples took with enthusiasm to the Spanish brand of Catholicism, which permitted Spanish colonization to take on a strongly cosmopolitan flavour.

Thus, apparently out of nowhere, Spain was suddenly a dominant power, capable of pushing aside France, England and anybody else to monopolize the Atlantic Ocean and make European affairs its tactical spin-off. But fortune was fickle. The two Trastámara branches died out, leaving a Habsburg heir, Charles I (1500–58), whose enthronement as Holy Roman Emperor Charles V coincided with the conquest of Mexico in 1519–21. Major revolts in Castile, Valencia and Mallorca in the early 1520s, in protest against foreigners in positions of power, only served to reinforce the strength of the Crown. Charles V also had to face Martin Luther's challenge of religious reform in Germany, which he did in the crusading spirit of his Spanish ancestors.

Charles failed in his vow to serve out his life as emperor and Crusader, and abdicated after making peace with the Protestant German princes in 1555. He split his inheritance: the Austrian lands went to his brother Ferdinand I, the Spanish realms to his son Philip II (1527–98). Philip tried to continue his father's policies, stamping out any trace of Protestantism in Castile and confronting Protestant protest in the Netherlands. The war with the Dutch, however, was a disaster: lasting eighty years (1568–1648), it drained Spanish income from the Americas and encouraged piracy, until finally Spanish control of the Atlantic sea-lanes collapsed and the treasure ships bringing the wealth of the New World back to the peninsula had to sail in convoy to defend themselves against enemy raiders. In the Mediterranean the Spaniards had fought the Turks to a standstill by the end of the 16th century.

Portugal brought Philip much-needed success. In 1581 he was able to annex the neighbouring kingdom. Now the peninsula was a single dynastic entity and the first true world power, stretching from Italy to Flanders and from Mexico to the Philippines. Spaniards were so confident that they actually thought they could take over China as they had done with Mexico and Peru. Perhaps the greatest expression of the new Spanish 'unipolar' system was the worldwide expansion of a new religious order, the Jesuits (established by a Castilian Basque in 1540), which brought an intense missionary to the Catholicism of the Counter-Reformation.

The fightback came from the Dutch and English, who managed to outmanoeuvre Philip's invasion attempt – the Great Armada – in 1588. There were other, later, armadas, but Dutch, English, French and even Scottish and Swedish corsairs broke the Spanish monopoly in the Atlantic and the Portuguese stranglehold in the Indian Ocean and the Pacific Rim. When in 1648 the Spanish king's representatives signed the European Treaty of Westphalia (and agreed to Dutch independence in the simultaneous Treaty of Münster), Spain was no longer hegemonic. Portugal split off in the war of 1640–68. Under the later Habsburgs of the 17th century, the Crown was served by chief ministers who, though powerful, were in no sense the equals of their contemporaries in France.

The period from the late 16th to the late 17th century was Spain's golden age, with major writers such as Cervantes, Lope de Vega and Calderón de la Barca establishing the Castilian language as 'Spanish', and painters, notably Velázquez, setting an aesthetic model for much of European posterity. Cultured protest took the form of economic writing called *arbitrismo*, erudite treatises that favoured simple solutions for complex problems, such as the construction of canals to stimulate internal trade.

Without effective leadership, and finally with an impotent king unable to produce an heir, Spain became a priceless pawn on the European chessboard after 1700. The War of

The Holy Roman Emperor Charles V at the Battle of Mühlberg in 1547, painted by Titian, his Venetian court painter, who portrayed Charles as the perfect Christian knight in battle against Lutheran heretics. In reality Charles was sick and gout-ridden; in 1555 he made peace with his enemies and abdicated in 1556.

Spanish Succession (1701–14) pitted the partisans of a Bourbon prince from France against another Habsburg as rival candidates for the throne. The French Philip V (1683–1746) finally won, but Spain's European possessions were broken up, and even Britain acquired toeholds on the peninsula (Gibraltar) and nearby islands (Minorca). Philip V's second wife was an ambitious Italian princess who bore her husband many sons and wanted Italian principalities for all of them. Enormous resources from the empire were now poured into endless dynastic wars. Philip's heirs (Ferdinand VI and Charles III, previously king of Naples) are usually presented as reforming monarchs among the mid-18th-century's so-called enlightened despots. Their main efforts were directed at a more efficient exploitation of imperial products and markets, and the recovery of status through a strong navy.

Portugal, Spain and France all expelled the Jesuits in the 1760s, but the Spanish Inquisition was still kept busy stopping books at the border, and Spain did not enjoy much of an Enlightenment. French style was observed in polite society but distrusted in popular terms. Despite territorial rivalries in North America, the American Revolution could be admired due to traditional animosity towards the British, but the French Revolution made it close to treasonable to be French in style (afrancesado), especially after the French attack on the Catholic Church in 1790. In 1795, however, Charles IV's chief minister Godoy restored the traditional French alliance in a stunning reversal. Spain was now drawn into French politics, and Napoleon took on the Royal Navy and lost both the French and the Spanish fleets at Trafalgar in 1805. He pushed for a general European embargo of British goods, which Portugal refused to join. A French attack on Portugal through Spain became an outright invasion of Spain itself, as Napoleon took advantage of a Bourbon family squabble and coup, dictating a constitution and setting his older brother Joseph on the throne. The Spanish administration acquiesced, but the lower and middle classes erupted and the entire country was consumed in a vicious conflict, part civil war, part war of national liberation, with British support for the 'patriot' cause. The French were expelled in 1813 and definitively defeated in 1814, but the 1812 constitution approved by a parliament held in Cadiz, under the protection of British naval guns, was disowned by Ferdinand VII (1784–1833), who had returned from French exile and was anxious to re-establish private cabinet rule. By then the effects on Spanish holdings in the Americas were decisive: by 1824, all the territory of the old empire now consisted of new republics independent of Madrid, and only the Antilles (Cuba and Puerto Rico) and the Philippines remained under Spanish control.

'Liberal' revolt in Cadiz in 1820 restored the constitution and set off the first of the European waves of revolution. The 'Holy Alliance' powers that had defeated Napoleon now asked for a new French invasion, this time to restore Ferdinand to absolutist rule. Where in 1808 French troops had met fury, they now had a military parade. The occupation lasted until 1827. By then protest was coming not from the Liberals but from the clerical Conservatives, who felt Ferdinand to be too indulgent.

Spain was almost continually at war with itself and had little energy for foreign adventures. Spanish Liberals opposed the ultra-Catholic, extreme-right 'Carlists' in a succession of internal wars (1846–49, and 1872–76). This internal strife was complicated after 1868 by Cuba, still Spanish territory: the island suffered thirty years of warfare until the military intervention of the United States in 1898, which definitively ended Spain's overseas empire.

There was a perennial obsession with the collapse of Spanish power in the Americas between 1810 and 1824, followed by the loss of the Caribbean islands and the Philippines in 1898. Spain's only major overseas efforts were directed at the invasion of Morocco, first attacked seriously in 1859–60, then with small border wars in 1893 and 1909. The sultanate became a co-protectorate split between France and Spain in 1912, with a cruel and costly

Generalíssimo Franco celebrating victory over the Republicans in Madrid in May 1939. His dictatorship was underpinned by the military and Rightists in a united 'National Movement'. Officially neutral but close to the Axis in the Second World War, due to the polarities of the Cold War he managed to stay in power until his death in 1975.

'pacification' struggle that lasted well over a decade. The upside of this internal rupture and instability was that Spain remained outside Europe's major conflicts between 1854 and 1871, and stayed neutral in the two World Wars.

Barcelona became the economic centre – in bitter rivalry with Madrid, the political capital – and blossomed culturally, with literature in Catalan rather than Castilian, and a sheer joy in architectural extravagance exemplified by Gaudí. Catalan nationalism facilitated the appearance of similar enthusiasms in the Basque Country and in Galicia. In general, the early 20th century saw a reflowering of Hispanic literature – especially essayism and poetry (most prominently that of García Lorca) – in what has been termed a 'silver age'. Even more important were the fine arts, with world-renowned figures such as Picasso, Miró and Dalí taking centre stage. The overthrow of the Bourbon dynasty and the proclamation of a new republic in 1931 (which included Catalan home rule) seemed linked to this sensation of cultural bloom. But the optimism did not last.

The Spanish Civil War (1936–39) was viewed with great excitement by the rest of the world, with the conflict between the Popular Front and the National Front symbolizing the wider struggle between revolution and fascism. But the conflict was in fact much more of an internal fight, a continuation of long-term confrontations within Spanish society, than a great ideological watershed. The victorious Franco dictatorship (1936–75) crushed the left, the Catalan and Basque nationalists, and all manner of what it viewed as cultural indiscipline. After the defeat of the Axis powers in 1945, the regime, although it held a firm grip, could not live down its bastard origins in the failed military coup that set off the Spanish Civil War in 1936 and was boycotted for its duration until Franco's death in 1975. This meant that economic recovery was slower than in much of the rest of the Continent, although it did take off in the 1960s. This facilitated ideological pacification and an apparently easy transition from dictatorship to democracy after 1975, under a re-established Bourbon monarchy. In 1977 the negotiated acceptance of Catalan autonomy led to a generalized redesign of the democratic political system (the new constitution of 1978), based on nineteen regional governments for all Spanish territory. What long-term form this compromise will ultimately take – as a full federation, and with what degree of devolution – remains the subject of intense political debate.

Spanish constitutional history has been bumpy: since 1808 no political system has lasted a full fifty years. Political division held back development of an efficient transportation system, and restrained production and the growth of internal consumption. The state played an excessively dominant role in Spanish society and the military had an overbearing importance in state affairs. Civil society was weak and polarized, tempted by revolutionary or counter-revolutionary movements with all-or-nothing attitudes. Parliamentary government was interrupted by army disquiet in the 19th century, while the 20th century was dominated by militarism.

A pedestrian walkway in Zaragoza. In many ways, Spain changed more between 1980 and 2000 than in the previous century. Now accustomed to being a wealthy, secularized society, Spain was hit by the global recession of 2008, which turned into a national depression with long-term effects.

By the mid-20th century, grinding rural poverty still held back what was already in essence an urban society rooted in out-of-date agrarian customs: indigenous *machismo* oppressed women, and traditional religiosity was strong and unfavourable to individual freedoms. Changes in the Catholic Church after 1962, together with the influx of non-Spanish tourists, would soon widen norms. The Franco-sponsored growth of consumer-oriented large-scale production provoked an impressive change, abetted by massive European funds after entry into the European Union in 1985. In little more than a generation, Spain went from being a family-centred, socially conservative country with a high birth rate to an extremely open society marked by one of the lowest birth rates in the world, with women participating in public life at higher levels than in Scandinavia. After the 1990s massive immigration from South America and Africa maintained population growth. Spain's future in the 21st century will depend on its capacity to sustain this kind of change, growth and openness in a much less favourable world economic climate.

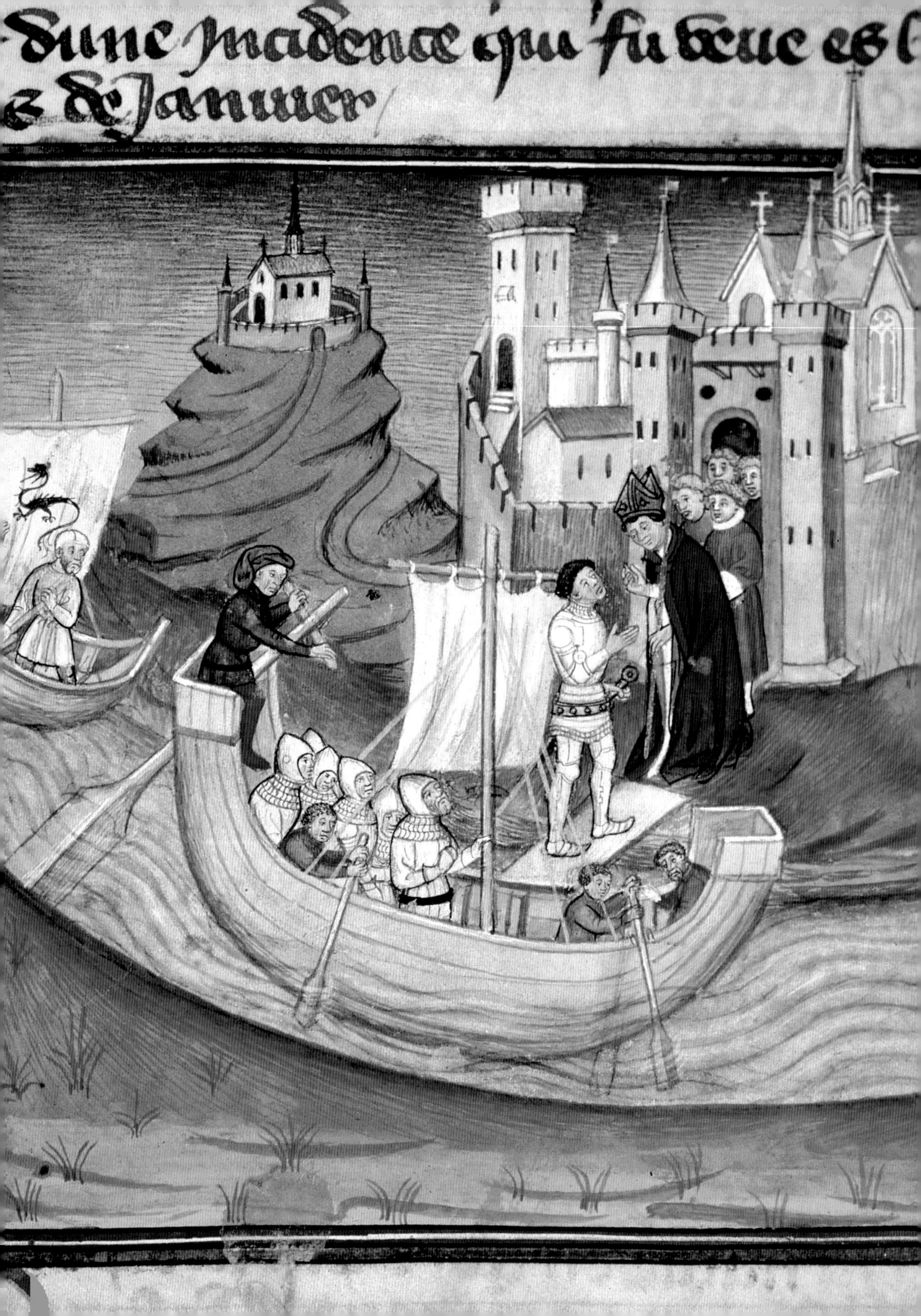

France

The history of the hexagon

I was born in Normandy and was brought up to believe that we were descended from the Vikings, a bunch of blond, blue-eyed ruffians who had invaded the region shortly after the reign of Charlemagne (r. 768–814): their Norse blood had turned us into Normans, the finest men in what had once been Roman Gaul and was now France. A second historical precept of my youth was that we Normans had conquered England in 1066 and brought civilization to that country. Eventually I had to give up this idea when I found out that, even before the arrival of William the Conqueror (*c.* 1028–87), the Saxons had small but pretty churches, so they were clearly not the savages I had believed them to be; and besides, the Domesday Book revealed quite a sophisticated level of housing and agriculture.

Nowadays all this is irrelevant. As far as my homeland of the Caen area of Basse-Normandie is concerned, the key historical event is now the D-Day landing of 6 June 1944. One day in late August 1944, I met my first British soldier and asked him for some sugar, a commodity in short supply; my English pronunciation was so appalling that he gallantly offered me a cigar. Since then, the anniversary of D-Day has become Normandy's biggest festival. The history of Normandy had spun on its axis, with its constant being sea landings: the 9th-century Vikings landing in Neustria (as it was then known), the Normans landing in England in 1066, and the British and their allies returning in 1944.

France may not always have been hexagonal in shape, but the hexagon has a particular symbolic strength. The country began as the original *Francia occidentalis* or Western Francia; then Louis XI (1423–83) absorbed the Duchy of Burgundy in the 15th century. In the 16th century Henry II (1519–59) made ridiculous attempts to invade Italy (although these did bring us cultural benefits), but then succeeded in conquering part of Lorraine; and a hundred years later Louis XIV (1638–1715) advanced into

The Normans, led by the Viking chief Rollo, besieged the town of Chartres in 911, but Bishop Gantelme succeeded in warding off their forces by displaying the tunic of the Virgin Mary, as seen in this miniature from The Chronicle of St Denis, *printed by Antoine Vérard in 1493.*

Alsace and the Nord and Pas-de-Calais, taking over a considerable area of the former Southern Netherlands.

Meanwhile the Occitan south (Toulouse, Montpellier and so on) was gradually conquered by the French from the 13th century onwards: through conflict in the case of Languedoc, more peacefully in the case of Auvergne and Limousin. Brittany became part of France in the 16th century. The Pays Basque became French in 1453, though without impinging on its ancient traditions – just as it had once been unwittingly English under the Plantagenets.

The hexagon of land that was now France was patiently reinforced. While not fixed, it defied the passing of centuries: although temporarily bereft of Alsace-Lorraine between 1871 and 1918, and again in 1940–45, it regained its canonical shape soon enough. To paraphrase Louis XV (1710–74), it could be said that it 'will last as long as I do' ('il durera bien autant que moi') or, in fact, even longer. If any element of the past remains present, it is the map of France that appears on the TV weather report every night.

Another indication of the past in modern France is its regions, or more precisely its ethno-linguistic areas. Ten such regions can be distinguished, relics of a distant past thrown into the national melting pot. The largest is the region of the *langue d'oïl* (the modern French language), which roughly makes up the northern two-thirds of the hexagon, consisting of some sixty *départements*. Born from the Roman invasion of the lands of Gaul, this region was later seasoned with a mixture of Germanic elements, and finally extended towards the south: the 'elite' culture of the Ile-de-France was carried

TIMELINE

58–51 BCE Gaul is conquered by the Romans under Julius Caesar

800 CE Charlemagne is crowned emperor

843 The Treaty of Verdun divides Charlemagne's empire between his three sons, separating France and Germany

1328 Start of the Hundred Years' War in which the English kings assert their claim to the French throne

1562 The French wars of religion begin, ending in 1598 when Henry IV asserts toleration of religion with the Edict of Nantes

1643 Louis XIV comes to the throne; by his death in 1715 he has expanded France's boundaries, increased the wealth of the nation and built his grand palace at Versailles

1685 Revocation of the Edict of Nantes

1789 The French Revolution begins, with a republic declared in 1792

1793 Louis XVI is executed; the Jacobin Terror begins

1799 Napoleon Bonaparte is appointed as first consul and crowned emperor in 1805

1815 The final defeat of Napoleon at Waterloo; the monarchy is re-established

1830 Revolution brings Louis-Philippe to the throne; he is overthrown in 1848

1852 A Second Empire is established by Napoleon III

1870 Defeat by Germany ends the empire and institutes the Third Republic in 1871

1904 The Entente Cordiale between Britain and France is signed

1914–18 The First World War, much of it fought on French soil

1940 Conquest of France by the Nazis; Charles de Gaulle sets up a French government in exile in London

1945 The Allied invasion liberates France and the republic is restored, with de Gaulle as president

1958 De Gaulle initiates the Fifth Republic in response to a crisis over the war of independence in the colony of Algeria

1968 *Les événements*, the student uprising in prostest against de Gaulle's conservative presidency

2003 French president Jacques Chirac leads European opposition to the invasion of Iraq

A portrait of Louis XIV in magnificent robes, by Hyacinthe Rigaud (1701). The emperor's aim was to impress not only his subjects, but also the distinguished foreigners who came to see him, including representatives of the British upper classes, who were only able to contemplate His Majesty during the short periods of peace between the two nations.

down to the southern parts of the country by policies of centralization and linguistic assimilation in the 19th and 20th centuries.

The other regions are mainly, but not solely, seen as peripheral. The oldest is the Pays Basque, heir to a language that may date back to the Palaeolithic era: it is linked to both France and Spain. Although the current economic crisis has led many Spanish Basques to embrace socialist politics, the nationalist impulse nonetheless remains strong south of the Pyrenees, with its terrorist wing ETA. The French Basque country remains closely bound to the rest of the French nation, but it nevertheless constitutes a 'reserve' base to which ETA's clandestine forces sometimes retreat.

With more recent, but still ancient, roots are the northern and northeastern regions, born of the Germanic invasions of the first millennium. These include the Flemish-speaking region of French Flanders, with Dunkirk and Cassel in the far north – a former part of the Southern Netherlands that was annexed in the 17th century. Some of its nationalist elements were temporarily tempted into collaboration with the Nazis, but now it is practically integrated into the dominant French culture. Further south, Lorraine and Alsace, or more precisely Moselle and Alsace, were annexed respectively under the reigns of Henry II (r. 1547–59), Louis XIII (r. 1610–43) and Louis XIV (r. 1643–1715), and to varying degrees suffered through difficult times between 1870 and 1945. Re-annexation to Germany, then back to France between the wars, was followed by the violence of Nazi occupation from 1939 to 1945, with the young men of Alsace-Lorraine known as the *malgré-nous* (lit. 'despite ourselves') forcibly conscripted and sent to the Russian front. Since the Second World War, Alsace-Moselle has led a double life, at once French and pan-European in outlook.

Weeping bystanders during the Nazi occupation of France (1940–44). Sadness was widespread, but the French soon showed they were still able to laugh at life. The period could well be called Shakespearean, combining bleak tragedy with light-hearted interludes. The figure of de Gaulle retrospectively dominates this five-year period, but does not encapsulate every aspect of it.

In the northwest is Brittany with its Celtic language, the fruit of late colonization by immigrants from Cornwall and Wales apparently fleeing from invading Anglo-Saxons. Brittany is an integral part of France but retains a distinctive personality, with a lively school of Breton history and ongoing attempts to resurrect the ancient language. In the south are the Romance-speaking areas. Their attachment to France, although not without tragedies, has been accomplished relatively smoothly because shared Latin roots unite them with the north of the country. Among them are the large group of Occitan speakers (occupying some thirty *départements*), famed for the poetry of their medieval troubadours, and for the poetic and linguistic rebirth inspired by the great writer Frédéric Mistral (1830–1914) in the early 20th century. Attempts to revive the Occitan or Provençal language are frequent, but face a double challenge as a result of immigration from both the northern French, many of them retired, and from those leaving former colonies in North Africa, who find the climate in Provence similar to the one they left behind.

There are Catalans in the *département* of Pyrénées-Orientales, the result of another annexation carried out by Louis XIII and Louis XIV, perhaps tempted by the prosperity

An image capturing the dawning of a peripheral form of nationalism in Corsica. Militants have vandalized signposts, crossing out the Italian-influenced place names traditionally used by maps and tourist guidebooks, and leaving only the Corsican names.

of Barcelona. And there is Corsica, with its own Italianate Romance language. This island is home to a strong nationalist movement, that has been responsible over many years for acts of terrorism which, although relatively mild in terms of the number of human casualties, have dissuaded financiers from investing in the 'Isle of Beauty', as Corsica is nicknamed. Less well known is the extensive Franco-Provençal region, which combines linguistic features of both French and Occitan, and covers the Rhône-Alpes: Lyon, Saint-Etienne, Grenoble, Savoie and – beyond the borders of France itself – the French-speaking part of Switzerland. The dialect of this area is well established but it has never had a great writer to bring a particular sense of character and unity.

The state is evidently a central part of any historical vision of France. Let us begin with Louis XIV's 'L'Etat, c'est moi' ('The state is myself'). In fact, there is no certainty that he ever uttered those words. At the most, one might say that the statement fits Louis's style of rule, particularly in the earlier part of his reign, when he encouraged a cult of personality and sycophancy up to about 1685. Later, however, beset by difficult circumstances, Louis grew more humble: 'Il faut se soumettre' ('One must submit [to the will of God]') he said, as he faced the terrible losses that devastated his family. The ageing

Louis's thoughts about statehood are encapsulated in the words spoken on his deathbed: 'Je m'en vais mais l'Etat demeurera toujours' ('I am leaving, but the state will always remain'). This echoes the medieval English idea of the king's two bodies: the body politic and the body natural. Louis was making a similar separation of his own mortal self and the extensive superstructure of the state.

Louis XIV's machinery of state was so full of potential that several generations later it would emerge definitively from the beheaded body of Louis XVI (1754–93) and survive the fall of several monarchical regimes, and even the disastrous defeat of 1870, to form the core of a future – republican – great power. Yet what did it comprise? The apparatus of his state was already powerful enough to maintain a degree of autonomy from the monarch himself. It included *officiers civils*, precursors of modern civil servants, who purchased their own posts and could pass them on to their sons, making each office-holder independent from central government.

The distinction between monarch and state had been asserted a quarter of a century before Louis XIV by Cardinal Richelieu (1585–1642) on his own deathbed. When asked if he forgave his enemies, he replied simply: 'Des ennemis, je n'en ai eu d'autres que ceux de

A triple portrait of Cardinal Richelieu by Philippe de Champaigne. Between 1580 and 1723 France was controlled by powerful statesmen, among them Richelieu who opposed the British at first and later supported the German Protestants despite his own Catholicism. Cardinal de Retz said that he used to 'thunder rather than govern'.

l'Etat' ('As regards enemies, I had none but those who were against the State'). This primary distinction was already embodied at the heart of the growing French nation.

What has changed over the centuries is not the idea of the state but its sheer size. In the 1520s, under the rule of Francis I (r. 1515–47), 15 million Frenchmen were governed in the name of the king by some 5,000 *officiers*. Under Louis XIV the number of *officiers* had grown to 50,000, and by the eve of the Revolution to 100,000. Today the public sector in France employs several million people. The central nucleus of the state is still present, but its dimensions have radically changed, having expanded to an extraordinary degree, although the efficiency of the system has not risen in proportion.

France's history includes many regrettable events, several of which are far from simple, including the St Bartholomew's Day massacre of Huguenots in 1572; the Revocation of the Edict of Nantes in 1685, which had offered toleration to Protestants; the Jacobin Terror of 1793,

This caricature reflects the realities of the Terror, which lasted from August 1792 until the summer of 1794 and beyond. The French Revolution as a whole was a larger process that lasted much longer, until 1877, from the monarchy to the rule of the French Republic, through years of anguish and upheaval.

which led to the execution of thousands of royalists; and the persecution and deportation of the Jews during the Nazi occupation (1940–44).

However, France has many achievements of which it is rightly proud – though far fewer than those of Britain, whose accomplishments across the world are immense. In this respect, France is closer to countries such as Italy, which is legitimately proud of the art of its Renaissance; Germany and its scientific advances in the 19th century; and Spain with the literature of its golden age. French achievements include its early literature, particularly from the early Middle Ages (the *Song of Roland* easily bears comparison with the Anglo-Saxon epic *Beowulf*); the Romanesque art that is original and unique to southern France; Gothic architecture, rooted in the Ile-de-France area and in Normandy, but spreading far beyond the modern borders of France; the medieval Sorbonne with its network of colleges; Renaissance literature and thought from Rabelais and Montaigne onwards; the religious tolerance established by Henry IV (1553–1610) in the Edict of Nantes (1598) at a time when nothing similar existed in Europe outside the Netherlands;

In the late 17th and early 18th century, the French capital was no longer Paris, but Versailles. The château, with its spectacular Hall of Mirrors, became an architectural icon for the whole of Europe. It was here that Louis XIV kept the aristocrats under his thumb, housing them in small palace rooms like tenants in a modern tower block.

and the support offered by Richelieu, a Catholic cardinal, to European Protestants during the Thirty Years' War, support that would protect France and perhaps the rest of Europe from falling under the rule of an inquisitorial Catholic Church. Another of the country's great achievements is its 17th-century classical literature. France may never have had a Homer or a Shakespeare, but la Bruyère, la Rochefoucauld, Saint-Simon, Molière, Racine and Tallemant des Réaux were all worthy authors.

More generally, Gallic achievements must include the entire reign of Louis XIV. Even though his brazen nationalism and institutionalized religious discrimination should be counted among the failures of our nation, the flowering of the luxury arts and the architecture of Versailles produced magnificent imitations right across the Continent and even among the British aristocracy. Nor should French science be forgotten, inspired by Jean-Baptiste Colbert, founder of the Paris Observatory and a driving force behind the development of the market in luxury goods. Indeed, the whole of the European 18th century was a French creation in many respects, including the universality of our language throughout the Continent, the philosophy of the Enlightenment, and the kingdom's economic growth under Louis XV and even Louis XVI.

The balance sheet of the French Revolution – a matter of pride or one of regret? – should be examined carefully. If it does not show an overall profit, this is because the toll of the Terror tends to be (wrongly) subtracted from the sum of benefits gained through the great event. But in the months between the Fall of the Bastille on 14 July 1789 and the storming of the Tuileries Palace by the mob in August 1792, the French have nothing to be ashamed of. After the end of the Terror the Directoire did what it could to safeguard the basic gains of the Revolution, such as the introduction of equal rights and the removal of power from the aristocracy and nobility.

Even Napoleon (1769–1821) should not necessarily be consigned to the dustbin of history. The countries of Latin America, at least, have often considered the Corsican general to be the catalyst of their liberation from Spain, a country weakened by the terrible Peninsular War waged under the reign of the emperor.

What the writer and journalist Léon Daudet called the 'stupid 19th century' was in fact a successful amalgam of French elements with English and German ones: the Romantic movement, for example, which began as a synthesis between a kind of medievalism rooted in the ancien régime and the emotional advances of the French Revolution. France adopted distinctly Anglophile policies in the first half of the century under Louis XVIII, Louis-Philippe, and Napoleon III, who was a close friend of Queen Victoria. The foundations of the Entente Cordiale, which was agreed in 1904 by Edward VII and Théophile Delcassé and which paved the way for the First World War, were laid down in the 1830s and 1840s by Louis-Philippe and his prime minister François Guizot.

The Third Republic, or *the* Republic as it was simply known, was born on 4 September 1870 and became a remarkably sturdy regime that has governed France under various numbers – Third, Fourth, Fifth – for almost 140 years (discounting the four years of German occupation). This long-lasting system is something of which our country can be proud, unlike the fragile monarchies and empires that existed between 1800 and 1870. It is worth mentioning the admirable resistance of the French working classes, together with the nation's elite, on the battlefields of the First World War. I cannot see what Europe would have gained from a victory of the armies of Kaiser Wilhelm II. After the Second World War, Charles de Gaulle (1890–1970) reintroduced a monarchical element into our republican constitution. This was overall a success, even if some of the presidents who succeeded him have been justly ridiculed.

France also led the way in the post-war creation of the new Europe. French statesmen played a key part: Aristide Briand (1862–1932), too little recognized, through the 1920s and early 1930s; the Catholic statesmen with links of varying strengths to German

Catholicism, including one great Frenchman, Robert Schuman (1886–1963); and the moderate layman Jean Monnet (1888–1979).

So there are many sources of pride among countless failures and missteps. They do not equal the achievement of Britain or the United States, but they have nonetheless given France a decent reputation in Europe.

Foreigners have had plenty of misunderstandings about France and its history; I would like to mention just a few.

Some historians have tried to draw comparisons between Napoleon and Hitler, but the differences are so fundamental as to render any comparison meaningless. They have also criticized Louis XIV's 1685 Revocation of the Edict of Nantes, which suppressed Protestantism and caused many Huguenots to leave, but they tend to forget that Britain's policy – if it can be so called – towards Catholic Ireland has hardly been more hon-ourable than that of the Sun King towards his Huguenot subjects. The Revocation was not an isolated case in European history.

It is from some Americans that misunderstandings of our history most often spring. Franklin D. Roosevelt (1882–1945), for example, did not understand de Gaulle (the same is true of Churchill, although he originally supported de Gaulle when he arrived in London in 1940). Perhaps the general's arrogance explains this: because he had an aristocratic-sounding name, went to Mass and behaved like a curt and authoritarian military man, some French in London mistook him for a man of the far right, and passed this impression on to their British and American friends. Roosevelt, unbelievably, planned a buffer state between de Gaulle's France and Germany, and between France and the Netherlands, fashioned out of Belgium and Alsace-Lorraine, that keystone of French patriotism. This was clearly foolish and it required all the tenacity of the British foreign secretary Anthony Eden, an inveterate Francophile, to dissuade him. Another Allied idea was the installation of AMGOT (Allied Military Government for Occupied Territories) following France's liberation. The tri-umphal arrival of de Gaulle in Paris was all that prevented this monumental act of folly.

Roosevelt had a tendency towards these kinds of misunderstandings. In fact, the British and American press often supported de Gaulle when he was facing hostility from Roosevelt and later from Churchill. This anti-de Gaulle attitude persisted to some degree after 1945: hence the temptation, particularly in Britain, to mistake de Gaulle for a Fascist when he took power again in 1958.

Another example of a misjudgment of France came at the start of the Iraq War in 2003. President Jacques Chirac (b. 1932) found himself virtually alone in Europe in opposing this act of pure aggression. I am no unconditional supporter of Chirac: his dissolution of the French Parliament in 1997, which allowed his opponents to come to power, was ill-advised; more serious still was his referendum on the European constitu-tion in 2005. His intention may have been to embarrass the French socialists, but the

If the whims of Hitler had decreed it, Paris could have been destroyed in 1944 as many other European cities were.
But thanks to the fortunate combination of the Allies, Generals Charles de Gaulle and Philippe Leclerc, and perhaps
a certain moderation by the Nazi forces, the City of Light managed to survive and remains as eternal as ever.

resulting disaster was a harsh blow to the European Union. None of this, however, was as important as his attempts to prevent war in Iraq.

A side effect of Chirac's initiative was an intense campaign of anti-French propaganda. United States National Security Advisor Condoleezza Rice spoke of punishing France. French fries were renamed 'freedom fries', a ridiculous episode that became the tip of an iceberg of American Francophobia. Did the departure of George W. Bush's regime in the United States make this Francophobia only a bad memory? I'm not sure. Recently a radio broadcast from across the Channel or across the Atlantic (I forget which) described a speech by a leading French politician as 'very confused, very French'. I cannot say that such a juxtaposition is fair to France or the French people.

DINA KHAPAEVA

Russia

Fractures in the fabric of culture

The Bolshevik revolution of 1917, according to the poet Josef Brodsky (1940–96), launched an epoch of 'permanent terror'. During the years of Soviet rule 50–55 million people became victims of repression and were physically and morally maimed; 11–13 million were executed or perished in prison. Lack of accurate data about the number of victims is a striking illustration of the neglect of humanity during the Soviet regime. The civil war of 1918, the forced collectivization, the deportation of nationals, the Great Famine of 1932–33, the purges of 1937, the Siege of Leningrad in 1941–44 and the Great Patriotic War are all symbols of the destruction of civilians and soldiers not only by enemies but by their own government and people. The regime lasted for seventy-four years and buried three generations as well as numerous age-old traditions.

Yet in 2007, when I conducted an opinion poll with the historian Nikolay Koposov in St Petersburg, Kazan and Ulyanovsk, we found that more than half of Russians considered the Soviet past to have had a positive impact on contemporary Russia. Over two-thirds referred to the years 1922 to 1953, when Joseph Stalin (1878–1953) was leader of the Soviet Union, as a golden age, when 'people were kinder, less selfish, and more sympathetic', and 'the country was kept in order'. Eighty per cent had no doubt that the history of their country should only stir feelings of pride, and over two-thirds of respondents admitted no guilt or historical responsibility. Nowadays schoolbooks increasingly regard Stalinism as a justified measure that was necessary for the modernization of the country, while historical monographs present Soviet history as a celebrated continuation of the glorious history of the Russian Empire. Yet people do not try to conceal the crimes or forget them – over 90 per cent of Russians are aware of the repressions and the enormous number of victims.

A Merchant Woman Drinking Tea, *by Boris Kustodiev, 1918. Kustodiev grew up in a merchant's house where he observed the way of life of a class that proved to be doomed. Later he used these memories to create his colourful paintings. He died in Leningrad in 1927.*

The attitude of my countrymen towards the Soviet past cannot be fully explained as a symptom of apathy or indifference. It reveals (and not for the first time in Russian history) a denial of fundamental cultural values, humanism and humane society.

Russia has undoubtedly created genuine cultural masterpieces and can still do so. But there has nevertheless been a constant and hostile attitude towards culture and civilization, manifested in two fundamental events: the founding of the Russian state and the adoption of Orthodoxy. Both are an expression of Russia's attitude towards the West, and initiated the leitmotif of Russian history: a steady fascination with the West, coupled with an urge to excel it in order to escape its influence. Russian history could be viewed as a chain of fractures in the fabric of culture, as a constant disruption of the elite's attempts to spread Western culture and civilization to the immense forests, boundless spaces and unpopulated areas of the vast country.

The first cornerstone of Russian national identity is the story of the founding of the state, and it questions the ability of Russians to create a state on their own, and to respect and keep order in it. The most ancient source on the history of the ancient Rus, the 11th/12th-century *Tale of Bygone Years*, also known as *The Russian Primary Chronicle*, conveys the following events. In 862 the Slavic tribes in the major centres of ancient Rus (Novgorod, Beloozero and Izborsk) refused to pay tribute to the Norsemen (Vikings, also known as Varangians) and fell into a state of brigandage and anarchy. Not being able to stop the unrest, they asked the Norsemen to be their masters and reign over them. The chronicler informs us that Rurik, the Varangian prince, did not respond right away,

TIMELINE

862 Varangian princes found the state of Rus centred on Kiev

988 Baptism of the Rus by Vladimir the Great

1230s The Mongol invasions destroy the state of Rus and raze Moscow

c. 1480 Moscovy's control over most of the Russian lands is confirmed; Ivan III adopts the title of tsar

1547–84 Ivan IV ('the Terrible') creates a despotic regime, using 'Oprichnina' as an instrument of terror

1598–1613 The 'Time of Troubles', a dramatic period of political unrest, natural disasters and foreign invasion

c. 1580–c. 1660 Russia expands across Asia to the Pacific

1703 Peter the Great founds St Petersburg as a European capital

1812 Russia is invaded and Moscow burned by Napoleon

1825 The Decembrist uprising demands the abolition of serfdom and the replacement of the monarchy by a republic

1861 The emancipation of the serfs by Tsar Alexander II

1905 First Russian revolution against tsarist autocracy

1917 Abdication of Tsar Nicholas II; the October Revolution begins Bolshevik rule, followed by civil war

1932–33 The Great Famine

1936–38 Joseph Stalin begins the Great Purges

1941 Invasion of the Soviet Union by Nazi Germany brings huge losses but eventual victory in the Great Patriotic War

1955 Formation of the Warsaw Pact, consolidating Soviet control in Eastern Europe

1956 Condemnation of the Stalin 'cult of personality', known as the Thaw

1991 Collapse of the Soviet Union; beginning of democratic reforms

2000 Establishment of an authoritarian regime of so-called 'sovereign democracy'

'being afraid of their feral appearance and temper'. Thus, according to legend, the Norsemen who came to Rus and founded the first state were not conquerors in the way that William the Conqueror was in England. They were freely invited by the people who thereby acknowledged their inability to govern themselves. Even the name Rus itself appears to be of Norse origin: according to the *Tale of Bygone Years*, 'The name Rus came from the Varangians, and nowadays the people of Novgorod belong to the tribe of Varangians, though initially they were Slavs'.

This story has long been remembered. The origin of Rus was a topical subject of debate between the Westernizers and Slavophiles in the 19th century, as well as Westernizers and nationalists in the Soviet era. 'Normanists' insisted on the dominant role of Scandinavians (Norsemen or Normans) in the formation of Kievan Rus, while anti-Normanists insisted on the exceptional role of the Slavs. An acknowledgment of the fact that Rus was founded by the Norsemen supported the idea that Russia should follow the Western path of development, while the opposite thesis supported the idea of Russia's unique mission and its independence from the West.

The sense of the Norman theory for Russian self-actualization was outlined in the *Course in Russian History* by Russian historian Vasiliy

This manuscript, copied in the 15th century, is the only ancient illuminated copy of the Tale of Bygone Years, *compiled in the 11th and early 12th centuries. Designed in the style of the Byzantine universal chronicles, it presents the history of ancient Russia.*

Klyuchevskiy (1841–1911): 'There was nothing extraordinary or unprecedented in the events, calling on princes for assistance. It is not something that happened only in our country – such events were quite common in Western Europe of those times.' The historian's desire to present the call to the Varangians as a military draft and to interpret this event as 'ordinary' in the history of any European state is evidence of how morbid this issue remained for Russia's national identity. Klyuchevskiy was, in fact, an advocate of the Norman theory: he emphasized the exceptional role of Varangian princes in the formation of Russian statehood, the princes comprising the ruling class or 'Rus' and turning

The Golden-Locked Angel, dating from the 12th century and depicting the Archangel Gabriel, is an outstanding example of icon painting. Like many icons of the period it was painted in the Byzantine style; the spread of Christian traditions from the Byzantine Empire resulted in Byzantine artists and architects coming to ancient Russia.

the Slavs into a subdued population: 'The Russian state was formed by the activities of Askold and later Oleg [Varangian followers of Rurik] in Kiev. Political consolidation came from Kiev and not Novgorod. The Varangian princedom in Kiev had become the kernel for unification of Slavic and Finnish tribes, which can be considered as an initial form of the Russian state.' The only thing that was unacceptable for Klyuchevskiy in

Norman theory was the implication that Russians were incapable of developing their own social order.

The second cornerstone of Russian history – the adoption of the Orthodox faith, which was to become a major source of opposition to the West – comprises three events. These were the conversion and mass baptism of the Rus by Prince Vladimir the Great in 988; the East–West Schism in 1054, when the Pope in Rome and the Byzantine Patriarch irrevocably cursed each other; and the fall of Constantinople to the Ottoman Turks in 1453, after which Moscow, known as 'the Third Rome', proclaimed itself the only bearer of the Orthodox mission and heir to the Byzantine Empire.

The ancient Slavs in Rus had barely been touched by Byzantine, Roman, Greek or Arabic culture. Byzantium was profoundly alien to the local population: its influence was limited to the transfer of religious beliefs and artistic styles brought by touring priests and artists from abroad. Irregular contact meant that the legacy of Byzantium could influence only the representatives of the educated elite.

The conversion of the Rus was implemented by the Varangian princes. According to legend, Vladimir the Great, after having been baptized so that he could marry Princess Anna, sister of the Byzantine emperors Basil II and Constantine VIII, forced his subjects to the River Dnieper and had them baptized. Traces of this forced conversion can be seen in the double religion and widespread pagan cults of Russian villages that still survive today.

The Military Gallery in the Winter Palace, St Petersburg, is one of the main monuments to the victory over Napoleon (1812–14). Built by the Italian architect Carlo Rossi, its walls are adorned with paintings by English artist George Dawe of the generals who took part in the campaign.

The first code of laws, the so-called *Ruskaya Pravda*, was probably created by foreign Christian judges – Greeks or Southern Slavs – in the 11th century in order to abolish, or at least soften, 'some indigenous customs particularly abhorrent to the moral and legal sense of Christian judges, who were cultivated by Byzantine ecclesiastical and civil law'. The fact that legend proclaimed these vital institutions to have emerged out of forcible intervention affected attitudes to law and order, culture and morality. People perceived culture and civilization as alien and adverse, something enforced by the foreign rulers.

The ensuing inferiority complex underlies Russia's national identity, and the country and its people have never been able to respond convincingly to it. It has generated the ambition not only to be like the West and Europe, but to surpass them. Hence the frequent themes in Russian history: Rus protected Europe from the Mongols in the 13th century, Russia rescued Europe from the yoke of Napoleon in the 19th century, the Soviet Union saved the world from fascism in the 20th century, and so on.

Profound uncertainty about national identity, which some tried to explain as Russia's intermediate position between East and West, was in fact rooted in the contradictory efforts to become as Europe, to surpass Europe and to deny the values of Europe. Repeated attempts of the ruling elite to exceed the West have resulted in disastrous counteractions. The long history of the oppression of culture and civilization and the failure of Westernization are woven into Russia's historical narrative, and have proven to be deeply embedded in national consciousness. On a personal level this conflict became a source of dilemma and psychological conflict. The debauchery and scandals described in the novels of Dostoyevsky (1821–81) are evidence of such conflict – small acts of rebellion in which an individual disputes the values of culture and civilization. In this respect Dostoyevsky is a truly Russian writer.

Another manifestation of this conflict between East and West was the reforms of Peter the Great (1676–1725), who tried to transform Russia using the model of advanced European countries of that time, notably Holland. Peter's reforms covered all aspects of society, from public and church administration to making the nobility wear European dress; from educational and cultural reforms (including the establishment of a university and an academy of sciences) to modernization of the economy and army; from building the new capital at St Petersburg to the formation of the navy. Yet all this was implemented via tyrannical measures. Peter's serfs paid for his reforms with thousands of lives, and in the forty years of his reign the population of Russia fell from 13 to 11 million. Even the introduction of European culture among the Russian nobility required force to achieve, which became the subject of unconcealed admiration during the Soviet era. Peter's reforms made the cultural divide within Russian society even deeper: the contrast between the lifestyle and behaviour of a tiny elite and that of the mass of illiterate peasantry was huge, as they remained culturally, politically and economically unaffected by the reforms and kept the lifestyle of old Rus until 1917. The reforms of Peter the Great evoked an increased hatred of cultural achievements and civilization in the 'simple folk'.

Debate about the role and significance of Peter's reforms began in 1836 with the publication of the *Philosophical Letters* by Pyotr Chaadaev (1794–1856), in which he criticized Russia's isolation and backwardness. It continued for the second half of the 19th century between Westernizers (eminent writers, composers and historians such as Ivan Turgenev, Nikolai Melgunov and Vasiliy Botkin) and Slavophiles, upholders of the unique and messianic path of Russian development based on orthodoxy and autocracy (Aleksey Khomyakov, Ivan Kireevsky and Konstantin Aksakov). In these debates the Norman theory acquired a special significance while Russian Orthodox chauvinism ripened into a denial of

Western civilization and culture. These debates also prepared the ground for a new denial of the West based on the Marxist theory of class struggle.

Another fissure in Russian society was often mentioned by Russian historians: that of serfdom, an institution that expressed a particular attitude of the ruling class towards its people as captured and colonized. The Decembrist uprising (14 December 1825) was an attempt to reform Russian society on a European model. The Decembrists demanded both the abolition of serfdom and the replacement of the monarchy with a republican form of government. The failure of the uprising was another painful rent in the thin layer of culture and civilization. Serfdom was perceived as an expression of Russia's attitude towards the West by both its supporters (the ruling elite, although usually educated in Europe and admirers of the Enlightenment ideals, were not willing to abolish serfdom until 1861) and its opponents. At the same time, serfdom had created among the peasants a powerful perception of government, law and culture as something foreign, hostile and imposed by force.

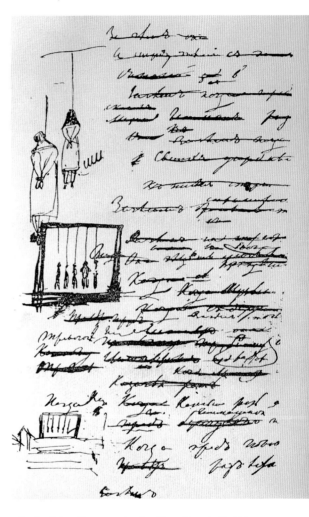

This sketch (1825) by poet and national hero Alexander Pushkin shows the execution of five of the Decembrist revolutionaries (Sergey Muravyov-Apostol, Mikhail Bestuzhev-Ryumin, Pyotr Kakhovsky, Pavel Pestel and Kondraty Ryleyev). Pushkin himself was in exile at the time, condemned for his radical verses.

This attitude towards culture and civilization reached its culmination in the October Revolution of 1917. It was not only the crowds of illiterate soldiers, sailors, workers and their power-hungry leaders who were overwhelmed by the feeling of heady excitement from the triumph of vandalism and the destruction of public order; so, too, were many eminent Russian intellectuals. Vivid examples are the famous poems 'Scythians' and 'Twelve' by Alexander Blok (1880–1921), in which the poet glorifies the ecstasy of 'casting off the chains' of culture and civilization. The atrocities of the first decades of Soviet rule and the destruction of Russia's modest cultural capital remain a tragic chasm in the 20th century.

This attitude could, to some extent, explain the destiny of the Russian intelligentsia. The themes of exile, imprisonment and execution have long been common in the

Vladimir Ilyich Ulyanov, universally known as Lenin, at the May Day demonstrations in Moscow, 1918, inciting the masses with slogans and exhortations to 'expropriate the expropriators'. The brutal mass executions of 'foreign class elements' together with the plundering of property known as the Red Terror laid the foundation for the Soviet regime.

biographies of top Russian writers and artists – to the point that not being harassed by the state could be regarded as a sign of marginality. The Soviets officially considered the intelligentsia a 'socially alien group', and the mass annihilation of intellectuals was a conscious Bolshevik policy. Murder of the country's best writers, poets, composers and artists was accompanied by an attack on intelligentsia cultural values and modes of behaviour. The state's distrust of intellectuals reflected popular attitudes towards better-educated compatriots. One episode reflecting this traditional mentality is especially telling. In the late 1880s the Narodniki 'back to the land' movement inspired several hundred noble Russians, who felt guilty about their privilege, to dress in traditional peasant fashion and move to Russian villages with a mission to educate and enlighten the peasantry. Yet the peasants felt nothing but mistrust and suspicion: most of the Narodniki were denounced to the police, beaten up or humiliated. Neglect of intellectual work and suspicion of intellectuals as unearthly fools or cowardly social parasites remains widespread today, even though almost one in three citizens of major Russian cities possesses a diploma of higher education.

Bolshevik ideology was built on an opposition between Russia and the West, between what was referred to as 'the Soviet state of workers and farmers' and Western capitalism. Soviet propaganda presented the bourgeois West as an embodiment of all evils. The determination of Soviet leaders from Stalin to Khrushchev to 'catch up with the West and to exceed it' in all spheres of life in order to prove the superiority of socialism over capitalism attracted the Russian people to the West hidden behind the Iron Curtain, and made it even more alluring and mysterious.

The last twenty years have seen another indicative break. Indeed, the idealization of the West has never been stronger than in the late 1980s and early 1990s. For a short time the West was the unambiguous choice as the model for transforming post-Communist Russia into a free democratic society, and this became a basis of government reforms that were strongly supported by the general public. The idealization of the West turned into a denial of everything Soviet, and all the drawbacks of socialism were explained in terms of Russia's deviation from the mainstream Western path of development for humankind after the Bolsheviks had come to power. The West became a new social project, creating a way out of the historical impasse into which the society had been driven by socialism. In the perestroika era of the 1980s Russia was consumed with denouncing Stalinism. It would have seemed logical to expect that Western-oriented intellectuals – leaders in the search for truth about the Soviet past – would strongly encourage post-Soviet society to contemplate how they should deal with this grievous legacy. However, the heated interest in the Soviet past died away as suddenly as it appeared. In early 1992 it was pushed into the background by the problem of choosing a suitable economic model. Western-oriented intellectuals now preferred to consider themselves and their society as victims of totalitarianism, and renounced any historic responsibility for, or connection with, the Soviet past.

However, the break with the Soviet past had an enormous impact on the consciousness of Russian Westerners: denying the significance of the Soviet period meant that it was no longer considered to be a historic era filled with landmark events. Instead, the Soviet years had ruptured historic continuity and left a gap in time, while those who still accepted Communist ideology were ostracized. According to a typical expression of the time, 1990s Russia was equated with the 1920s United States, a land at 'the dawn of capitalism'. In those years the word 'present' disappeared: in social journalism and everyday language it was ousted by the term 'transitional period', emphasizing the yearning to rush through the present and find a future, modelled after the idealized West, as soon as possible. The future and the past converged, denying the right of Russia's present to exist.

Belief in progress would guarantee Russia's arrival into this happy future. And since the path that Russia was supposed to follow had already been traversed by the West, all Russia

Unlike the Nazis, whose crimes have been well documented, the perpetrators of the crimes committed under Soviet rule were able to conceal the evidence for seventy years. Scattered across the wide expanse of the former Soviet Union, the wooden barracks of the camps decayed along with the countless bodies of the victims, among them poets, artists, teachers and doctors.

had to do was quickly follow in its footsteps. The market economy was considered by Russians the vehicle they could use to reach the future. Yet this trip to Western modernity would become problematic: memory of the Gulag undermined faith in progress and had to be suppressed in order to give Russians, even briefly, the confidence that they would achieve a happy Western tomorrow.

This Russian image of the West as an embodiment of their expectations for a perfect society caused significant psychological discomfort. Russian Westerners of the early 1990s, tormented by political instability, economic crisis and consumer shortages, were anxious about their own imperfection as well as the imperfection of their everyday life. Idealization of the West therefore intensified the national inferiority complex, rather than helping Russians to reinforce their own identity which had been undermined by the collapse of the Soviet regime.

Within a very short time attitudes started to transform dramatically. This can be illustrated by comparing the opinion surveys of 1990 and 2007. In 1990 residents of Leningrad ranked Peter the Great as their most admired statesman and Lenin fifth; positions two to four were filled with the names of three American presidents: Roosevelt, Lincoln and Washington. However, in 2007, of all the American presidents, residents of St Petersburg named only Roosevelt. Even he was only listed seventeenth, while the top five were all national heroes: Peter the Great, Catherine the Great, Stalin, Lenin and Stolypin.

In 1990 four fifths of the residents of Leningrad repudiated the founding dogma of the official Soviet propaganda about the social and political superiority of the Soviet Union. However, in 2007 the idea of Russia's pre-eminence over the West had returned. Whereas in 1990 only one tenth of the residents of Leningrad believed that Muscovite Rus was superior to Western Europe, in 2007 the number of such respondents had gone up to one quarter. The change in assessment of the Soviet era is even more vivid. In 1990 only 5.5 per cent of Leningrad residents thought that Soviet Russia was superior or equal to the West, but in 2007 their number increased to more then 40 per cent! In 1990 the question 'Do you consider yourself a European?' was answered positively by more than two-thirds of the respondents; in 2007 this number fell to one third. Asked 'In which country would you prefer to be born?', half the respondents chose Russia in 1990, but

A military parade in Red Square, Moscow, in 2006, celebrating the anniversary of victory over Nazi Germany. The Stalinist myth of the so-called Great Patriotic War reframed the tragedy that people lived through under Soviet rule as patriotic heroism and formed the basis of nationalistic propaganda of the post-Soviet authoritarian regime.

three-quarters in 2007. More than half of the respondents thought that there was a foreign threat, and three-quarters named the United States as a potential aggressor.

The refusal to condemn the Soviet past and the desire to embrace the Soviet regime in the epic of 'glorious national history' have added to the practice of the successful and unpunished struggle against culture and civilization, and transformed the denial of the West into a *modus vivendi* of the current political process. However, the West has not lost its crucial significance for Russian national self-consciousness. It remains a determining factor for the cultural anxiety and ideological concerns of the Russians – it is here, at the core of national identity, and it has to be denied and surpassed over and over again.

PAVEL SEIFTER

The Czech Republic

National history and the search for identity

The most recent incarnation of the Czech state, proclaimed on 1 January 1993, was formalized in a hurry, and history was called upon to justify it. The prime minister chose a symbolic place to deliver his founding address: a national cemetery, where he stood beneath statues of the mythical heroes Záboj and Slavoj, who had been invented almost two centuries earlier to add flesh to medieval foundation myths. The new parliament immediately began to debate whether the birth of the nation should be observed on 1 January, the day the present republic was declared, or on 28 October, when the independent Czechoslovakia first came into being in 1918. Another proposed date was 28 September, the day on which St Wenceslas, patron saint of Bohemia, was murdered in 935. Parliament eventually settled on 28 October, asserting the new state's continuity with Czechoslovakia; meanwhile the 9 May holiday, which had been celebrated for almost fifty years to commemorate the liberation of the country by the Red Army in 1945, was moved to 8 May, marking the end of the Second World War in Europe. Although something of an arcane shift to outsiders, the latter decision was crucial to Czech self-understanding, for it revised the country's role in European history since 1945. No longer a Communist state bound to celebrate the arrival of the Red Army in 1945, it was now one of the victors in the Second World War. This in turn justified the mass expulsion of Czechoslovak Germans and Hungarians from its territory after 1945, perhaps the most controversial action in its 20th-century history. It was a case of parliamentarians re-making history on the hoof.

Two forces dominate the Czech marketplace of history: contemporary Czech pragmatism and would-be traditional conservatism. Although people are no longer as nationalistic as they once were, they tend to ignore their own historians in favour of a

A page from the Codex Manesse (1305–40), depicting King Wenceslas I of Bohemia. Wenceslas was considered a martyr and a saint immediately after his death in 935. A Wenceslas cult developed in Bohemia and in England, which still has a Christmas carol dedicated to 'Good King Wenceslas'.

residual patriotic sentiment that has remained unchanged since the 'national revival' of the 19th century. So politicians return again and again to the romantic national narrative, which goes like this:

The Czechs are the ancient (Slav) inhabitants of the Bohemian lands; their history is thousands of years old and Christian. When forged Czech medieval manuscripts were 'discovered' at the beginning of the 19th century, they seemed to confirm that Czech history was even older, replete with ancient heroes and even Bohemian Amazons. Among the first dukes, Wenceslas (*c.* 907–35) today holds an exclusive position in Czech history (although his fratricidal brother in fact did more to establish the state). From the start, however, the Czechs had a problem with Germans, who began settling in the Bohemian borderlands during the 13th century. The Czechs achieved glory when the 'Father of the Country', Charles IV, acceded to the Bohemian throne in 1346 and made Prague on the River Vltava the centre of the Holy Roman Empire; in 1348 he founded the first university in Central Europe there. A decline followed Charles's reign; less than a century later came the Hussite Revolution, when the cleric Jan Huss (*c.* 1369–1415) spoke out against the moral decrepitude of the Church of Rome, for which he was burned at the stake and came to be regarded as a martyr (a recurrent motif in Czech history). The pope sent in Crusaders whom the Bohemians defeated in several battles 'against all comers' (that is, *Proti všem*, the title of Alois Jirásek's classic nationalist novel of 1894). The radical wing of the Hussites was finally defeated at the Battle of Lipany in 1434, as a result of treachery (another recurrent Czech motif). Prague once again became a centre of European culture under Rudolph II (1576–1611) and the Czech language continued to flourish, closely linked to the Protestant Unitas Fratrum (Moravian Church). The next historical disaster came in 1620, when the Bohemians were defeated by a coalition of Catholic and Habsburg imperial forces at the Battle of the White Mountain. Twenty-seven of their leaders were executed; many other members of the Bohemian nobility and intelligentsia, including the famous scholar Jan Comenius, chose to leave the country. This marked the

TIMELINE

***c.* 885** CE Foundation of Prague by Duke Bořivoj

935 Murder of Duke Wenceslas, patron saint of Bohemia

1355 King Charles IV accedes to the throne of the Holy Roman Empire

1415 Jan Huss is burned at the stake for heresy

1618 The Defenestration of Prague starts the Thirty Years' War

1620 Bohemians are defeated by imperial forces at the Battle of the White Mountain

1918 Declaration of Czechoslovak independence (the First Republic)

1938 The Munich Agreement paves the way for the German invasion of Czechoslovakia

1948 The Communist Party seizes power in Czechoslovakia

1968 The Prague Spring is overthrown by a Soviet invasion

1989 The Velvet Revolution overthrows Communist rule in Czechoslovakia

1993 Creation of the Czech Republic

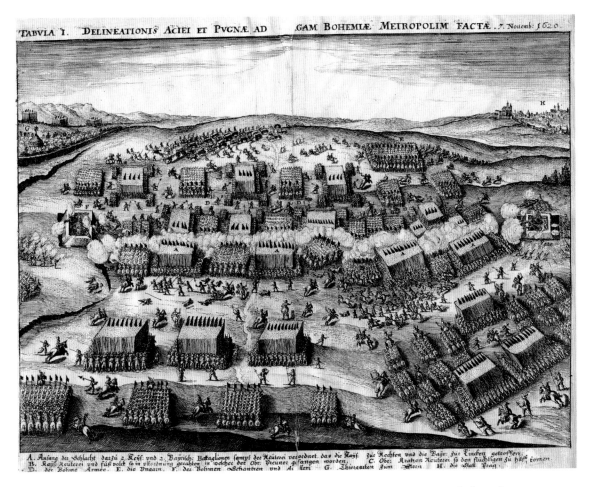

An engraving depicting a scene from the Battle of the White Mountain (1620), where a tiny army of exhausted Bohemian noblemen lost a relatively small battle in two hours. This defeat constituted the end of the 'Czech episode' of the Thirty Years' War: the Czech lands were relegated to the edge of Europe for the next 300 years.

beginning of 300 years of suffering, the Baroque 'Age of Darkness' (or *Temno*, the title of another Jirásek novel published in 1915). The nation was brought back to Catholicism by force, almost lost its language, and was in danger of fading away. Beginning in the late 18th century, however, the National Revivalists awakened the slumbering nation and set about reviving its language, encouraging the development of Bohemian *belles-lettres*, scholarship, and, eventually, history. The Revival succeeded, and in 1918 the state of the Czechs and Moravians (and their Slovak brothers) was restored.

This Revivalist model of national history corresponds to the nation's 'childhood'. What is important here is not history itself, but the building blocks on which the nation was constructed. The small, weak nation needed something to lean on and it found this

The first Czech translation of the Bible, known as the Bible of Kralice, dating from the 16th century. The Revivalist movement of the 19th century used its vocabulary to help restore Czech as the official language, which was to represent a highly educated, spiritual and cultured nation.

in its Slav beginnings; the Hussites provided the idea that Bohemians were 'warriors of God', and Huss himself suggested the idea of a nation of martyrs. By contrast, the Baroque period was seen as an age of suffering, associated with an alien nobility, the 'un-Czech' Roman Catholic Church and 'German' Habsburg Austria – the Germans emerge from Czech history as the age-old enemy. Throughout all of this, the common people – the smallholder, the artisan, the priest, the schoolmaster and the writer – are portrayed as the bearers of Bohemian/Czech history, giving the nation its 'plebeian' character, which some mistake for a democratic character. This nationalist model of Czech history has been immortalized in the national pantheon at Vyšehrad Cemetery, Prague, the equestrian statues of St Wenceslas and the Hussite leader Jan Žižka (*c.* 1360–1424), the twenty outsized canvases of the Art Nouveau *Slav Epic* by Alphonse Mucha (1860–1939), the symbolic ornamentation of the National Theatre, and the operas of Bedřich Smetana (1824–84).

Yet the patriotic version of Czech history is not the only one. The Czechs have shared their history with many other nations in the Bohemian lands – when ruled under the Habsburg monarchy, and later when they had their own state, Czechoslovakia, together with the Slovaks. The historian Jan Křen sees Czech history through a European lens, and places it in the wider framework of Central Europe. In doing so it becomes clear that the Bohemian lands were at a great disadvantage from the beginning, being far from the sea and from the leading centres of classical civilization. The country therefore got off to a late start in history compared to the rest of Europe and was forced to catch up. This is the most important feature of Czech history, although it was also the fate of much of Central Europe. Other important themes, such as the discontinuities of history, and the country's perception of itself as a victim, are also not unique to the Czechs. These are shared by their neighbours the Slovaks, Hungarians, Austrians and, especially, the Poles and the Germans, for whom the interruptions have been incomparably more disastrous.

Between the Turanian Whip and the Sword of the Goths, *a painting by Alphonse Mucha (1912) showing the spirit of the nation ascending into the realm of the sacred. It forms part of the* Slav Epic, *a cycle of twenty canvases illustrating the history of the Czech people.*

In spite of its late start, Central Europe was also fortunate. Greater Moravia, an empire of the Western Slavs, disintegrated in the late 9th century, and so, unlike the the situation among the Germanic tribes, no sense of belonging developed among its peoples, and no counterweight to the empire of the eastern Franks therefore emerged. Czech history has not, however, been completely separate from Western European history. In about 885 Duke Bořivoj founded Prague and built a castle there. Prague has remained the undisputed centre of the Bohemian lands and the capital of the state for over 1,100 years, and to this day the head of state has his seat only a few yards from the place that the founder of the city selected. Czech international relations were determined by the fact that the state was part of the Holy Roman Empire, but in the territory of the Bohemian state the sovereign lacked any immediate rights, and could not intervene significantly in policy-making.

From the end of the 12th century and into the 13th century the Bohemian lands underwent radical modernization. Boroughs and villages were established in the form they would retain until the mid-19th century or later. The cultural landscape was thus for all practical purposes complete. Germans arrived, chiefly as the burghers of the new boroughs, and from the 14th century they increasingly moved into the borderlands. They became part of the native society, and until the 19th century did not constitute a group separate from the Czechs. Central Europe – and the Czech lands – thus became a transitional zone between West and East.

Bohemia had a unique opportunity to step into the heart of European history with the Czech Reformation, the first in Europe, initiated by Jan Huss. Yet it was Germany that became the true cradle of the Reformation a century later, as Hussitism remained isolated. The Bohemian state eventually ceased to be the centre of the Holy Roman Empire that had linked it with the West. Meanwhile it was edged out by developments of a different order. In the 15th and 16th centuries, as Ottoman expansion undermined Mediterranean trade and Iberian voyages of discovery shifted the centre of events to the Atlantic coast, the Bohemian lands were left on the sidelines of a rapidly globalizing European economy. The Thirty Years' War, which started in Prague with an uprising of the Bohemian Estates against the Habsburgs in 1618, did the rest. When the war ended the country was exhausted, the population greatly reduced, and the state, now definitively controlled by the Habsburg monarchy, faded into insignificance. While Western Europe stood on the threshold of a leap towards pre-industrial modernization, Bohemia stagnated under the Spanish absolutism and Roman Catholicism imposed by the Habsburgs. It became a territory on the fringe of Europe, no longer its core.

This map dating from 1570 shows Bohemia as the heart of Europe. Bohemia was indeed at times at the heart of Europe's history but more frequently, and for long periods, the Czech people found themselves on the periphery of Europe.

Modernization did not start until about 1800, and with it came nationalism. Among all the social, economic and intellectual changes, one stands out: only now did two ethnic groups begin to form in the Bohemian lands as two national units: Bohemia and Moravia. Germans of the same period had to make the difficult decision between a marginal existence in a future German state and a privileged position in the multinational Habsburg monarchy. For the Czechs it was easier: they preferred autonomy in a federalized Austria to being a minority in Germany. The dilemma was solved by František Palacký (1798–1876), historian and leader of the nation. His preference for autonomy opened up a range of political possibilities, from a territorial sub-state inside the Habsburg Empire (like Hungary) to limited autonomy as a Czech-speaking land, and to a share in the administration of the Austro-Hungarian Empire in Vienna. His *History of the Czech Nation* was an interpretation of this strategy.

Czech historical narratives, some patriotic, some more partisan, often represent strategies for interpreting the nation as, for instance, having a Central European or more broadly European past. In interwar Czechoslovakia they converged. The First Republic, founded after the end of the First World War and the collapse of the Habsburg Empire in 1918, is often regarded as the highpoint of 20th-century Czech history. Its founder and first president was Tomáš G. Masaryk (1850–1937). As an open-minded scholar and politician well acquainted with modern Europe and the United States (his wife was American) he opened Czechoslovakia to Western modernity. On the other hand, Masaryk concentrated his own interpretation of Czech history and statehood on Huss and the Unitas Fratrum. Thus 'Masaryk's model' carried a version of the 19th-century National Revival into the 20th century. In his role as the 'philosopher king' at Prague Castle he bolstered Czech self-confidence: his republic was modern, skilled at diplomacy, economically developed and the only functioning democracy in Central Europe. But the republic perished not only as a result of defects in interwar Europe, but also through its own defects, namely the nationalistic selfishness of its political parties and the superficiality of its immature democracy. Masaryk talked about 'democracy without democrats'. The Czechs, however, for the first time identified themselves with their state; aside from the National Revival, the First Republic has left the strongest mark on their historical consciousness. It was highly esteemed, even mythologized, by Czechs and Jews for its tolerance, but damned by Communists, Germans and Hungarians for its opposition to their own political ends. The Slovaks both praise and damn it.

The events that followed were, and clearly remain, even more questionable. After the Munich Agreement of 1938, by which Britain and France effectively handed the nation to Hitler, an extreme right-wing, fascist-leaning Second Republic emerged. The Nazi German occupation followed and with it both Czech resistance and collaboration. The post-war restoration of would-be democratic Czechoslovakia and a welfare

Czechoslovakia, August 1946: the German occupation during the war claimed 350,000 victims, 280,000 of whom were Jews. In 1945 there were nearly 3.5 million Germans on Czech territory. The following year the Czechoslovak government began the process of deporting over 2.5 million of them to Germany.

state coincided with the expulsion of over 2.5 million Czechoslovak Germans and 600,000 Hungarians, an action the Czech state would later be called upon to justify. Three bitterly politically contested post-war years ended in 1948 with the Moscow-oriented Communist takeover and subsequent forty years of Communist Party rule. The Czechs, subjected to Soviet civilization, lost contact with the West again. Paradoxically, it was the fact that the Czechs shared a long tradition of Marxist socialism with Western Europe, and the strength of a Communist Party (founded in 1921) on a par with the French and Italian Communist parties, that contributed to Czechoslovakia's post-war isolation from the West via its immuring in the Eastern Bloc. In 1946 half the country voted Communist, apparently freely choosing a fate they later came to despise.

Historical traumas were piling up: Munich and the end of the Czechoslovak dream; the war years with a limited history of resistance and military heroism along with collaboration under German occupation; the post-war expulsion of the Germans; the 'class war' and its terror, show trials and new concentration camps of the Cold War in the 1950s. A strong disillusionment and reaction to this in the 1960s (the 'Prague Spring') moved Czechoslovakia to the centre of European affairs for a brief moment again, in the turbulent year of 1968.

When the Soviet Union led a military intervention in Czechoslovakia in August of that year to put down the reform movement, the whole nation, Communists and non-Communists, united against it. After the defeat, however, only a handful of dissidents openly resisted the restoration of a hard-line Communist regime. When the Moscow-led Eastern Bloc of Communist countries unexpectedly collapsed in 1989, these dissidents, led by Václav Havel, were swept to power in a non-violent (hence 'Velvet') revolution and inspired – again for a brief moment – great hopes in the West, especially on the Left. As a result of the events of 1989 and the years that followed, the whole of Central Europe reintegrated with Europe. The Czechs entered the full range of Western institutions, including NATO in 1999 and the European Union in 2004. How near to the centre and how far from the European periphery this shift will eventually lead the Czechs is still uncertain.

The 20th century has been especially traumatic for the national psyche, to which all of Czech history has to keep coming back. The Communist past became embarrassing. People rushed into a belated fight against Communism, reducing the past to the files of the secret police and a history of culprits ('the others') and victims (themselves). Of the more distant historical events, the 'trauma of Munich' is indelibly imprinted on the Czech psyche. The Munich Agreement of 1938 remains a wound that will probably never heal. Should they have defended themselves against the Germans? Were they betrayed? Was their state ever viable? The Soviet invasion in 1968 and even the Communist putsch in 1948 tend to be seen through the same lens: should we have taken up arms?

A Czech protest poster from 1968 against the invasion and Soviet occupation that put an end to the 'Prague Spring', when post-war culture climaxed in a golden age of film and literature and new hope for democratic reform. The invasion was met with passive resistance by the people, in ways that showed characteristic creativity and humour.

129

The non-violent Velvet Revolution of 1989 overthrew Communist rule following numerous demonstrations and street protests. Masses of people engaged in carnival-like celebrations – the dream of a free and democratic nation was coming true at last.

It can of course never be clear what the Czechs should have done. Unsurprisingly there is no period, no event, no king, no hero and no place that has not become controversial. Even the moment of triumph in late 1989 lost its shine within weeks. Incomprehensibly to the outer world, once free of Soviet control the Czechs and Slovaks broke their joint state into two lesser ones. The Slovak state forged confidently ahead, but the Czech state seemed to lose its bearings, drawing the very concept of the Czech nation into question. This blasphemous notion had been raised as early as the end of the 19th century, when it was asked whether it might not have been better for the nation to join some more meaningful, developed society and do more for humanity than was possible in the constrained circumstances of the Czechs. Masaryk wrote a work in 1894 called *Česká otázka* (The Czech Question); Milan Kundera (b. 1929) gave a speech at the 1967 Congress of Czechoslovak Writers called 'Nesamozřejmost existence českého národa' (Doubting the Existence of the Czech Nation); and the philosopher Jan Patočka (1907–77) called one of his historical essays 'Co jsou Cesi?' (What Are the Czechs?).

The present-day Czech intelligentsia no longer formulates the aspirations of the nation as it did in the 19th and 20th centuries; Czechs have given up their tradition of listening to national elders and teachers for the answer to who they are. The market, the media and politicians today break off unconnected fragments of history and use them for their own entertainment and political purposes. The price of such reductionism is the loss of a unified historical narrative and judgment. The attitude of the man in the street today is that history has lost its authority: Czechs can get by without it.

The Czechs also have a more congenial way of escaping history: they have ironic, invented and frivolous history, in which fiction becomes reality and vice versa. Czechs identify with the Good Soldier Svejk (hero of the eponymous 1923 book by Jaroslav Hašek) and long ago stopped perceiving him as merely the main character of a novel about the Great War. They have a similar attitude towards the imaginary inventor and traveller, Jára Cimrman, whose memorial plaque is affixed to the building of the Czech Embassy in London. The statue of St Wenceslas in Wenceslas Square, Prague, where the nation has traditionally assembled when under threat or celebrating a triumph, today has its double a few hundred yards away: he sits in his armour astride the belly of his dead horse, suspended by all fours from the ceiling of a shopping plaza.

The problem faced by Czechs today is not in their attitude to history. It is in their concept of the present and the future, for which they have no ideals. If there is no point to a national community, there is no point to national history either. Probably every Czech historian – the National Revivalist, the Masarykian, the Marxist, the anti-Communist dissident, the European and the postmodern – would agree on that.

Poland

Tragedy and heroism in the
face of powerful neighbours

When I was a university student during the 1980s, history was a popular subject of study. This was due to the peculiar situation in Communist Poland where politics was intermingled with one's attitude to the past. History was a force that united those opposed to the regime, strengthening the image we already had of Poland as a country betrayed by the West.

This feeling was the legacy of the past, of bitter stories told at home about grandparents arrested, imprisoned or shot during and after the Second World War. The Communist system seemed as strong as ever, and the feeling of hopelessness turned many young people towards the study of the past. History could tell us why we had lost our independence again after the Second World War and how to react. Our generation was the next in a long line of Poles reliving the scenario of occupation and illegal opposition movements.

From this point of view the partitions in the 18th century were crucial events in Polish history. The weakness of Poland's internal political system, and the strength and greed of the neighbouring countries Russia, Prussia and Austria, meant that, despite domestic reforms, Poland lost its independence. In three partitions between 1772 and 1795 this large country of around 12 million people completely disappeared from the map of Europe – not to return for over 120 years. The name Poland only survived in the form of the 'Kingdom of Poland', a semi-autonomous state in union with Russia between 1815 and 1831.

From 1569, before the partitions, Poland was a country with an unusual political system that was often perceived in the West as anarchic. Known as the Kingdom of Poland and Grand Duchy of Lithuania, it was a kind of noble democracy in which the political class controlled the legislature and limited the power of the kings, who were

A poster from the 1950s produced by the Polish Communist Party for 1 May. International Workers' Day was transformed into a ritual of support for the Communist system as the masses were forced to march before their leaders to keep up the myth of a joyful state of workers and peasants.

chosen by election. The nobility was strongly opposed to any restriction of personal freedom, and the very concept of an absolutist state was abhorred. It is possible to see this system as a forerunner of modern constitutional monarchy and democracy. Despite the fact that only the nobility had political rights, they comprised about 10 per cent of the population, which was still the largest percentage of population in Europe with such privileges. The Poles like to see their Polish–Lithuanian Commonwealth (as the Kingdom and Grand Duchy was sometimes known) as a tolerant, multi-ethnic state with the populace enjoying comparative freedom.

This tradition of tolerance before the partitions is always mentioned with pride. It is important to remember that, during the centuries of religious persecution in Europe, Poland was a safe place not only for Christians of all denominations but for Jews as well. The Statute of Kalisz of 1264 guaranteed personal and religious liberties to Jews. The traditional policy of tolerating Protestant denominations and all radical Christian sects acquired a legal basis in 1573 under the articles of the Warsaw Confederation. These became part of Poland's constitutional provisions in the 16th and 17th centuries, and this peaceful co-existence of all denominations was a theory that was only violated in practice from time to time. Yet Poland was a country that did not make use of the burning stakes – something that could not be said of many other 16th- and 17th-century European countries.

From the middle of the 17th century Poland started to experience a slow decline in its political and economic system, which was eventually one of the causes of the partitions. Just before its final disintegration Poland tried to implement a series of reforms which, in a bold attempt to reverse the current of fate, culminated in the constitution of 3 May 1791.

TIMELINE

966 Conversion of Poland to Christianity by Mieszko I

1333–70 Reign of Casimir the Great, ruling from Krakow

1386 Foundation of the Jagiellon dynasty when Władysław Jagiełło, Grand Duke of Lithuania, became king of Poland (after the Union of Krewo, 1385)

1569 Creation of the Polish–Lithuanian Commonwealth; rulers were chosen by the Sejm (parliament)

1655–60 Poland is devastated by a Swedish invasion

1674–96 Rule of Jan III Sobieski; victories over the Turks

1772 The first partition of Poland by Prussia, Russia and Austria; two more follow, in 1793 and 1795, after which Poland ceases to exist

1918 Poland is declared an independent state, confirmed by the Treaty of Versailles in 1919

1919–20 Poland defeats the Soviet invasion

1939 Poland is invaded by Germany and the Soviet Union

1941 Germans build concentration camps in Poland, including Auschwitz, which becomes the largest death camp during the Holocaust

1944 Warsaw Uprising against the Germans, defeated despite the presence of the Soviet army nearby

1945 The Yalta Conference leaves post-war Poland in the Soviet sphere of influence

1978 Election of Karol Wojtyła as Pope John Paul II

1980 Beginning of the Solidarity trade union and pro-independence movement

1990 Post-Communist elections; Solidarity leader Lech Wałesa is elected president

2004 Poland joins the European Union

2010 President Kaczynski dies in an aircraft crash in Russia while commemorating the 1940 Katyn massacre of Polish troops by Russians

A British map of the Partition of Poland, dated 1799. The complete elimination of an entire state was an unprecedented event in European history, breaching the principles of international relations. The indifference of other European states surprised the Polish elite, who never reconciled themselves to the loss.

Since 1990 this date has been restored as a holiday to commemorate the first European modern constitution, which was based on the principles of popular sovereignty and a separation of powers between legislature and executive. It was a short period of hope for Poland and despite the speedy demise of the state – the constitution was overthrown by the Russians just a year after it had been introduced – it is still a source of pride for Poles today.

135

Russian soldiers capturing Polish children in Warsaw. After the November Uprising of 1831, severe repressions afflicted even the families of the participants. These children were enlisted by force into special battalions preparing them for future military service in Russia.

The reaction of the Polish political class – the nobility – to the partitions was twofold. Acceptance of the political realities coexisted with a strong desire to rebuild the state. A series of unsuccessful and tragic uprisings (the largest took place in 1794, 1830–31 and 1863) and the failure of European diplomatic interventions on behalf of Poland left the Poles convinced that the world was against them. The insurrections were followed by severe repressions. Long prison sentences, exile to Siberia and confiscation of property were typical punishments inflicted by the Russian authorities on their rebellious subjects.

The Polish insurrections of the 19th and 20th centuries showed certain common traits. The rebels were usually not very well equipped, and enthusiasm for the cause and a belief in the possibility of winning against all odds were more important than rational preparations. Organized by visionaries, the uprisings were the Polish response to a seemingly hopeless situation. But these uprisings are a source of dispute among present-day Poles. The hopeless attempts to gain freedom in reality weakened the population, and the mostly young idealists were either killed or exiled. Some Poles today consider these to be great heroic deeds, while others regret the uprisings because of their heavy cost.

Despite the fact that Poland was divided into three parts, it was Russia who was and still is in the popular imagination the main culprit of the partitions. The empire of the tsars gained most from the partitions – over 80 per cent of Polish territory was in its hands. The biggest and most tragic uprisings were organized against Russian occupation. Although Germanization was forced on the Poles at the end of the 19th and beginning of the 20th centuries, in popular memory it is not remembered as much as the forced Russification. The feeling of superiority of the 'civilized' Pole over the Muscovite 'barbarian' was intermingled with the fear and hatred of the weak towards the oppressor.

Probably the most debated historical event among Poles is the Warsaw Uprising of 1944. The Polish Home Army struggled for sixty-three days to liberate Warsaw from the Nazis before the Soviets arrived, but their efforts ended in defeat. The price of their hope and heroism was terrible: about 16,000 Polish fighters were killed in the combat and 6,000 wounded. The civilian death toll was enormous: about 200,000 were killed by the Nazis and a large part of the capital was completely destroyed.

The majority of Poles believed and still believe that the Soviet army deliberately stopped on the left bank of the River Vistula to wait for the Nazis to finish off the uprising. In this way they used the Germans to get rid of the most active and independent elements in the Polish capital, making it easier for Polish Communists to take power in the country. This not unfounded belief strengthened anti-Communist and anti-Soviet feelings in post-war Poland.

The Warsaw Uprising can be seen as symbolic of the entire history of Poland of the last two centuries. Tragic and heroic, it was poorly

A patrol of soldiers of the Polish resistance movement on the streets of the temporarily liberated city during the Warsaw Uprising of 1944. The largest anti-Nazi revolt in Europe became the subject of a masterful 1956 film by Andrzej Wajda called Kanał (Sewer), *which depicted the tragic fate of the insurgents and civilians.*

organized yet carried out with the utmost devotion by patriotic youths. For my generation it was legendary. In the gloomy times of Communist rule it was the ultimate example of patriotism. That was the Polish dilemma of later generations: is fighting the only way to serve the country?

After the Second World War Poland was forcibly turned into a vassal of the Soviet Union. This powerful neighbour was perceived by many as a more dangerous incarnation of Russia. The post-war arrangements were seen as a new partition because Poland lost not only its sovereignty but a large part of its territory as well. The new Polish–Soviet frontier established in 1945 pushed Poland much further west. Although some lands that had been German before the war were added to Polish territory, this did not compensate for the loss. Poland was now smaller and the millions of Poles who moved westwards from the territories taken by the Soviet Union brought with them resentment towards their eastern neighbour.

The Communist system in Poland was not a monolith: it evolved as conditions changed in the Soviet Union itself. Extremely repressive in the 1950s, it grew milder in the 1960s and 1970s. The anti-Communist resistance movement had been formed just after the Second World War, but it was quickly eliminated as a military and political force, leaving the Poles with no outlet to express their dissatisfaction. Social unrest grew, and demonstrations and strikes among the workers of large factories began to take place. In 1956 and 1970 the army and militia used brutal force to quell huge demonstrations, killing over a hundred protesters and bystanders. The demands of the workers were mostly economic, but were quite often perceived by many Poles and those in the West as a sign of fundamental opposition to the oppressive political system. Non-violent opposition groups started to emerge after 1976 – a year in which severe measures were brought in against workers taking part in a strike.

The opposition formed after 1976 was based on the belief that Poland, as a member of the Soviet bloc, needed gradually to create an autonomous society which would defend its human rights by legal means. Activities such as collecting signatures for letters of protest, and organizing legal and economic help for the families of the political prisoners were undertaken semi-openly. Lectures were held in private homes on historical and literary topics, aiming to deepen knowledge about Poland and its culture, which was perceived as essential to its survival as a distinct nation. Another opposition activity included the printing of books, brochures and leaflets.

This non-aggressive action was reserved for small groups, but information about the existence of the opposition travelled fast around the country and many Poles started to believe in the possibility of liberalization. Radio programmes broadcast from the West had been listened to since the 1950s. The Polish sections of Radio Free Europe and the BBC kept their audiences informed about all the actions of the opposition and the repressive tactics of the government. Listening to forbidden and often jammed radio was a safe and popular expression of resistance that could be practised at home. Yet it was quite common even for Communist Party members who officially supported the system to derive basic political information from this source. It was a classic Orwellian double-think common in totalitarian countries.

Despite the strong anti-Communist and Catholic traditions in Poland, the Polish United Workers' Party was a large organization with 3.5 million members by the end

7 June 1979, Oświecim, Poland: Pope John Paul II enters the gates of the Auschwitz concentration camp. The sign above the gate reads 'Arbeit Macht Frei' (Work Makes One Free). The Pope visited the cell in block 11 where Father Maximilian Kolbe died giving his life in exchange for one of the prisoners.

of the 1970s. Belonging to the Party was necessary for promotion rather than a question of ideology: all the key posts in state-run organizations required membership. Nevertheless even party members were dissatisfied with the effects of Communist rule. Economic problems, permanent shortages of certain foodstuffs and industrial products, and queues in the shops were a fact of life. Apart from short periods of full shop shelves and relative but superficial prosperity, everyday life in Communist Poland was dull, drab and difficult.

The ailing political system was dealt a severe blow by the election of Cardinal Karol Wojtyła (1920–2005), from Krakow, as Pope John Paul II in 1978, the first non-Italian pope for centuries. When he visited Poland in 1979 millions of Poles went to see him and returned home with a feeling of victory: this was the first time that Communist Poland, which officially professed atheism, had allowed such huge religious gatherings. Many of those who went to see the Pope were not practising Catholics, but participating in his visit was for them a way of expressing their dissatisfaction with the ruling ideology and lack of freedom, and their belief in Poland's continuity with its past and traditions.

The connection between being Polish and being Catholic had been finally established in the 19th century after the partitions, when the two main aggressors were Russian Orthodox and Protestant. Catholicism was an important way of confirming the nation's self-image in opposition to the dangerous foes. Protestant and Orthodox Poles also existed, but they were a small minority. After the Second World War the status of Polish Catholicism took on a strongly anti-Communist character.

Solidarity, the first officially acknowledged independent trade union and the pride of Poland, was set up in August 1980 after a series of strikes. It proved that the Communist authorities were weak and that the opposition forces had reached a point of mass support. In the 1980s Solidarity was much more than just a trade union: it was a very broad anti-Communist social movement containing different political views. The international implications of Solidarity became paramount: this first independent organization in the Communist bloc proved that Communists could be forced to accept liberalization of their system.

Polish tanks after the introduction of martial law in 1981. Such images were shocking for the older generation as they brought back the worst memories from the Second World War. Nobody realized that this demonstration of power was actually a sign of the weakness of the Communist regime.

In an act of despair on the part of the authorities, martial law was introduced on 13 December 1981. Several years of repression followed, but these did not destroy the opposition. After the initial shock, the underground activities resumed, repeating an already established pattern. The printing and distribution of books, brochures and leaflets were familiar activities to the Poles. Small meetings were held in private homes and large gatherings in churches, all devoted to the defence of human rights. There were occasional strikes and growing social unrest. Solidarity existed underground within a well-organized local and national structure.

The Communist authorities ultimately had no power to suppress Solidarity and eventually in 1988 decided to open negotiations. The recent changes in the Soviet Union – Mikhail Gorbachev (b. 1931) had become the First Secretary in 1985 – facilitated the possibility of success for these negotiations. Round-table talks in 1989 led to the agreement which brought the legalization of Solidarity and other independent trade unions, semi-free elections and real changes in the political structure of the state. Solidarity's landslide victory in the elections of 4 June 1989 paved the way for a final dismantling of the Communist system, leading to a free and democratic country.

The so-called 'Solidarity Revolution' hastened the collapse of the whole Communist bloc, thus introducing enormous changes in Central and Eastern Europe. The region's

Members of the Solidarity trade union welcome Pope John Paul II to Poznan in June 1983. Despite the Polish-born pope's emphasis on dialogue rather than confrontation, his very presence united Catholic patriotism with political opposition to Communism in a manner that ultimately proved devastating to the regime.

peaceful transfer from totalitarianism to democracy is a source of pride for Poles: it proved that they were able to use opposition as a positive, creative force.

For the last 200 years Poland has had little chance for independent development, apart from a short period between 1918 and 1939. The fall of Communism, the growth of freedom and joining the European Union have all played a role in Poland's transformation into a normal democratic state. History is very important to the Poles as it forms part of the nation's self-image. Despite this, it does not provide a pattern of behaviour for the younger generation to start anew, free from the burden of failures and defeats.

erét vt sic sibi saluté τ corpú suoₓ ħuarét itegritaté. Illi igit
ꝛi ꝑsilio scī regis acꝗescétes a facie maloₓ τ doloₓ i bohem
erút. De moꝛte scīssimi regis stephani. τ ð electióe petri

LÁSZLÓ KONTLER

Hungary

The thousand-year realm

Hungarian statehood is ancient, but Hungary's integrity and sovereignty have been precarious throughout much of its history. The combination of these factors explains Hungary's preoccupation with the 'foundation of the state'. The coronation in 1000 CE of King Stephen I, instituting a Christian monarchy in the country, is a major landmark. Depending on one's opinion, Stephen's exertion of his iron will over his own subjects and powerful neighbours could be regarded as an act of either shrewd statecraft or Christian piety, or as the first manifestation of a larger vision to associate Hungary's fate with 'Western civilization'. Whichever view is accurate, the creation of the polity has been celebrated to an extent without parallel in any other European national history.

King Stephen's antecedents are the subject of much discussion and caricature among rival nationalist camps. One side considers the conquering Magyars, who had arrived from the steppe a century earlier, to have been a horde of savages speaking an isolated language, whose only skills were pillage and plunder. The other views them as glorious warriors, a people of refined material and spiritual culture, who taught Europeans how to cook meat, use forks and wear trousers. Yet it is clear that Stephen and his successors transformed Magyar society beyond recognition. Territorial organization replaced a society based on kinship, while devotion to the Gospel replaced the ancient pagan cult. The substance and speed of those transformations also defined much subsequent Hungarian history.

Accommodation and adaptation are central to Hungarian history. The question of how much independent scope for action Hungary has had throughout history has been a cherished topic of discussion. Was this a small nation struggling for survival against hostile powers and their regional clients, or one making efforts to retain its hard-won identity as a member of the European family? There are countless possibile answers.

Stephen I, the first king of Hungary (1000–38), represented in Chronicles of Hungary *by János Thuróczy (1488). A scion of the last nomadic chieftains who permanently settled in Europe, he was canonized in 1083. In modern national consciousness Stephen is still an emblem of the Hungarian 'capacity for statehood'.*

'We've got something. We've indeed got *something*… But maybe not the real thing.' The phrase recurred, in engagingly broken Hungarian, in the performances of Arkady Raikin, a popular Soviet comedian during the 1960s. Many listeners interpreted it as a bittersweet piece of self-deprecating humour expressing the malaise that the people of 'goulash Communism' felt upon contemplating that they were after all content having 'something' rather than the 'real thing'. Since 1000 CE the 'real thing' for many Hungarians has been a putative (Western) European standard, perhaps in the form of noble assemblies that kept medieval kings in check; Latin Christianity and its reformed offspring; humanist philology and Enlightenment ideals; market capitalism; and parliamentary constitutionalism. And often the Hungarian 'something' has resembled these standards: the Golden Bull of 1222, establishing the right of the nobility to resist the monarch, was near-simultaneous with the English Magna Carta (1215) in laying the foundations for medieval constitutionalism; from the late 1460s King Matthias Corvinus (1443–90; r. 1458–90) built the first Renaissance court north of the Alps. Between these dates, the medieval *regnum Hungariae* was a sound unit that survived the devastating Mongol (Tartar) invasion of 1241, as well as the extinction in 1301 of the House of Árpád (which had ruled since 896 when the Magyars had first arrived). It also asserted itself as a regional power and escaped the calamities of the Black Death in the 14th century.

At the same time, however, the towns were small and few, their representatives missing or relegated to ancillary roles in the representative assemblies, and their merchant communities more concerned with providing luxuries for the royal court and aristocracy than with an expanding internal market. Hungary avoided the economic and demographic 'crisis of the 14th century', but only because its cause – over-expansion – was missing. Thus she also missed the dynamic recovery from the crisis that Western

TIMELINE

896 CE Conquest of the Carpathian Basin by Magyar tribes led by Árpád

1000 The coronation of Stephen I

1222 The Golden Bull records the privileges of the nobility and restricts royal power

1241–42 Mongol (Tartar) invasion

1458–90 The reign of King Matthias Corvinus

1526 Ottoman triumph in the Battle of Mohács; Hungary is divided into three zones

1526–1918 The Habsburgs rule Hungary

1699 The Ottomans are expelled from the territory of Hungary

1703–11 Anti-Habsburg revolt led by Francis Rákóczi II

1848–49 The attempted Revolution and War of Independence, led by Lajos Kossuth

1867 The dual monarchy of Austria–Hungary is formed

1920 After defeat in the First World War, Hungary is dismembered by the Treaty of Trianon

1941 Hungary enters the Second World War as an ally of Germany against Russia

1945 The Germans are expelled from Hungary by the Soviet Red Army

1948 Communist rule under Soviet domination

1956 Anti-Communist uprising results in Soviet invasion

1989–90 The collapse of Communist rule; democratic elections and the departure of Soviet troops

2004 Hungary joins the European Union

Europe enjoyed. Attempts to establish a permanent university in Hungary proved futile until
1635 because university-educated literati were
happy to travel abroad. Matthias's lavish
patronage of the arts and learning was a tip
without an iceberg: the initiative of a towering
individual, inspired by an isolated intellectual
elite amid general backwardness.

Matthias's splendid residences at Buda and
Visegrád are now archaeological sites where
stone fragments indicate the original layout.
This suggests the next theme in the grand narrative of Hungary's past: that of decay. It was
initiated by the triumph of the Ottoman
Suleiman II in the Battle of Mohács (1526),
which caused one of the great ruptures in
Hungarian history. It resulted in the tripartite
division of the country into the residue of the
Kingdom of Hungary, inherited by the House of
Habsburg, to the west; a triangle-shaped zone
occupied by the Ottomans in the centre; and a
fledgling Principality of Transylvania, reduced
to a permanent diplomatic oscillation between
her powerful neighbours, to the east. The once-
prosperous regional power became a frontier
zone between two world empires. The spread of
the Protestant Reformation in each of the three

*The Battle of Mohács (1526) in a Turkish miniature from 1588.
Suleiman II can be seen on a white horse, in a golden robe. The
ensuing 'Ottoman yoke' amplified tendencies of socio-economic
backwardness and heralded a long period of domination by
neighbouring imperial powers Austria and Turkey.*

territorial units added to the sense of being wedged between, this time, two 'paganisms':
Islam and the Catholic Counter-Reformation of the Habsburgs.

Compromises were made. There were infrequent episodes of repression on the
Habsburg side during the 17th century (evoking constitutional protest, conspiracy
and/or armed resistance), but they were neither a chief cause of religious re-conversion
nor an impediment to progress and prosperity. Nor can 'decay' be exclusively ascribed to
the Ottoman presence, and the depletion of human and material resources by
internecine warfare. Yet the cumulative effect of these wars was dramatic. When a
Habsburg-led international effort expelled the Ottomans at the end of the 17th century,
just 2 per cent of Hungary's land was cultivated, and it was inhabited by roughly the
same number of people as it would be two centuries earlier. Resettlement (especially of

Northern and Southern Slavs, Romanians and Germans) transformed the ethnic composition of the Carpathian Basin. While the medieval kingdom had also been ethnically colourful, by the end of the 18th century the proportion of Hungarians dropped to about 40 per cent.

But just as the Ottoman presence had long-term consequences, the 'Hungarian decay' associated with it had some longer-term causes. Even with the Ottomans close and the Atlantic remote, international cycles of prosperity stimulated the Hungarian economy up to the end of the 16th century, but they failed to lead to the capitalization of agriculture and the rise of industry. One reason is that, even before the Ottomans arrived, Hungary's nobility was able to reap the benefits of the agrarian boom without embarking on such transformations, simply by strengthening its hold over the land and the peasantry.

That same nobility gloried in defending 'the liberties of the land' against exertions of arbitrary power, and at times proved a committed leader of national revolts. This was the case after the expulsion of the Turks in 1699 by Leopold I (1640–1705), when the excesses of the new Habsburg administration provoked an eight-year war, led by Francis Rákóczi II, scion of the 17th-century princes of Transylvania. In 1711 this effort ended in failure, but a compromise peace restored the ancient Hungarian 'constitution' and integrated the country as an autonomous unit within the Habsburg monarchy. In spite of frequent complaints about 'colonial status', Hungary obtained domestic peace and more favourable conditions for a gradual recovery than had been available earlier. Much depended on the ability of the elites to respond to a world of accelerated change, sometimes imposed from the Vienna of the enlightened despots Maria Theresa and Joseph II in the later 18th century, to employ improved methods of cultivation and administration, and to absorb notions of the public good and social responsibility. Their failure conserved some ossified structures and relationships, and made it hard for the country to cope with the challenges of modernity. Their successes prepared, and to a great extent constituted, one of the most vibrant chapters in the history of Hungary: the age of reform and its cathartic culmination, the Revolution and War of Independence of 1848–49.

An ethos of pragmatic improvement, which aimed to enhance competitiveness based on education and social emancipation, was suppressed in the atmosphere created by the late 18th-century French Revolution. However, it resurfaced in the 1820s and became combined with the ancient pursuit of constitutional defence by the political elite and a new preoccupation with vernacular culture. The product was a general liberalism and 'national awakening', a programme of civil and national emancipation coupled with material progress – not only among the Hungarians, but also the Slovaks, Croats, Romanians and other ethnic minorities. But Hungarian liberals asserted the idea of the 'unitary political nation', implying that civil equality for individuals would cancel the

A painting by Alexander Bogdanovich Villevalde, dating from 1881, depicting a skirmish during the Hungarian Revolution of 1848–49. The Hungarian reforms of the 1830s and 1840s culminated in a 'lawful revolution', which turned into an anti-Habsburg war and was subdued by the intervention of tsarist troops.

need for special community rights, and tension was inevitable. Nevertheless, a dynamic seemed to develop that could break Hungary out of its narrow confines. Amid bitter debates about 'the fatherland and progress', notably between Count István Széchenyi (the leading proponent of progress) and Lajos Kossuth (the nationalist hero), there was a growing euphoria about civilizational advances. There followed an overhaul of laws and administration to foster market relations and extend constitutional rights to those not previously covered, or, as Kossuth described it, to 'extend the bulwarks of the constitution'. This phrase implied the abolition of serfdom, equality before the law, and representative government based on liberal suffrage in a Hungary tied to Austria only through the person of the monarch.

These were exactly the achievements of the bloodless revolution of March 1848. They were, however, nullified within a year and a half when Vienna recovered its strength after

the embarrassment of revolutionary upheaval in several corners of the monarchy. Austrian troops, backed by the Russians, proved too much for the freshly raised Hungarian forces. An additional challenge was the magnitude of the tasks facing the revolutionary government, in particular with regard to resolving peasant emancipation to the satisfaction of all parties, and the mutual distrust between the Hungarian elite and minority ethnic group that resulted in bloody exchanges and enduring resentment.

Hungary carried these liabilities beyond 1867, when the non-cooperation of the Hungarian elite with a repressive regime and the difficulties that Austria was experiencing on the international scene created the conditions for another compromise, the creation of the joint Austro-Hungarian monarchy. Largely thanks to the prudence of a few veterans of 1848, such as 'the sage of the nation' Ferenc Deák (1803–76), the Austrian emperor Franz Joseph I (1830–1916) was transformed from a foreign autocrat into the constitutional king of Hungary, now an equal partner of Austria within the Habsburg monarchy. Together with a liberal parliamentary system, burdened as it was with anachronisms, came industrial capitalism (in a predominantly agrarian country, where the relations of authority within rural society preserved much of their old feudal character) and urban modernity with all the flamboyance of the belle époque. Emancipated and assimilated Jews played a prominent part in the country's economic and cultural life. Progress and prosperity appeared to make great strides, and most people believed in the resurrection of Hungary's past 'greatness'.

However, Franz Joseph's Hungary differed from that of Matthias I's in one crucial respect: its ethnic composition. Even the maximum of concessions that could be expected from the Hungarians would have been unsatisfactory for the minorities, who tended to challenge the integrity of the Hungarian state. The Compromise of 1867 was forged between the elites of the two strongest national groups of the Habsburg monarchy at the expense of the other minorities; although realistic at that time, the system based upon it collapsed after 1918 because no satisfactory solution existed to all the constitutional issues.

The 1920 Peace Treaty of Trianon, which sealed the dismemberment of 'historic Hungary' – giving two thirds of her territory and total population, including one third of ethnic Hungarians, to her neighbours – is remembered as the greatest tragedy of the country. It still provides flammable ideological and political material, and even overshadows such horrors as the Hungarian Holocaust of 1944 (which cost the lives of several hundred thousand citizens, the state authorities willingly cooperating with the German occupying forces) and the suppression of the 1956 revolution. By one reckoning, Trianon

Succeeding to the throne at the age of eighteen during the revolutionary times of 1848, Franz Joseph I was still regarded as a foreign autocrat in Hungary at the time of this portrait (1855). With the Compromise of 1867, he came to be seen as a constitutional ruler.

Hugh Wallace, United States Ambassador to France, signs the Peace Treaty with Hungary at the Grand Trianon Palace in Versailles in 1920. Given the conditions imposed on their country, the Hungarian signatories no longer wished to participate in political life. The treaty reduced Hungary's population from 20 to just 7.6 million.

was the outcome of the narrow-minded and repressive politics of the Hungarian elite towards the minorities. By another, it arose from the strategic interests of hostile great powers, who used ethnic tensions as part of their war effort, and were willing to listen to the claims of the aggressive new nation states that allied with them.

The real tragedy of the Trianon Peace Treaty lies in the fact that it contributed to the survival of structures that had steered the country towards war in the first place. Hungarian national consciousness imagined a medium-sized state where Magyar primacy was based not on statistical majority and racial identity, but on historical and political achievement. It was bewildered at being forced within the confines of a much smaller country. Internally, the flaws of the settlement justified the general sense of outrage and revenge. In the eyes of its neighbours and their patrons, Hungary was transformed from a nation of haughty oppressors into one of petty troublemakers, and a threat to international stability.

Hungary predictably drifted into the Second World War in alliance with Germany again. True, the regime of Regent Miklós Horthy (r. 1920–44) was a reluctant ally, trying to preserve the goodwill of the Western powers. It is also true that anti-Jewish legislation was introduced in Hungary in the 1920s, before the world had even heard of Hitler. Parliamentary trappings did little to hide the authoritarian character of the regime, which suited the Christian middle class that provided its main leverage, nor was this class inoculated against the temptations of right-wing radicalism. The figures that became international brand names of Hungarian culture during this period – László Moholy-Nagy (1895–1946), Robert Capa (1913–54) and Béla Bartók (1881–1945) – emigrated. The Hungarian Holocaust has already been mentioned. If this were not enough, by the autumn of 1944 Hungary became Nazi Germany's last ally, and Horthy's belated and blundering attempt to leave the sinking ship only opened the door to Hungary's indigenous national socialists. Soviet tanks swept away these as well as the last post-feudal structures that had been saved in 1918–20. But what was to replace them was beyond the control of the Hungarians themselves.

Hungarian Jews on the platform at the Auschwitz–Birkenau extermination camp; women and children were separated from the men. About half of the one million Hungarian lives lost in the Second World War were victims of the Holocaust.

Budapest, October 1956: Hungarian freedom fighters walk past the corpses of state security servicemen. After some ephemeral success, the anti-Communist revolution was ruthlessly suppressed by Soviet intervention. The ensuing retaliation was followed by the rise of a 'soft dictatorship', also known as 'goulash Communism'.

Even without the presence of Russian troops, the astonishing depletion of resources and the near-complete tabula rasa by the end of the war, the situation favoured the Communists. Their confident activism, simple solutions and organization seemed to answer the spirit of the times. Political strategy and military pressure, violence, manipulation and opportunism helped to transform the burgeoning democracy of 1945–47 into a totalitarian regime dependent on Moscow by 1948. But slogans like 'We shall have turned the world around by tomorrow' also won willing collaborators. The period of Sovietization and Stalinism during the 1950s was a painful test of social and political morality for Hungarians, which they stood with varying success.

During the revolution of 1956, when a short-lived Hungarian regime under Imre Nagy (1896–1958) was suppressed by Soviet tanks, besides the outrage at the crimes of the

Soviet regime and the plight it brought to the people, a new, albeit vague, democratic consensus seems to have been dominant, and the anti-Stalinist rage was not accompanied by any serious possibility of the recovery of conservative authoritarianism. The events of 1956 became an episode in Hungarian history comparable in its pathos to 1848–49, and it also restored much of the country's lost international prestige.

And 1956 repeated the pattern of 1849, 1918–20 and 1944–48 in the sense that international contingencies once again, and more shockingly than ever before, deprived Hungary of the opportunity of deciding its own future. After 1956 a pattern also well known from post-1849 (or post-1867) and post-1920 domestic history repeated itself: a regime born out of naked terror consolidated itslf by means that were acceptable to a broad segment of Hungarians. Also similarly to 1848–49, the revolution of 1956 could be viewed as creating the basis for a compromise by compelling the Hungarians to make a realistic assessment of their predicament, and Moscow to recognize that there were limits to their subjection. The latter circumstance opened up the opportunity for Hungary's new leaders – primarily János Kádár (1912–89) – to win the acceptance of most, though the devotion of few, Hungarians by benefits that were not available to citizens of other countries in the Soviet bloc. These included a cautious freedom of expression and access to cultural goods – carefully steered processes of upward mobility and consumerism. They reconciled people to the rule of the party bureaucracy, the Communist nomenklatura under Soviet tutelage, and to certain taboos such as the one-party system or

Soviet soldiers prepare to leave Hungary in May 1989 as the Cold War winds down. Having previously lived an isolated life in assigned barracks, most of the c. 70,000-strong occupying forces were just as happy about the start of troop withdrawals as the Hungarian population.

the qualification of 1956 as a 'counter-revolution'. However, neither the liberalization nor the increasing foreign loans that supplemented it were sufficient to maintain the standards reached by the early 1980s; so the regime was unable to keep its part of the deal. Even so, by 1989, when Communism was finally overthrown, Hungarians had developed diffidence as their second nature, and were lulled into political laziness by the little compromises required in return for modest comforts. Few were prepared for this new chance to establish democracy, this time as apparently unlimited masters of their fate and succeeding or failing entirely on their own account. Distance will help posterity to judge how well they have fared.

Turkey

The land with a lost empire

The immediate ancestors of Osman (1280–1324), the founder of the Ottoman dynasty that endured until 1922, came to Anatolia in the second of two great waves of Turkish migration from Central Asia, following the Mongolian expansion across that area in the early 13th century. The enterprise started quite modestly, with nothing to suggest its subsequent triumphs. A small tribe of 400 tents deployed in the fringes of Bithynia managed to take advantage of political disturbances in the region and establish itself as an autonomous entity. It was not the biggest or the noblest of the many other Turkish principalities of the time – the Seljuks, for instance, were considered the 'family of the kings' – but the Ottomans succeeded in becoming the major power in the region.

Ottoman success was such that, after conquering Constantinople in 1453, Mehmet II (1432–81) felt confident enough to say (in Troy, appropriately) that 'it was the Greeks and Macedonians…who ravaged this place in the past, and whose descendants have now through my efforts paid the right penalty…for their injustice to us Asiatics at that time and so often in subsequent times'. This echoed the idea endorsed by some in Europe that the Turks, like the Romans before them, were vengeful Trojans paying back the Greeks for their defeat in the Trojan War. In 1517 Martin Luther declared that it was wrong to fight the Turks, since to do so 'amounted to challenging God's judgments upon men's sins'. By the time the Ottomans reached Vienna in 1529, the once-modest principality had become an empire spanning three continents, controlling much of southeastern Europe, western Asia and North Africa. As late as 1683 it was still inspiring dread in the hearts of Europeans who expected that 'the executioner of God's vengeance' would be in Rome before the winter.

But something went terribly wrong in the following century. Order vanished, prestige dimmed. By 1817 the French Comte Auguste de Forbin was expressing amazement at

A 19th-century portrait of Osman I, the founder of the Ottoman dynasty. The Ottoman Empire was named after him ('Ottoman' or 'Otman' being Western corruptions of 'Osman') and dominated most of the former lands of the Eastern Roman Empire for centuries.

An illustration of the Siege of Vienna, 1529, which was orchestrated by Suleiman I, also known as Suleiman the Magnificent. The failure of the campaign is considered one of the defining moments in Ottoman history.

the empire's continued existence; British prime minster Lord Aberdeen (1784–1860) spoke of a 'baffling occult force' that seemed to keep Ottoman power alive. Across Europe people said the 'Turks could conquer but not rule'. There were even rumours about their possible extinction, which was seen as a historical opportunity by scientific-minded people such as philologist Hyde Clarke (1815–95) who invited the public 'to the spectacle of the extinction of a mighty and numerous people, such as took place with the ancient Greeks and Romans'. The story of the Turkish people lies in the nation's swift transition from being the executioner of God's vengeance to the 'sick man of Europe', the 'proud empire trying to maintain its dignity in frequently undignified circumstances'.

The 19th century proved to be the longest of the Ottoman Empire. Decline in the political arena and humiliations on the battlefield left permanent marks on the well-protected domains of the sultans. The physical map of the empire was not the only thing to change dramatically; the mental map of its people also altered as a result of financial and political setbacks. Throughout the centuries all ranks of Ottomans had believed in the invincibility of their imperial project. Despite accidents such as the Battle of Lepanto in 1571, which, according to Cervantes, revealed 'the fallacy of the prevailing opinion that the Turks were invincible', in general what was seen as 'mortifying Turkish pride' survived well into the 19th century. But in a couple of decades all the references to Ottoman arrogance vanished. In literature the cliché of the lustful Turk who could command the vulnerable captives of his harem was reduced to impotence; in travel

TIMELINE

1299 Osman, founder of the Ottoman Empire, comes to power in Anatolia

1389 The Ottomans defeat the Serbs at the Battle of Kosovo

1453 Mehmet II conquers Constantinople

1526 The Ottomans conquer Hungary at the Battle of Mohács

1529 Suleiman the Magnificent besieges Vienna

1571 The Ottoman fleet is defeated by a Catholic coalition at Lepanto

1683 The Turks besiege Vienna for a second time

1699 The Ottomans lose Hungary following the Treaty of Karlowitz

1832 Greece wins its independence from the Ottomans

1914 The Ottomans enter the First World War as allies of the Central powers

1915–17 Turkish troops begin a sequence of massacres of Armenians

1919 The Young Turks begin a war of independence from the Ottomans

1923 Foundation of the Turkish Republic with Mustafa Kemal as president

2004 Turkey applies to join the European Union

writing the obstinate locals, begrudging a simple salute because of their 'Turkish pride
and austerity' (in the words of Sir Frederick Henniker in the early 19th century), were
replaced by meek compatriots who admired the Western lifestyle.

Ottomans themselves started to think along the same lines. The Ottoman position in
comparison to Europe, said an Ottoman journalist in 1872, was 'like that of an unedu-
cated child beside an accomplished scholar'. The state-sponsored modernization
programmes of the late 1830s accelerated this process. Even though the Ottomans tried to
come up with their own syntheses (when Western furniture was the rule, pashas, longing
for the good old days on divans, sometimes sat tailor-fashion on their desks while their
subordinates crouched on the armchairs), the admiration for the 'Frankish' way of life
created a sense of inferiority that proved to be one of the most important legacies of the
Ottoman Empire in her later incarnation as Turkey.

The 'cultural cringe', however, was not the only bequest of the 19th century to modern
Turkey, and the discovery of the awe-inspiring West in the East coincided with the inven-
tion of a diametrically opposite East in the West. Writers comparing Ottoman and
European politics presented separate worlds with minimal interaction. Even as early as

*A postcard commemorating the Young Turk Revolution of 1908. A group of young Ottoman officers, inspired
by the ideals of the French Revolution, fought against Abdülhamid II to reinstate the Ottoman Constitution
of 1878. The revolution restored the parliament, which previously had been suspended.*

6037. P. Z. - CONSTANTINOPLE, PONT...

At the end of the 19th century Istanbul was a cosmopolitan city despite the decline in political power of the Ottoman Empire. Galata Bridge across the Golden Horn was built in the middle of the century to link the non-Muslim areas with the city centre.

1863 Hyde Clarke pointed out that 'things and institutions, common in Europe [with the Ottoman Empire] are daily marked out for censure against the Turks and represented as in opposition to European standards'. This picture was not completely different from the Turkish perspective. The Ottomanists tried to promote the idea of a unique empire and produced chauvinistic, ultranationalist history writing. Hence in their view a kind of 'iron curtain' appeared, separating the Ottoman and European worlds before the heyday of 19th-century imperialism. But this approach was unfounded. Throughout history there were vibrant trade relations between Europe and the Ottoman Empire, along with strong intellectual and cultural contacts. For the realists of Europe the Ottoman Empire, as one historian put it, 'was a power like any other and even a European power'. For the Ottoman sultans, on the other hand, this was only natural as they considered themselves, among many other things, the legitimate inheritors of the Roman emperors: *Kayzer-i Rum* was a title they carried proudly.

When the sultanate was abolished in 1922, the young republicans understood that Ottoman history was too controversial a subject: glorification of the 15th and 16th centuries was not ideologically convenient, while memories of the 19th and early 20th centuries were too close to forget. The central role of religion in Ottoman society was also an uncomfortable topic for the secular nationalists of the young republic. Moreover, the multicultural structure of the Ottoman Empire was at odds with the tenets of the new state that highlighted national purity. The republicans needed a clear break, so they discarded the Ottoman-Islamic past and came up with what is known as the 'official history thesis', based on a very liberal understanding of pre-Ottoman Turkish history. It was a defensive thesis against, as one of its theoreticians put it, 'slanders and arrogations such as the Turks belong to the "yellow race", [are] inferior to Europeans…[and] do not have any historical rights on Anatolia'. According to this theory, 'the cultural habitat of this race [the Turkish people] was Central Asia. The climate [of the region] changed in the order of things…[hence] this mass of people…had to emigrate.' While maintaining that the Turks were members of the Aryan race and had founded many civilizations including the Sumerian, Akkadian, Assyrian, Hittite, Egyptian and Aegean, the thesis also aimed to inform the public about the detrimental effects of Islam on Turkishness. The emphasis on ancient Anatolian civilizations was deliberate. In a strange way, the theory combined the

Mustafa Kemal Atatürk, founder of the Turkish Republic and its first president. He became famous as a talented commander during the Gallipoli campaign of 1915. Following the British occupation of Istanbul in 1918, he organized a resistance movement against the Allies. He set up a National Assembly in Ankara that would eventually abolish the sultanate in 1922.

Central Asian past of the Turkish people with the classical heritage of the land. Anatolia, said Mustafa Kemal Atatürk (1881–1938), founder of the Turkish Republic, 'has been the cradle of the Turks for seven thousand years'. In this understanding of the past, there was little place for the Ottomans. Even though this view never gained widespread recognition among intellectuals, it served quite well as the ideological fountainhead of the young republic between two world wars.

With the advent of the multi-party system in the late 1940s, the 'official history thesis' faded into oblivion. This period also witnessed the 'normalization' of religious affairs by the governing party to maintain its hold on power. While academics concentrated on the so-called golden age of the empire – the 15th and 16th centuries – the political world saw increasing references to the Ottoman past. The empire was striking back. A new perception of the empire, based on diligent archival work, was promoted by historians such as Halil Inalcık and Ömer Lütfi Barkan in the 1960s. According to this new view, the Ottoman Empire was a *sui generis* political entity rooted in an elaborate understanding of justice. It was entirely different to medieval Europe where peasants had no freedom.

A portrait of Abdülhamid II c. 1890. He was one of the most controversial Ottoman sultans, ruling his empire with an iron hand for more than thirty years. His emphasis on Islam and his efforts regarding modernization left a rather complex legacy.

Just as fascism had had a bearing on the republic's perception of its own history, so Marxism also created new discussions. Many researchers were preoccupied with the question of whether an Asiatic mode of production existed in the empire, or whether some kernels of capitalist development could be found.

After the military coup of 1980, the state started to draw upon Islamic education to fight leftist movements, and this promoted a new understanding of Ottoman history. Article 24 of the 1982 constitution reads: 'education and instruction in religion and ethics shall be conducted under the supervision and control of the state. Instructions and religious culture and moral education shall be compulsory in the curricula of primary and secondary schools.' This resulted in the equation of the Ottoman Empire with Islam. The Turks, disregarding the details of their Central Asian past, were now presented as the defenders of Islam, especially during the reign of Abdülhamid II (1842–1918; r. 1876–1909) when an unprecedented emphasis on religion gained a new momentum and the 'Turkish–Islam' synthesis was officially created.

Since the 1980s the empire had increasingly gained importance as a point of reference in internal and external Turkish affairs. In 1999 the 700th anniversary of the establishment of the Ottoman state by Osman was celebrated throughout the country. Schools were established and books written to commemorate the event. In January 2009, after a

January 2009: supporters of Prime Minister Recep Tayyip Erdoğan greet him with Turkish flags during a subway opening ceremony in Istanbul. Erdoğan walked out of a debate on the Middle East at the World Economic Forum in Davos after a confrontation with Israel's President Shimon Peres.

heated debate over Gaza with Israel's president Shimon Peres (b. 1923), Turkey's prime minister Recep Tayyip Erdoğan (b. 1954) stormed off the stage at the World Economic Forum in Davos. When he got back to Turkey he was welcomed by an overexcited cohort calling him the 'last Ottoman sultan'. A phrase that could have been used as a political insult during the first years of the republic now had a totally different connotation. Months later, when Erdoğan visited Syria, he gave a long speech about the common heritage of the two countries; he was again welcomed with the same slogan in both countries. This common heritage that the young republic tried to deny proved to be inescapable. Considering all these points, I cannot help wondering if Jason Goodwin was right to start his *Lords of the Horizons: A History of the Ottoman Empire* (2003) by saying 'this book is about a people who do not exist'. The empire, as a political entity, has long vanished in history, but its spirit is going to stay with us for some time to come.

Brazil

The legacy of slavery and environmental suicide

Two aspects of history have made Brazilians who we are today. First, for three quarters of our history since the Portuguese explorer Pedro Cabral landed at Porto Seguro in Bahia in 1500, Brazilian society comprised slaves and slave-owners, or the beneficiaries of slavery. Brazil was by far the biggest importer of slaves in the old colonial system and it was the last country in the Western world to abolish slavery, in 1888. Second, ever since the arrival of the Portuguese, but over the last half century in particular, the fundamental social and economic structures of Brazilian society have been determined by the predatory destruction of its environment, moving from the eastern coastal region towards the interior. By the 1960s the process had reached the major biomes of central and northeastern Brazil, the Pantanal wetlands, the Cerrado savanna and the Amazon region.

These two features are the underlying premises for the existence of Brazil, past and present. Their significance has been enormous, even on a global scale, and they are constants in Brazilian history. The other variables of Brazilian society have also continually depended on them and been derived from them.

From the 16th to the 19th centuries a total of 10.7 million slaves survived the Atlantic crossing from Africa to the Americas, and (according to recent calculations by historians David Eltis and José Flávio Motta) nearly half of them were shipped to Brazil. Thus, over 350 years, nearly 5 million slaves landed in Brazil. The British colonies in North America and the United States of America probably imported only around one tenth of this number. By 1850 there were 2.5 million slaves in the country and the 1872 census reported that around 58 per cent of the population were of African descent (whether slaves or free men).

Brazil's economy required a lot of manpower, but it did not require a strong and growing internal market as colonial Brazil's basic products – sugar cane, gold in the 18th

An aerial view demonstrates the extent of deforestation in the Amazon rainforest. The forests of the Amazon, the Pantanal and the Cerrado have been slowly destroyed since 1964, mostly by the agro industry. More than 15 per cent of the Amazon rainforest has disappeared and the Brazilian government seems unable to stop this ecological suicide.

century and coffee from the 19th century onwards – were in great demand in Portugal and the rest of Europe. In addition, the slave trade itself was highly lucrative and, in a country where land was abundant and not extensively tradeable, slaves were often the largest share of one's patrimony.

Indeed, slaves were not only used for plantation work. In Bahia, for example, fewer than a tenth of the slaves were used on sugar plantations. In the late 18th and early 19th centuries, between 13 and 39 per cent of households in the *capitania* of São Paulo owned small lots of slaves. Slave-owners might include tobacco planters, fishermen, owners of stills, craftsmen, church dignitaries, members of the liberal professions, small business-men or gang foremen.

The slave was thus a ubiquitous figure in Brazilian society and crucial for the functioning of the economy, but not only to produce surplus. Slavery permeated society, affecting its forms of saving, its imagination, religiosity, sexuality, collective mentalities, status symbols, the modus operandi of its family life and much more. The figure of the slave was so necessary for non-slaves that it became a 'natural' fact for them, a given feature of their automatic and unconscious approach to life and living. Brazil is the most comprehensive manifestation in Western history (both ancient and modern) of the ancient Greek philosopher Aristotle's notion of a society that regards slavery as natural. Slavery is such a given feature of this society that it goes as unnoticed as the harmony of the spheres (which Pythagoras said we could not hear because it preceded our birth). And just as this celestial music can only be detected by hearing its opposite – silence – the legacy of slavery is apparent to the contemporary Brazilian mentality only through its opposite: 'racial democracy', the belief proposed by sociologist Gilberto Freyre in 1933 that Brazil suffers no racial prejudice or discrimination. If Brazil has succeeded in exporting this myth so well, it is primarily because it truly believes in it.

The enslavement of one part of society by another leaves the indelible mark of Cain. The most acute result is that Brazilians have not created a full civic society. The chasm

TIMELINE

6000 BCE First recorded inhabitants of the Minas Gerais region

1500 CE Portuguese explorer Pedro Cabral reaches the Brazilian coast

1630–61 The Dutch set up a colony on the northern coast

1808 The Portuguese royal family, fleeing Napoleon, settles in Brazil

1822 Portuguese regent Prince Pedro proclaims Brazil independent of Portugal, appointing himself Emperor Pedro I

1888 Slavery is abolished

1889 Pedro II is deposed and a republic set up as a constitutional democracy

1930 A military coup ends the republic and Getulio Vargas takes power as dictator until 1945

1964–85 Military rule in Brazil

2002 Luiz Inácio Lula da Silva is elected president on a left-leaning platform

2011 Dilma Rousseff is elected Brazil's first female president

Between c. 1530 and 1850 nearly five million Africans were enslaved and taken to Brazil; about 40 per cent of the victims died during the trip. On arrival, those who tried to escape were submitted to the kind of punishment pictured above. Slavery in Brazil lasted until 1888 and the extreme social inequalities of the country are part of its heritage.

separating the social strata impedes the development of a sense of individual responsibility or a feeling of belonging to a community. The descendants of slaves continue to serve the heirs of non-slaves. The two continue to live in separate social spheres and symbolic units, a separation that differs from apartheid only in that the legal framework contains much 'egalitarian' legislation. Thus, typically, a plaque must be displayed in elevators in apartment buildings assuring domestic servants of their right to use the same elevators as the proprietors. But the law is ignored: as descendants of slavery, the subaltern classes do not actually claim what is theirs by right.

The absence of a sense of social belonging leads to extreme individualism. Economic and political corruption is seen as normal and pervades society; it is under the skin of business and found at all levels of the executive, legislature and judiciary. The public is resigned to corruption scandals, and blatantly corrupt politicians are re-elected. Antisocial behaviour is the norm. Major infrastructure investments are designed to line the pockets of the automotive industry rather than enhance collective transportation. Roads and streets are a sort of no-man's land. Trucks burn diesel oil with lethal levels of sulphur, polluting cities while exacerbating aggressive behaviour. Demand for bulletproof cars with darkened windows has soared. What is referred to as 'Brazilian informality' – another export that meets with ready acceptance abroad and in which Brazilians take great pride – is less a sign of appreciation for individual freedom than a privilege enjoyed by those who can bend the law in their favour. Meanwhile, those without the power to do this are submitted to bureaucracy and formalism.

Like slavery, bureaucracy is a part of the sombre legacy of the Iberian origin of Brazilian society. Other aspects include the influence of the Inquisition (which lasted in Portugal until 1821) and of Jesuitic patterns of education. A pro-agrarian and anti-industrial mentality was introduced, sanctioned by the Methuen Treaty of 1703 between England and Portugal, which had the effect of discouraging industrial development in the latter. Portugal severely forbade the existence of publishing houses and even the presence of printing machines in Brazil until 1808, resulting in an extremely weak tradition of the printed word in Brazil's colonial history and thereafter, and producing the deep-rooted illiteracy and anti-intellectualism of Brazilian 'elites'. Last but not least, a steady tradition of Iberian absolutism explains why Portugal and Brazil fell back so many times into authoritarian regimes during the 19th and 20th centuries (with no fewer than five coups in Brazil: in 1889, 1930, 1938, 1945 and 1964) and also why left-wing parties have been so sympathetic to Stalinism.

Residents of the Betania slum in Manaus use a makeshift walkway to avoid litter floating on floodwaters from the Rio Negro, a major tributary of the Amazon. There has been an uninterrupted population increase in this region since the dictatorship (1964–85), as the military believed the Amazon should be occupied for 'national security reasons'.

A float of the 'Beija-Flor' samba school bearing a giant statue of Luiz Inácio Lula da Silva during the 2003 carnival parade in Rio de Janeiro. Although educational and ecological conditions did not improve during his two terms in office (2002–10), social inequalities lessened, which explained the president's popularity.

The social inequality that arises from slavery is on the decline, at least in terms of the distribution of income. Unfortunately, this does not apply to the second theme of Brazilian history: predatory and devastating occupation of the land. The Atlantic forest vegetation that once skirted the coastline and covered 15 per cent of the nation's land mass barely exists today. In 1993 just 7 per cent of its original extent remained; another 100,000 hectares were lost in the three years between 2005 and 2008, and there are no signs that the last remaining vestiges will be saved. From the end of the 18th century a kind of precocious ecological conscience arose among Brazilian intellectuals educated in Europe. Through their critiques of deforestation – which echoed the Enlightenment ideals of harmony between culture and nature – we can follow the momentum of the destruction of the Atlantic forest.

The same fate awaits the Amazon region. For millennia human occupation of the Amazon caused no major change in its vegetation – until 1964, when a military coup ushered in a dictatorship powered by torture and chainsaws. The regime triggered huge social and environmental imbalances: new roads were built; there was rampant destruction of forest coverage and expansion of lands used for agricultural purposes; settlements were constructed for colonists from other regions of the country; river

Brazilian natives protest in front of the Supreme Court in Brasilia in December 2008 about the boundaries set by the government for the Raposa-Serra do Sol reservation, an Amazon forest territory which is home to 18,000 natives. The policy of creating such reserves has been controversial and seen as a threat to Brazilian territorial integrity and growth.

basins were disrupted by large hydroelectric dams; open-cast mining and gold rushes were instituted; rivers were polluted by mercury; wild species were endangered, made extinct, or smuggled and traded; and so on.

The dictatorship ended in the 1980s, but the ideology of 'national integration' that had been promulgated by the Higher School of War (according to which the military had the right of rule in order to guarantee national sovereignty) represented, and still represents, the interests of wide sectors of Brazilian society. These include the entities that have immediate interests in destroying what remains of Brazil's forest: landowners; pharmaceutical companies; manufacturers of industrial equipment, fertilizers, pesticides and transgenic seeds; timber companies and construction firms; meatpackers and retailers; the financial and administrative system irrigating this structure; and, finally, political parties and lobbyists. In short, the whole fabric of Brazilian economic and political power.

Nationalist intellectuals from extreme right to extreme left have been deployed to argue that the destruction of the forest is the price to be paid for economic growth, and that any attempt to hinder this process only serves the interests of the leading global economies, who now covet profits from 'our' forests, having destroyed their own in the past.

In addition, social movements tolerate occupation of the forest by surplus urban or rural populations. Since land in southeastern Brazil is for the most part in productive use, these movements advocate the moral right of landless workers to take over 'unproductive' land – that is, forest.

The ideologues of 'sustainability' on the other hand – agricultural economists and engineers – have produced a whole library of publications to show that economies of scale may be reaped by integrating the Amazon region with local and international markets without destroying the forest.

Since the 1980s Brazil's biomes have been destroyed at a faster rate than ever before. Between 1977 and 2005, 16 per cent of the Amazon forest formations in the region known as 'Legal Amazonia' were eliminated, an area far greater than that of France. There has been no let-up since. From the colonial era onwards, cattle-ranching has been the main driving force behind deforestation in Brazil – even now it accounts for 80 per cent of the destruction of the Amazon – making Brazil one of the world's largest beef exporters, with the domestic market also consuming huge amounts.

The desperate need for the conservation of Brazil's biomes has failed to arouse the nation. Its only advocates are the native Amazonian communities and small groups of academics and environmentalists, none of whom bear sufficient weight in terms of the balance of forces within Brazil and internationally. If the world community really wants to save the Amazon it must act quickly and forcefully. Historically Brazil has tended to evolve 'from the outside in'. Slavery was not abolished until very late, and only under heavy pressure from international interests. The fascist-like 'Estado Novo' regime, established in 1938, would have joined the German-Italian Axis had it not been for North American pressure. The dictatorship installed in 1964 was promoted by the United States Department of State, and would probably have lasted longer had President Jimmy Carter (1977–81) and the European democracies not put the dictators under pressure to re-establish democracy.

The same goes for saving the forest. Bound by the authoritarianism and property-first customs of its colonial past, this huge country, so inert and archaic by vocation, will only step back from the brink of environmental suicide if forced to do so by international pressure. Whether such pressure will be exerted is doubtful. By the time Brazilians realize that submitting forests to the logic of profit will only make them poorer, or the world becomes aware of the catastrophic effects of Brazil being reduced to savanna or desert, it will be too late.

tenochtitlan

ELIZABETH BAQUEDANO

Mexico

The land of the eagle, the cactus and the snake

A visitor to downtown Mexico City might be amazed at the beauty of the Mannerist buildings, Baroque churches and Art Nouveau hotels without realizing that this was once a lake where, in 1325, the wandering Aztecs found their promised land. In 1978, while an electrical transformer was being installed, the staff of the electricity company hit a big stone decorated with reliefs. Rescue archaeologists uncovered a sculpture of the moon goddess Coyolxauhqui. President José López Portillo (1920–2004) ordered that the buildings be torn down to reveal his people's past. 'I had the power', he said, perhaps consciously echoing the authority of his predecessors the Aztec emperors, even though part of his own family background was from Spanish Navarra.

It was foretold that the Mexica (as the Aztecs called themselves) would find a home when their priests saw an eagle perched upon a cactus and devouring a serpent. This was the promised land where they would be the masters of a great empire. The island was called Tenochtitlan ('place of the prickly pear fruit' or 'place of the fruit of the cactus') and it was here that the Templo Mayor (the great temple of the Aztecs), their most important religious precinct, was built to honour both Huitzilopochtli, god of war, and Tlaloc, god of rain.

It was at this temple that the most lavish ceremonies took place and the power of the Aztecs was manifested. Many cities paid tribute to the Aztecs with a variety of products – jewelry, masks, terracotta vessels and sculptures – while conquered people gave their blood as sacrifice to the gods. Other finds here indicate the Aztecs' awareness of and respect for earlier cultures: for example, an Olmec jade mask from 1200 BC was found, while the pyramid architecture of Teotihuacan, the great city in highland central Mexico built around 50–800 CE, was emulated. The Aztecs clearly recognized their own debt to the past.

A page from the Codex Mendoza, showing an eagle perched on a cactus and eating a snake, as predicted in an Aztec legend. The Aztec capital of Tenochtitlan was founded in 1325 on a site said to have been selected where the eagle was sighted. Tenochtitlan housed more than a quarter of a million people at the time of the Spanish conquest.

The Olmecs, whose civilization flourished on the Gulf Coast between 1500 and 400 BCE, laid the foundations for all later Mexican civilizations. Their gods, calendar and jaguar cult all spread far inland where they were adopted by the people of Teotihuacan and the Toltecs who flourished between 900 and 1150 CE, during what is now viewed as the golden age of pre-Columbian Mexico. It was their achievements, and their gods, that the Aztecs honoured in their own capital.

Among these legacies was the myth of Quetzalcoatl, the feathered serpent god. The symbol of the feathered serpent was adopted in particular by the last Aztec emperor, Moctezuma II (c. 1466–1520; r. 1502–20), who commissioned many serpent sculptures with his carved glyph that included a tiara and a nose-plug. According to myth, the fair-skinned Quetzalcoatl was tricked by his adversary Tezcatlipoca (Smoking Mirror) and as a result committed incest. The next morning he was so ashamed that he set sail towards the east, promising to return – in the very year the Spanish conquistador Hernán Cortés (1485–1547) arrived in Mexico.

This myth has been used to explain why Moctezuma initially vacillated when Cortés suddenly appeared in Tenochtitlan in 1519. After the conquest Mexican history presented this episode as if Moctezuma was waiting for Cortés to arrive, and was ready to give up his seat and allow Cortés to rule. But this has turned out to be a post-conquest construct: Moctezuma believed Cortés to be the emissary of a great king, but not a king himself.

It took just two years for the Spaniards to take Tenochtitlan. Their success was not down to the European conquistadors alone but also to their native non-Aztec allies. It is common to read – especially in European and American books – that the Spaniards conquered Mexico with only a few hundred men. It is true that there were only approximately 650 men with firearms, horses and fighting dogs; but fighting with them were thousands of Mexicans who preferred to help the new arrivals than the imperialist

TIMELINE

1500–340 BCE The Olmec culture flourishes

50–800 CE The great city of Teotihuacan is built in the Valley of Mexico

500–800 Monte Alban, one of Mesoamerica's first cities, is the political and cultural capital of the Zapotecs

900–1150 Climax of the Toltec Empire (the capital Tollan is now Tula in the modern state of Hidalgo)

1325 Traditional date for the foundation of Tenochtitlan as the Aztec capital

1519 Spaniards arrive in Mexico; the conquest of the Aztec Empire by Hernán Cortés takes place two years later

1535 The viceroyalty of New Spain is established

1551 Foundation of the University of Mexico

1767 Expulsion of the Jesuits from Mexico

1810–21 The Mexican War of Independence from Spain

1846–48 War with the United States; loss of California to the United States

1857–61 A liberal constitution is introduced by Benito Juárez

1862 France invades Mexico and Maximilian of Habsburg becomes emperor; Juárez seizes back power in 1867

1910–20 The Mexican Revolution results in a left-leaning, secular state

1994 Mexico joins the North American Free Trade Agreement

Enslaved natives building the Spanish capital Mexico City on top of Tenochtitlan in the 16th century. Soon after the conquest New Spain was built according to the ideas of the conquistadors. Cortés had much of the old city razed and many Aztec sculptures were reworked as bases for columns. Most of the remains were lost until the 1970s.

Aztecs. The choice they made marked the end of the old Mexico and the beginning of 'New Spain'.

Once the conquest was over it was considered important by the Spanish to end the old religion and introduce a new Christian faith. In 1524 Cortés welcomed the arrival of a Franciscan mission to convert the natives. In 1535 the king of Spain established the viceroyalty of New Spain in Mexico. The first viceroy, Antonio de Mendoza (1495–1552), created a Spanish city on the site of the old Aztec capital, most of which had been razed. Mexico City was not merely the capital of New Spain, it was also the seat of the archbishopric of Mexico.

The first viceroy asked the Spanish Crown to endow a university: the Royal and Pontifical University of Mexico opened in 1551 with a noted scholar, Francisco Cervantes de Salazar, as rector. Antonio de Mendoza and Juan de Zumárraga, first bishop of Mexico, also jointly approved the foundation in 1536 of the College of the Santa Cruz in Tlatelolco. This was administered by the Franciscans to provide an education for the children of the Aztec elite, and it was here that the first 'anthropologist' of the Americas, Bernardino de Sahagún (1499–1590), aided by his native informants, wrote the most

173

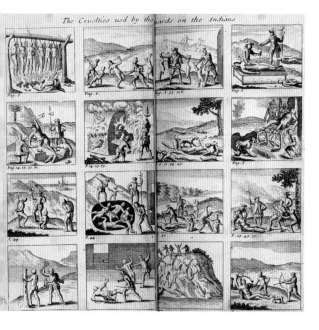

Bartolomé de las Casas (1484–1566), bishop of Chiapas and known as the 'defender of the Indians', catalogued the cruelties imposed on the enslaved native Americans by the encomenderos and petitioned the Spanish king on their behalf. His work was widely circulated, especially among Spain's enemies.

comprehensive work on Aztec culture, *The General History of the Things of New Spain* (1540–85). This was written in both Spanish and the native Nahuatl, and accompanied by illustrations. It remains an important source on anything to do with the life of the native peoples, from religion to pastimes.

From 1522 the Spaniards established a formal relationship of domination over the Mexican lords. Every major town (*señorío*) was given to one of the conquistadors. This system later became known as the encomienda (from the Spanish word *encomendar*, to entrust). Encomiendas gave the estate-owners control over indigenous labour and produce, resulting in ill-treatment of the Mexican commoners. The Dominican friar Bartolomé de las Casas, seeing the abuses, denounced them before Spain's king Philip II (1527–98; r. 1556–98). An example can be seen in the 16th-century *Codex Kingsborough*: four Mexican noblemen are shown being burned alive for late payments to the Spanish encomenderos. The demands imposed by the Spaniards were without doubt harsher than anything the natives had ever known.

By the 17th century many young Creoles (Spaniards born in the New World) were proud of their Mexican identity, but eager to create a Spanish-looking capital. In the late 18th century the Count of Revillagigedo (viceroy 1789–94), an exponent of the enlightened despotism favoured by Spain's Charles III (1716–88; r. 1764–88), embellished the great square of Mexico City, the *zócalo*. This involved digging into the foundations of the old city, in the process of which two native treasures were uncovered: the colossal statue of the goddess of the earth, Coatlicue, and the so-called Calendar Stone, a large sculpture commissioned by Moctezuma II, depicting the present era, the symbol for movement (a St Andrew's-like cross) leading to earthquakes, at the centre the face of a deity (possibly the sun), the previous eras that ended in cataclysms, as well as the twenty day signs.

Yet the values of the old civilizations would not be appreciated for another hundred years. The Creoles were more preoccupied with European style and despised the religious objects of the native Mexicans, being more interested in the religious symbolism of the Virgin of Guadalupe, an appearance of the Virgin Mary to an indigenous

Mexican in 1531; the image of the Virgin was also miraculously imprinted on a farmer's mantle, and became the most important Christian symbol in Mexico.

However, European cities, values and culture were not enough. The majority of the population was not European and there was inevitable dissatisfaction with the Spanish authorities. Two priests, Miguel Hidalgo y Costilla and José María Morelos, called for independence from Spain. In 1810 Hidalgo denounced European exploitation and sought a redistribution of land. He organized a revolt against the Spanish, buoyed by religious fervour under the banner of the Virgin of Guadalupe. When Hidalgo was executed in 1811 Morelos took over the revolution but suffered the same fate. These uprisings were led by Creoles fighting against the abolition of slavery and for Mexican sovereignty. Whereas during the 16th-century conquest the Mexicans fought for the Spaniards, Mexico's fight for independence – which was eventually achieved in 1821 – was orchestrated and organized by the Creoles. This apparent contradiction has characterized two important chapters of Mexican history.

A 16th-century shrine in the Basilica of Our Lady of Guadalupe in Mexico City, dedicated to the Virgin of Guadalupe who was said to have appeared on the cloak of a peasant in 1531. Known as the patron saint of Mexico, she became the symbol of the independence movement led by Miguel Hidalgo y Costilla.

Independence did not bring much change to the European cultural hegemony, although it did gradually see a move to build a fairer, more just society. The first dominant figure was General López de Santa Anna (1794–1876), who initially rebelled against the new presidency and then set up his own dictatorship, taking the country into a disastrous war with the United States in 1846–48. Santa Anna was overthrown and a new liberal constitution was promulgated in 1857. Though not radical, it was based on the principles of human rights and liberalism, with a clear division between state and church. No longer could the clergy interfere in the affairs of the government.

The new president Benito Juárez (1806–72) – a Mixe speaker from humble stock – forced the church to sell its land and to stop interfering in political affairs. This was one of the most important acts in Mexican history, shaping the country very differently from other Latin American countries, where politics and religion tend to go hand in hand.

In 1862 France invaded Mexico hoping to establish an empire. The French supported Mexican conservatives in offering the Crown to Maximilian of Habsburg (1832–67), in the hope that he would overturn the liberal reforms of Juárez. However, the new emperor did not oblige and consequently lost support from the conservatives; he was captured and executed by forces loyal to Juárez in 1867. The whole episode has been treated in Mexican history as one best forgotten. The avenue that connected Maximilian's imperial

Mexicans pose on a hilltop during the revolution, c. 1911, when a complex struggle for power developed into a civil war that continued until 1920. The revolution came about, among other reasons, as a reaction to Porfirio Díaz's long regime. With its nationalist and populist overtones, it became a key factor in the framing of modern Mexican identity.

residence with the centre of Mexico City had originally been called Paseo de la Emperatriz (Promenade of the Empress), but Juárez renamed it Paseo de la Reforma. New ideals of freedom, order and prosperity were preferred to European royalty.

Mexican history can be characterized as a series of disputes between basic human rights and the interests of a restricted few. 'Give everyone what they are entitled to' was the motto of Porfirio Díaz (1830–1915) when he took the presidency in 1876. Unfortunately his ideals were not to last, and he soon favoured the elite, both Mexican and foreign. During his thirty-five-year rule the city was heavily influenced by French trends. Many beautiful buildings in the country followed the European style. The Opera House (Bellas Artes) in Mexico City, begun in 1904, shows a mixture of styles that reveal the ambitions of a dictator obsessed with grandeur. Díaz was convinced that the country's healthy national economy justified it.

In 1911 Porfirio Díaz was driven out of the country after promising free elections but failing to deliver them. His opponent, Francisco I. Madero (1873–1913), adopted the powerful slogan 'Effective suffrage and no re-election', which set Mexico apart from other Latin American countries in the 20th century. Yet Madero's rule was challenged by General Victoriano Huerta (1850–1916), who then faced peasant revolts led by Francisco (Pancho) Villa in the north and Emiliano Zapata in the south, which turned into a long and messy revolution. Peace did not return until 1920.

Post-revolutionary Mexico was built on the concepts of anti-clericalism, land reform, protection of workers and nationalism. In 1930 the oil fields were nationalized. Mexico's national identity was now consciously constructed from the fusion of cultures, and was most powerfully expressed in the mural paintings of Diego Rivera (1886–1957), José Clemente Orozco (1883–1949) and David Alfaro Siqueiros (1896–1974). The country's indigenous roots were re-evaluated and the past became an inspiration for modern artists who used the walls of public buildings as books to indoctrinate the population of Mexico about its past. Though mostly dating from the 1920s and 1930s, these murals were still being produced by Siqueiros as late as the 1970s, and were imitated all over Latin America.

Since the revolution anthropologists and historians have played a crucial role in framing Mexican identity. The motto of the National University is 'Through my race, my spirit shall be revealed'. But this is not a racialist view: the attitude that deplores every Spanish contribution to Mexico's past is very much a minority one, and Mexico's past has been described by poet Octavio Paz (1914–98) as 'polycultural and polyfaceted'. Mexicans with Spanish ancestry look back with pride on the country's native past, and those of native backgrounds look to Europe, while many important government and cultural posts are in the hands of individuals with European backgrounds (many, too, are in the hands of women).

Zócalo Square, the heart of Mexico City's historic centre. Mexicans have struggled to emerge from the American stereotype of a lazy people despite the vitality and internationalism of contemporary Mexican culture.

However, the North American stereotype of the sombrero-clad Mexican as lazy, drunken and leaning on a cactus still endures. Originating in the 19th century in an Anglo-Saxon Protestant dislike of Spanish Catholicism, it has little grounding in reality: Mexicans are just as industrious as their neighbours, or even more so – or in history: the Aztecs honoured hard work, and reserved a special hell for those who died in their beds. It is true that the native population was demoralized after the conquest, but the adoption of alcohol by peasants was tolerated by the Spaniards, while the Aztecs had allowed it only for honoured warriors and the elderly.

The anti-clericalism of the post-revolutionary years was matched by their anti-capitalism, especially towards American capitalism. The 20th century saw a love–hate relationship with Mexico's northern neighbour, especially following the North American Free Trade Agreement of 1994, which hardened feelings of exploitation. Yet, in contrast to many other Latin American countries, modern Mexico is prosperous, cosmopolitan and outward-looking, with particularly strong cultural connections to Europe.

WILLEM FRIJHOFF

The Netherlands

Facing the challenges of water

Ask any Dutchman what force has shaped his country and he will answer: water. Or better: our struggle with water. *Luctor et emergo*, 'Struggling I overcome', as the device of Zeeland, the most watery province of the Netherlands, proudly states. Man is the country's second force, always competing with nature, managing physical adversity and creating new forms of land design. Although he may sometimes be forced to concede ground, the key words that permeate his country's history are safety, design and a quest for perfection: they form the core of Dutchness.

The Dutch live in a land of transit, for commodities as well as people. They have always looked for perfection elsewhere: previously in heaven, then in nations they considered exemplary. They were once captivated by France, their first ally during the 16th- and early 17th-century revolt against Spain, but now admire (and follow rather blindly) the United States of America. Small wonder that the Dutch Calvinists obsessively pursued the spiritual certainty of predestination. Or that, ever since the early Middle Ages, Dutch merchants have sought prosperity abroad, in their neighbours' economies and in countries overseas. Colonization and emigration, international commerce, trading companies and foreign investment have historically been the Dutch answers to the limits of their country's development and the threats of nature.

For some countries, water divides. In the spirit of the Dutch, however, water unites the country from within, and challenges it to expand its limits outside. The North Sea unites Holland with England, Scotland, the Frisian area and Scandinavia in a much stronger bond than that between the eastern Netherlands and neighbouring Continental Germany. As soon as the Dutch had won their independence, their merchant discoverers looked for new avenues for trade and settlement. Dutch names such as Cape Horn, Spitsberg, the Barents Sea, Arnhemland, Tasmania, New Zealand and Mauritius bear witness

A view of a Dutch riverside by Jan van Goyen (1596–1656). The many Dutch riverside paintings of the 17th century not only represent the landscape as it was perceived but speak also of the delicate harmony between land and water, including a moral message on man and nature.

Dutch people taking a Sunday walk in Yokohama, 19th century. The Dutch settlement was confined to the little island of Deshima in the harbour of Nagasaki. Dutch scholars influenced the rise of modern science in Japan.

to their expansion. For two centuries (from 1641 to 1853) the Dutch had a complete monopoly on trade with Japan. Other Dutch conquests were eventually lost but still bear the marks of their presence, such as Malacca, Ceylon (Sri Lanka), South Africa, the Gold Coast (Ghana), New Netherland (New York) and New Holland (the east coast of Brazil).

It was, however, the commercial organization of the Dutch East India Company, founded in 1602 as the first great semi-public shareholders' venture in Europe, that created the Dutch colonial empire. Before long it came to embrace the whole, immense Indonesian archipelago. The Dutch were efficient but often ruthless colonial administrators, profit always prevailing over civilization, in spite of huge missionary efforts. Their role in the slave trade of the Americas, still palpable in the architecture of the historic centre of Willemstad on the island of Curaçao (in the Netherlands Antilles), continues to fuel resentment in the last Caribbean remnants of its colonial empire and in former Dutch Guyana, now independent Surinam.

Water really has been the *materia prima* of Dutch history. Seven out of nine Dutch monuments on the UNESCO list of World Heritage sites involve water management: the Beemster Polder, the first of the great polders, created in 1609–12 by investors from nearby Amsterdam, then the booming centre of the world economy); the 18th-century Kinderdijk windmills; the former Zuiderzee island

TIMELINE

1543 Holy Roman Emperor Charles V, king of Spain, unites all the northern provinces of the Netherlands under Habsburg rule

1568 Start of the revolt against Spanish rule

1579 The Union of Utrecht establishes the United Provinces

1581 The United Provinces proclaim their independence from Spain

1602 Foundation of the Dutch East India Company

1648 Dutch independence is confirmed by the Treaty of Westphalia

1795 The Batavian Republic is established

1806 The (Napoleonic) Kingdom of Holland is established

1810–13 Annexation of the Netherlands to the French Empire

1815 The Kingdom of the Netherlands is established as a constitutional monarchy under the Orange-Nassau dynasty

1830 The southern provinces proclaim their independence as Belgium (confirmed in 1839)

1848 The adoption of a new constitution establishing a parliamentary monarchy

1914 The Netherlands remain neutral during the First World War

1932 Enclosure of the former Zuiderzee by the 'Afsluitdijk' (enclosure dam)

1940–45 German occupation of the Netherlands during the Second World War

1949 The independence of Indonesia (former Dutch East Indies) is confirmed

1957 The Netherlands are a founding member of the European Economic Community

1975 The independence of Surinam (Dutch Guyana) is proclaimed

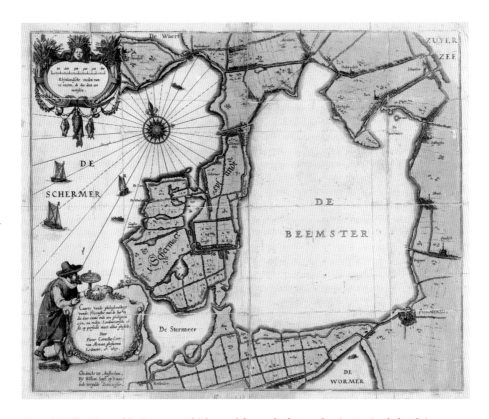

A map by Willem Jansz of the Beemster and Schermer lakes north of Amsterdam in 1607, just before their reclamation as polders for agricultural use. Dutch merchants invested their new wealth in land reclamation, also using the polders for building country houses.

of Schokland; the water defence line of Amsterdam (1880–1920); a pumping station opened in 1920; the Wadden Sea; and the historic canals of Amsterdam's city centre (the *Grachtengordel*). Centuries of shaping their land have made the Dutch excellent designers, witnessed in the Rietveld Schröder House in Utrecht and the Van Nelle Factory in Rotterdam. The image of Holland as a land of dykes, polders and windmills may be a cliché but it echoes the historical reality of the country's survival, even that of its inner, more secure regions.

Water has not only been the substance of Dutch history, but is also at the core of its national self-image and a powerful instrument of collective imagination. The riverscapes of Jan van Goyen (1596–1656), the cloudy skies of Jacob Ruysdael (*c.* 1628–82), and the marine paintings of the Van de Velde family from the 17th century all reflect the intense interplay of nature and culture in the minds of the Dutch, and their steady attempts at adjusting its physical forces to their benefit.

The threat of rising sea levels destroying the lower, western half of the country has recently revived ancient fears and memories of cataclysms, and left many people stricken

The 'Watersnood' or great flood of 1 February 1953 inundated a considerable part of the southwest of the Netherlands, destroying dykes and villages and claiming over 1,800 victims. In its wake the so-called Delta Plan was conceived, which involved damming the estuaries and restoring the dykes.

with panic. The menace is anything but hypothetical: in January 1995 more than 200,000 inhabitants of the central river area were evacuated due to the rising level of the Rhine and Meuse (Maas) Rivers. The prospect of climate change strikes the Dutch more vitally than other Europeans, and explains their huge involvement in environmental protection, planning and ecology, the more so as the Rhine and Meuse carry to the Netherlands the physical, chemical and nuclear waste of the whole of northwestern Europe.

After the disastrous flood of 1 February 1953, in which over 1,800 people died, the former archipelago of Zeeland and its hinterland were given protection by the Delta Works. That icon of modern Dutch engineering illustrates the old maxim: God made the world but the Dutch made their country. It is no coincidence that, running through polders and along river banks from southwest Zeeland to northeast Overyssel, there exists a large Bible belt in which Dutch pietism displays, in its most orthodox and steadfast form, its belief in God's election. Unsurprisingly the Museum of Netherlands History, recently commissioned by the Minister of Education, intends to put the theme of 'land and water' in second place among its five major historical items, between the sense of national identity, and the universal themes of 'rich and poor', 'war and peace' and 'body and mind'.

Dyke building, polder drainage, irrigation and mill technology were the first export products of the Dutch from the late Middle Ages, and harbour construction continues to be a Dutch skill recognized throughout the world. Technical innovations were at the basis of Dutch commercial supremacy in the 17th century, not only in shipbuilding, harbour provisions and urban layout, but also in engineering, mathematics and town fortification. In this century painters such as Frans Hals (*c.* 1580–1666), Rembrandt (1606–69) and Vermeer (1632–75) developed techniques for new forms of visual representation; cartographers made the world available to Dutch explorers; the telescope, the microscope and the pendulum clock were Dutch inventions that changed the perception of nature, space and time; print techniques made the Dutch universities, especially Leiden, the new centre of European science; and it has been argued that early 17th-century Amsterdam was able to grow into the very centre of the world economy through

Girl Reading a Letter at an Open Window *by Jan Vermeer, c. 1659. Vermeer's carefully designed and masterfully coloured paintings form a beautiful expression of the harmonious union of domestic burgher culture, the perfection of craftsmanship and the mathematical approach to reality during the Dutch golden age.*

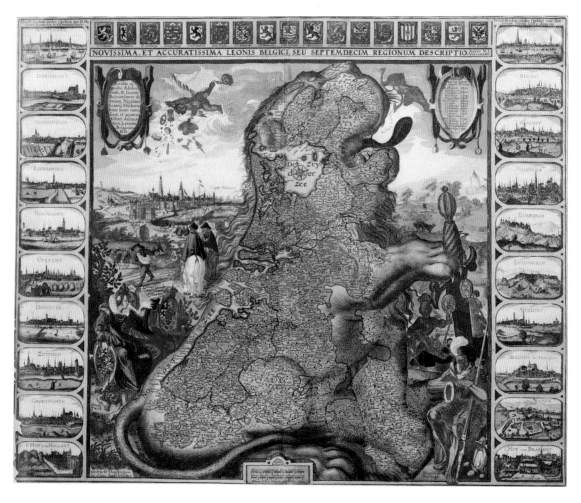

A map of 1609 representing the Netherlands in the form of the heraldic icon of the lion – symbol of courage in the face of the enemy. The urban character of the country and its government is emphasized by the cityscapes and the coats of arms of the main voting cities.

innovative communication techniques fostered by the town authorities, including daily newspapers, the stock market, shared risk management and actuarial science. The huge town hall of Amsterdam – now the Royal Palace on the Dam – begun in 1648, was celebrated as the eighth Wonder of the World. Its original decorative programme expressed all the virtues of Dutch burgher society: the freedom of an egalitarian society, peace for commerce to flourish, tolerance in the community, equal justice for all and trust in God.

Nowhere on earth is water management as instrumental as in the Netherlands. In 1809 Louis Bonaparte (1778–1846), the first real king of the Netherlands, following his brother Napoleon's conversion of the Batavian Republic into the new Kingdom of

Holland (1806), created a ministry for water management. In the Middle Ages, water boards and dyke councils had been the first elective organizational structures of the country, involving representatives both of the landed gentry and of the common landowners and farmers. Still playing a vital role today, they are considered to be at the heart of Dutch democracy. The so-called 'polder model' remains a structure of decision-making that, by taking into account the interests of all parties involved, has to arrive at a workable solution for everybody, including in politics, in the corporate culture of the great Dutch companies, and in trade unionism.

The ancient water boards correspond to some basic features of Dutch society throughout history. They are egalitarian structures managing the community's interests, in which differences of opinions, ideals and agency are tolerated, meritocracy is valued, and negotiation prevails over authority and power. The fragmentation of particular interests that they embody is recognized as a legitimate characteristic of the country's historical organization. It prevents the formation of any majority acquiring a controlling interest, and obliges constant coalition-making in virtually all fields of political, social and cultural life.

The *materia secunda* of Dutch history is man. In antiquity the frontier of the Roman Empire passed through Nijmegen and Utrecht, but Rome has left just a few ruins, place names and funeral monuments. It is almost forgotten now, except for the enduring myth of the Batavians, the country's first historical inhabitants, mentioned by Tacitus. From the modern perspective, the medieval legacy consists of the stories of counts and knights in the west, the myth of Frisian freedom in the north, and nostalgia for the Hanseatic League in the east. Some great monuments from this period have been conserved, such as the majestic cathedrals of Utrecht and Bois-le-Duc (now called 's-Hertogenbosch), many country and town churches, and a row of impressive castles such as the Muiderslot and Loevestein.

The towns, duchies and counties of the Netherlands were part of the Holy Roman Empire in the medieval period and remained so until the formal acknowledgment of Dutch independence at the Treaty of Westphalia in 1648. As early as the 15th and 16th centuries, however, they were united under the duchy of Burgundy. The revolt against the duke's successor, the king of Spain (the Eighty Years' War, 1568–1648), led to the independence of the northern part of the country (present-day Netherlands) and its separation from the south (the present-day Belgium). The rebels, nicknamed Beggars (*Geuzen*), were driven by a desire for freedom as well as for reformation of the church and evangelical renewal. Since their most prominent leaders professed the Calvinist creed, Calvinism became the public church of the new Dutch state, although a plurality of other important confessional groups, including the Catholics, survived, setting the tone for the country's future religious diversity and tolerance.

The rebellious state founded at the Union of Utrecht in 1579 was ruled by a republican oligarchy until it was democratized after the Batavian Revolution of 1795. It was, in fact, a confederation of seven small independent republics, the 'provinces', governed by local elites. Although not anti-monarchical from the start, the decentralized political organization of that urbanized society with its bourgeois culture, not to mention some awkward experiences with foreign rulers, swiftly brought the Dutch to decide against having a king. The *Staten-Generaal* (states general) at The Hague united them for warfare and other common interests, but there was no real head of state. Usually a member of the Nassau family and prince of Orange (France), the *stadtholder* was a curious anachronism. Heading army and navy as a servant of the republic, he had no formal political power, yet he enjoyed an immense moral prestige among the masses that made him a quasi-sovereign.

In 1815, after the Napoleonic era (1806–13), the country became a constitutional monarchy under the Orange dynasty, called the Kingdom of the Netherlands, which until the Revolution of 1830 included present-day Belgium. This evolving state structure anticipated the slow but unavoidable formation of a true Dutch nation out of the union of the sovereign 'provinces': at first seven, then eleven, at present twelve. Quite recently the province of Flevoland was added, really a bunch of reclaimed polders with its capital Lelystad, named after the visionary engineer Cornelis Lely (1854–1929).

The constitutional reform of 1848 produced a liberal state with a modern parliamentary regime that opened the country to its second golden age of commerce, industry, colonialism and science. Yet it also revealed the congenital weakness of Dutch 'particularism': the nation found itself segmented into competing confessional and ideological bodies – the Protestant, Catholic, socialist, liberal 'pillars' among others – claiming full autonomy and self-determination within a distant state. Since the Netherlands remained neutral during the First World War, the Second was the first real challenge for national unity. Beside the delicate, enduring divisions between 'good' and 'bad' Dutch, collaborators and resistance fighters, it brought the profound trauma of the Holocaust to a nation that had once boasted of being the New Israel and a haven for the persecuted Jews of the whole of Europe. After the war, decolonization was quick and crude. Indonesia was lost as early as 1949, and the 'pillarization' of Dutch society collapsed in the 1960s to make way for an ever more centralizing, invasive and secular welfare state dominated by some of the world's greatest companies (Philips, Royal Dutch Shell, Unilever) and a powerful financial sector inherited from the past.

However, the legacy of Calvinism continued to express itself in the conviction that the Netherlands was an elect nation, a moral compass for the world, a *gidsland* ('guiding country'): against nuclear warfare, in favour of peaceful agency between states, tolerant towards all minorities, an asylum for political victims, and – somewhat paradoxically –

always ready to expand the legal and actual limits of drug consumption, homosexuality and euthanasia. It is only during the last decade that the permissive society of the Dutch has been obliged to cope with a double, unexpected problem: mass immigration from Mediterranean countries with a non-Western culture, and the appearance of an intolerant Islam, not to mention the economic problems that challenge the welfare state. Utterly unprepared, Dutch society has been shaken by the strength, speed and suddenness of these challenges, and is still working towards new formulas for integration, diversity, multiculturalism and participation. For the moment, Dutch politics have fallen back on a form of conservative nationalism and the country has lost its unconditional faith in European integration.

Yet, ask any Dutchman what is his nation's major contribution to humankind, and he will most probably answer: tolerance, democracy and religious freedom. Some, mindful of the work of sociologist Max Weber (1864–1920), may say Calvinism, in terms of its work ethos and moral probity. The result of Calvinism, even in its purely cultural present-day variety, is not only a profoundly individualistic attitude, but also a liberal state with a moral mission and a sense of global responsibility.

On the other hand, water and the need for shared agency and continuous negotiation between man and nature have made Holland a matter-of-fact society: physical survival precedes the flourishing of the mind. In science, as in everyday life, Dutch people tend to think of

The Dutch humanist scholar Erasmus of Rotterdam (c. 1469–1536) and the Islamic philosopher and poet Rumi (also known as Mevlana, 1207–73) are represented on a mural next to a mosque in Rotterdam as icons of the universal need for toleration between religions and cultures.

practical initiatives, problem-solving and techniques, before developing abstract ideas, broad values and universal perspectives. Their main philosopher, Spinoza (1632–77), was a perfect rationalist; his near contemporary, the French mathematician Descartes (1596–1650), felt profoundly at home in Holland, and in the early 20th century the painter Piet Mondrian (1872–1944) evolved a purely geometric conception of forms and colours. Dutch Nobel prize-winners have always excelled more in physics, medicine and economics than in literature. Yet literature there is – unfortunately, however, in an old and rich language that most Europeans ignore. And alas, few Dutch are proud enough of their mother tongue to speak it with foreigners.

PETER ARONSSON

Sweden

From Viking community to welfare state

The Swedes, like other Europeans, were overcome after 1945 with tremendous relief at the apparent end of war and crisis. War, violence and occupation had led many countries to develop a sense of their historical fate; Sweden, on the other hand, began to believe that history belonged to the past, and that poverty, dirt, disease and gender and class divisions were coming to an end. The world would be governed by benevolent and inventive politicians, engineers and experts who could be trusted to manage all possible problems. Sweden's wartime neutrality was projected into both the past and future as the country set itself up as the conscience of the world and the spokesman for human rights. Swedish inventions and design conquered the world. The invention of dynamite by Alfred Nobel (1833–96) was now eclipsed by the brilliance of the prizes set up in his name, which made Sweden the global home of reason. The celebration of modernity created a national pride far removed from the former emphasis on historical glories. The end of ideology and history was at hand.

Each era has its own understanding of the past. The Swedes have not always seen themselves in this way, nor do they wholly do so today. Sweden, or Svea Rike, is the name of the state that took shape at the turn of the first millennium out of the prolonged fighting between the Geats of Göta Rike in the southwest of the modern country and the Swedes of Svea Rike in the east. According to the medieval chroniclers the Geats were associated with the Gothic conquerors of the Roman Empire. The fertile imaginations of medieval historians turned this brave people, better known as the Visigoths, into the direct descendants of Noah's grandson Magog; they had moved south to the Black Sea, occupied Rome in 410 CE and conquered Spain. This story was well known to the educated elites of Europe. A thousand years later at the Council of Basel in 1434, when the Swedish delegation revived the story to demand the best seats alongside the Pope, the

A girl in a cowshed, Kalmar County, southern Sweden. Kalmar County belongs to the historical province of Småland which is rich in lakes but largely unsuitable for agriculture, with the exception of the Kalmar Plains. Småland was also the site of several peasant rebellions during the 16th century.

English responded that while the story may have been true, it would have been the brave ones who left Sweden while the cowards stayed at home – so the Swedish should remain seated far down the table.

This grand vision of Swedish history, which mixed Tacitus's 1st-century CE *Germania* with biblical stories and Icelandic sagas, inspired the Swedish conquest of much of northern Europe, from the reign of Gustavus Adolphus (1594–1632; r. 1611–32), whose intervention in the Thirty Years' War changed the course of Eastern European history until 1718, when Charles XII (Karl XII, 1682–1718; r. 1697–1718) died in battle. There is still some controversy over whether he was killed by his Norwegian opponents or by members of his own army who had grown weary of fighting. During this so-called 'golden age', the combination of a centralized government, personal qualities of the monarchs and Protestant convictions, together with innovative techniques in warfare, mobilized the nation to an unprecedented extent. This small, poor country was transformed into a major power in northern Europe, disrupting the long tradition in which the other powers had played Denmark and Sweden against each other to prevent a single power from monopolizing Baltic trade.

The piecemeal loss of Sweden's Baltic empire to the rising power of Russia began at the beginning of the 18th century and continued until the early 20th century. In 1809, during the Napoleonic Wars, Russia conquered Finland, which had been the eastern part of Swedish territory. This trauma was temporarily alleviated when Norway was forced to abandon its union with Denmark and adopt a loose alliance with Sweden between 1814 and 1905.

The nationalist historians of the 19th century primarily looked back to the era of Swedish greatness during the 17th century, and counterposed the gradual loss of territories thereafter with the rise of science, led by great intellects such as the botanist Carolus Linnaeus (1707–78), and industrial progress, both of which restored Sweden's sense of national pride, albeit within reduced borders. In this they tended to emphasize the history of the people more than that of their kings.

TIMELINE

700s Swedish adventurers (Vikings) begin to move west across the North Sea and east into Russia

995 King Olof (d. 1022), the first undisputed Christian king of Sweden, comes to the throne

1397 The Union of Kalmar unites Sweden, Norway and Denmark

1521 Gustavus Vasa overthrows Danish rule and in 1527 introduces the Protestant Reformation

1542 The Dacke War peasant uprising against the rule of Gustavus Vasa

1611–32 The reign of Gustavus Adolphus initiates Sweden's 'age of greatness'

1648 The Treaty of Westphalia confirms Swedish dominance in northeastern Europe

1718 The death of Charles XII puts an end to the Swedish Empire

1809 Finland is conquered by Russia

1814 The union of Norway–Sweden is founded

1905 Norway gains its independence from Sweden

1986 Murder of Prime Minister Olof Palme

Death of Gustavus Adolphus at the Battle of Lützen *by Carl Wahlbom (1855). The 'golden age' that began under Gustavus Adolphus in 1611 became an important focus for Sweden in regaining national self-esteem after the loss of Finland in 1809 and Norway in 1905. Many monuments and paintings were created until the First World War.*

These 19th-century historians depicted the farmers as representing stability and having an absolute right over the land, with the Vikings contributing a touch of brutality – at a comfortably safe distance from the present. The story of the nation's history that emerged from this school began with the Ice Age, when glaciers covered the whole of Scandinavia. When the ice withdrew a little over 10,000 years ago, a virgin land was revealed, ready for human habitation. The various tribes that arrived left traces in the form of archaeological objects from this period. As the first cultures were conquered by more advanced ones, a farming culture emerged that gave its name to the Neolithic Age, the empire of the settlers. The Neolithic tribes sowed the first seeds in a Swedish nation that for ever afterwards has farmed the land and manufactured with iron: the evidence can be seen in objects left in the ground and carved in stone. The Vikings were the first to speak to posterity through runes carved on stones, which tell of family relations, places of residence and noble deeds: 'The good farmer Holmgöt let rise [the stone] after his wife Odendisa,' reads one, 'There will never be a better housekeeper at Hassmyra to care for the farm. Rödballe carved these runes. To Sigmund was Odendisa a good sister.'

The era of the Vikings was hailed in the early 19th century as a source of national pride and an idyllic society in which rustic Nordics gathered at the courthouse to make decisions and administer justice. Families were united by concepts of honour for men and women alike that had to be defended at all costs. The energetic Vikings set off for adventures on western and eastern trails to trade or plunder, according to circumstances. Respect and fear of the Norsemen spread throughout Christendom, and intensified following the widely reported Viking attack on the Anglo-Saxon monastery of Lindisfarne off the northeast coast of England in 793 CE. 'A furore Normannorum, libera nos Domine' ('from the fury of the north-men, God deliver us'), monks are said to have prayed. The horror stories were most likely exaggerated in order to demand fidelity to the church and personal sacrifice in defence of the homeland: fear of the Vikings was a potent source of domestic political strength for Anglo-Saxon rulers during the 9th century.

The Vikings were ascribed different roles in the national memories of the various Scandinavian countries. The beautiful Viking ships discovered south of Oslo during the early 20th century were important to the assertion of a distinctive Norwegian heritage and cultural identity at a time when Norway was claiming its political independence. The colonizers of Iceland were compared to contemporary Norwegian polar scientists, and Vikings were admired as explorers rather than pirates. In Denmark, as agriculture was modernized, Vikings were viewed as early predecessors, farmers with an eye as much for agriculture as for sea travel. In Sweden, where industry was of supreme importance, the Vikings were portrayed as skilled craftsmen and pioneering merchants who traded with the Orient. Finally, Finland had to invent non-existent Finnish Vikings in order to be seen as a proper Nordic nation at the end of the 19th century.

Aside from the drama of the Viking period, and the aesthetic value of the castles and cultural treasures of the 'age of greatness' created mostly by a small group of immigrant European nobility, the focus of Swedish history was dominated by the importance of the country's farming culture. In Sweden the role of the farmer acquired a political signifi-cance far greater than elsewhere in Europe. The large number of independent farmers demanded, and gained, political representation at local, regional and national levels. This representation was formalized religiously, judicially and politically from the 17th century onwards. The four-estate parliament was regulated from 1617, interrupted by shorter periods of absolute monarchical rule to counteract the House of Lords. Gradu-ally the uniform channels for social integration that had been instituted by the Protestant Church (the Reformation had been introduced in 1527) were complemented by schools, council authorities and national culture. This created a sense of pride in the freedom of the Swedish *allmoge*, the independent farmer, as the nucleus of the vital state-building force in the 19th century. By contrast, the urban middle classes and the aristocracy were small. The monarchy struck important political alliances, sometimes with the nobility, but at other times with the tax-paying country people.

As the framework of social democracy and the collective welfare state emerged, historians of the early 20th century played down the role of the independent farmers and national movements. Instead, the working-class, revivalist and temperance movements were increasingly seen as forces for community building, democratization and citizenship. The strong power of the state initiated under the reign of Gustavus Vasa (1496–1560; r. 1523–60) in the 16th century and the successful bureaucracy of the 17th-century golden age were emphasized. The transformation of the people from coarse rebels to obedient subjects in an efficient social and political machine now became the dominant view of Swedish history. Strong political coalitions between the farmers' and workers' parties in 1933 prevented the radicalization of politics and, together with strong collective agreements between employers and unions in 1938, created a stable framework for modernization.

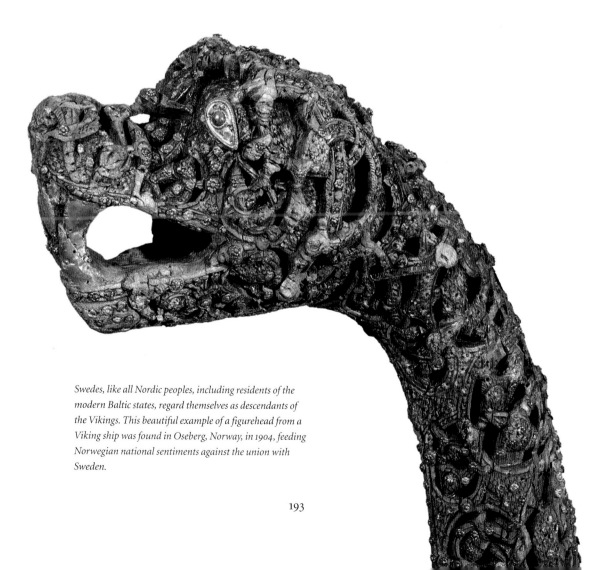

Swedes, like all Nordic peoples, including residents of the modern Baltic states, regard themselves as descendants of the Vikings. This beautiful example of a figurehead from a Viking ship was found in Oseberg, Norway, in 1904, feeding Norwegian national sentiments against the union with Sweden.

The 'Million Programme' social housing initiative (1965–74) testifies to the ambition of the Social Democrats to provide everyone with good housing at a fair price. However, some areas quickly turned into ghettos, which became symbolic of the difficulty of devising effective welfare policies.

After 1945 the feeling that society had passed into a modern age of pure ahistorical reason began to grow.

A stagnating economy at the start of the 1970s threatened this belief in the end of history. At the end of the 1980s – with the murder of Prime Minister Olof Palme in 1986, accelerating globalization, the fall of the Soviet Empire, the application to join the European Union and the emerging cracks in the Social Democratic ruling elite – history was rediscovered. In 1993–94 a large countrywide exhibition project called 'The Swedish History' tried to present a unified picture of the country's history. Many Swedish characteristics such as quietness, shyness, consensus-seeking and the concept of *lagom* (meaning not too much, not too little, just the right amount) surfaced in the debates of the early 1990s as essential qualities of both the political and the individual Swedish character. Prime Minister Göran Persson took the initiative in calling a large international conference on the Holocaust in 1999; he also set up an authority to educate Swedish schoolchildren and the general public about genocide, a subject that had disappeared from the secondary school curriculum and which was generally lacking from public consciousness. At the same time a number of studies questioned the legendary benevolence of the Swedish state. Were the Swedes not among the first to establish an institute for racial biology in 1921 – and rather late in closing it down in 1959? Did not forced sterilization of 'undesirable' women still take place as late as the 1970s, based on all-too-shaky science? Was Sweden too quick to comply with Hitler's demand for pure-race business contacts and transit of troops? Was it late in supporting the Allies? After the war was it quick to satisfy the Soviet demands for recognition in the Baltic? Did the state not continue to supervise its citizens in secret and unconstitutional forms, as still happens now? These uncomfortable questions threatened Sweden's cosy image of itself during the 1990s. However, when the neo-liberal conservative party Moderaterna decided to give up the traditional image of the people's home as its rallying cause, and instead presented itself as the new workers' party and the new defender of the welfare state, the political and ideological base for an alternative history fell apart.

Today everyone unites around a nostalgic description of the good welfare state, but with a slightly nagging feeling that its time has passed. In 2010 he king inaugurated the first permanent museum exhibition making a full chronology of Swedish history available to the public, in conjunction with the publication of the first new complete history of Sweden in fifty years, supported by television productions and commercial patrons. Today we find ourselves at a historical crossroads, without any indication of which direction to choose. Is Swedish history for leisure consumption alone, or should it become a vital framework for the community and for political integration?

In Sweden, as in the rest of the Western world, cultural heritage and museums have become increasingly important components of the economy. Many countries want to develop their medieval towns as well as their industrial wasteland into cultural centres. In Sweden, a country with relatively few recent traumatic memories, it has been especially easy to appeal to history as a simple way to unite people, and historical tourism as a pleasant holiday activity.

The medieval town of Visby on the island of Gotland was included on the list of World Heritage sites in 1995. Today energetic re-enactments of medieval culture are held there, including the dramatic re-creation of a cruel (Danish) invasion in 1361, encouraging civic pride and enterprise among the 57,000 inhabitants of the island. More than 800,000 visitors now come every year to engage in time travel, as well as bathing and the consumption of a fair amount of good food and drink. A new industry has been established, with history as its raw material. Visby is now more 'medieval' than it has been in 500 years, with the support of strong heritage institutions.

The Knight Templar (1998–2000), a trilogy by Jan Guillou about the fictional crusader Arn Magnusson, updated the Swedes' views on Arabic culture at the end of the 1990s. Returning to Sweden after twenty years spent both befriending and fighting Saladin in the

Holy Land, Arn shows a capacity both to fight for and to develop his homeland, thereby evoking the old twin values of military glory and modernization. Arn's fictional home is Västergötland in Western Gothia, and the author has found some evidence that a person of Arn's description may have actually existed. The absence of irrefutable proof has not hindered the development of Medieval World, a historical theme park based on the books that has become the most successful in the country. There the Middle Ages seem real, yet different from our own time; the park functions as a fairytale-land in which visitors can play with their expected social roles. Swedish men – normally champions of equality – can pretend to be knights, while working women allow themselves to curtsy at a fictional court.

The 17th-century wars of the golden age arouse the most enthusiasm among specialists of the arts and crafts of the time, although they also serve as political models for the xenophobic extreme right. This is ironic, given that most of the army's officers were immigrants and Charles XII, the most celebrated king of the Swedish golden age, was comprehensively defeated. The *Vasa* ship in Stockholm provides the perfect opportunity to explore this sense of enthusiasm about Sweden's great past. It is a well-preserved, fully equipped warship that sank on its maiden voyage in 1628 without ever firing a shot. In 1961 it was salvaged, a triumph for Swedish engineering skill, and can now be admired near the open-air museum of Swedish peasant life in Skansen.

The *Vasa* ship (built in 1626–28) is a war monument for a country that has claimed neutrality in war since 1814 and maintained this position during the Cold War. The ship sank on its maiden voyage in 1628, before it could do any damage, and was rescued in 1961. It is one of the most popular sights to visit in Sweden.

Sweden's rusty industrial heritage does not capture the imagination in quite the same way. Although it has a certain aesthetic, sometimes called 'industrial cool', this more recent element of the country's past is not as exciting, or sufficiently nostalgic, to attract much of a following. It has been easier to exploit the Swedes' well-known love of nature and peasant traditions. Today, however, Sweden's best-loved cultural product is probably Astrid Lindgren (1907–2002), whose children's books, notably *Emil in Lönneberga* and *Pippi Longstocking*, have been exported to many countries. Her home town has even changed its name from Vimmerby to Astrid Lindgren's Vimmerby.

If other Europeans have any concept of Swedish history, it probably merges with that of Scandinavia as a whole. The Vikings turn up all over world as a violent people, used to market everything from hamburgers to car tyres. The period of Swedish superpower is probably best known across northern Europe for its contribution to the Thirty Years' War that devastated the German population by a third during the 17th century, although the Baltic states remember Swedish rule of this period as characterized by great law and order compared to that of the Russian autocracy that followed.

The concept of the Swedish welfare state is one that has spread far and wide. The world believes that in Sweden the state takes a greater responsibility for the individual's welfare than in many other countries, a belief that interacts with stereotypes about Sweden's unbridled sexuality and free women. The career of Alfred Nobel reminds people that Sweden experienced the world's fastest industrial growth during much of the 20th century. The films of Ingmar Bergman (1918–2007), meanwhile, have provided an international showcase for Swedish melancholy.

These stereotypes are not entirely misleading. Sweden's identity springs from having been a society with strong independent farmers who were already politically aware in the pre-modern era. Industrialization and urbanization occurred late, and made Sweden one of the world's richest countries, with a strong state and a stable coalition between labour and capital. The fact that Sweden had not been at war since 1814 greatly contributed to this.

Less well known, both within Sweden and outside, is the age-old tradition of successful negotiation between an ambitious state and a well-organized people. One might describe Sweden less as a society brought to obedience by the power of the state than as an organized society that invaded the state. The result is a country in which the concepts of society and state are interchangeable. The values associated with this are better captured by foreign stereotypes than by the country's own impressions of itself. The Swedes, for example, regard themselves as shy and *lagom*, while foreigners stress

Alfred Nobel made his fortune with the invention and manufacture of dynamite. His name is forever connected with the Nobel Prize, which every year gives credit, fame and remuneration to scientists, authors and promoters of peace for the greatest service to mankind.

Swedes' individualism, especially in sexual matters. If we look below the surface, the Swedes are extreme in several respects. Swedish society is one of the most secularized in the world and Swedes place a very high priority on the development of individuality. Yet, in order to choose an education, career, spouse or home freely, and not be dependent on parents and family, these individuals need partners. Hence the wider paradox: Swedes need a strong state to guarantee the freedom of the individual.

Great Britain

The confected nation state

'Rule Britannia, rule the waves, Britons never will be slaves.' James Thomson's lines for the masque *Alfred* (1740) remained resonant while Britain was the world's leading maritime power. They looked towards 1902 when Arthur Benson's words for 'Land of Hope and Glory' were first heard as part of the Coronation Ode for Edward VII (1841–1910; r. 1901–10). As with Thomson's lines, which were produced at a time of war with Spain, much of the expression of Britishness was focused on antipathy to what was presented as a quite different world, that of Continental autocracy and Catholicism. National identity was moulded during war with France and Spain. In a period of a little over a hundred years, from the early 18th to early 19th century, there was declared war with the former no less than seven times and undeclared war twice, with hostile relations existing at other times.

This was the context in which British identity was created and the empire expanded. English identity had owed a lot to the Hundred Years' War with France in the 14th and 15th centuries, the hostility towards Catholicism stemming from the Reformation in the 16th century, and to war with Spain in the 16th and 17th centuries. In the same way the values of Britain, newly created as a state in 1707, were cemented when it was at war with France. The experience of the early 19th-century Napoleonic Wars, in particular, under-scored a patriotic discourse on British distinctiveness, while simultaneously creating a new iconography of national military heroes focused on Admiral Nelson (1758–1805) and the Duke of Wellington (*c.* 1769–1852). In the 1800s 'God Save the King' was named the national anthem.

The resonance of these wars was longstanding for London, which was both the national and imperial capital, as well as the setting for a memorialization of identity through victory. Nelson's Column, Waterloo Station, the tombs of national heroes in

The death of Admiral Nelson in 1805, painted here by Daniel Maclise in 1864, served as a central image of bravery over the following century. Despite important victories on land, the British saw themselves as a naval power. Much applauded in his day, Maclise (1806–70) produced epic historical paintings for the Houses of Parliament.

St Paul's Cathedral, Wellington's funeral: these sites and occasions contributed directly to a sense of national exceptionalism.

The 19th century also saw a fleshing-out of a sense of national greatness that did not focus so closely on triumph in war. Victorian Britain displayed a sense of uniqueness, self-confidence and contempt for foreigners, especially Catholics. This xenophobia was not a matter of hostility towards foreignness itself, but rather towards what was seen as backward and illiberal. The latter were defined in accordance with British criteria, but these criteria were also considered to have wider applicability. Freedom of speech, a free press and – despite distrust of Catholics – religious tolerance were regarded as important.

Parliamentary government was viewed as a key characteristic of Britishness, one that Britain exported to its dominions overseas. This was appropriate because, as a unitary state, Britain was created by act of Parliament, and thus by the politics that led to that act. The United Kingdom of Great Britain was established on 12 May 1707 as a result of the union of England and Scotland. This was intended to be more permanent and far deeper than the union of the Crowns that had occurred on the death of Elizabeth I (b. 1533) in 1603, when James VI of Scotland (1566–1625) became James I of England as well. It was believed that this earlier union could dissolve if the Crowns of England and Scotland went different ways – as was expected to happen after the death of Queen Anne (1665–1714), who had no surviving children.

It was Great Britain, though, that came into being in 1707 and not the much older kingdoms of England or Scotland or the principality of Wales, which had been incorporated into the English realm as a result of an act of Parliament in 1536. (Northern Ireland, which today forms part of the United Kingdom of Great Britain and Northern Ireland, is a relict of a different Act of Union – that of 1801 between Britain and Ireland.) In this

TIMELINE

43 CE The Romans successfully invade Britain and establish the province of Britannia. They eventually make their presence felt as far north as Inverness

410 The withdrawal of the Romans causes Britain to break up into many kingdoms

1066 The conquest of Anglo-Saxon England by William of Normandy begins

1216 The establishment of the principality of Wales

1284 The principality of Wales is subject to the English Crown

1320 The Declaration of Arbroath asserts Scottish independence from England

1603 The Scottish and English Crowns are united by James VI and I Stuart

1707 The Act of Union of Scotland and England forms Great Britain

1801 The Act of Union creates the United Kingdom of Great Britain and Ireland

1807 Act for the abolition of the slave trade

1815 British forces under the Duke of Wellington defeat Napoleon at Waterloo

1877 Queen Victoria becomes empress of India

1921 The Anglo-Irish Treaty confirms Irish independence, but Northern Ireland remains part of the United Kingdom

1940–45 The wartime premiership of Winston Churchill takes Britain to victory over the Axis powers

1973 The United Kingdom joins the European Economic Community (later the European Union)

2003 Prime Minister Tony Blair joins United States President George W. Bush in invading Iraq

2011 The Scottish National Party wins a decisive victory in elections to the Scottish Parliament, promising a referendum on devolution

A map of the British Empire from 1886. Maps conveyed a potent sense of imperial power, showing maritime links to colonies across the world. Henry Teesdale's New British Atlas *(1831) was one of the first examples to show British possessions in red, a convention that came into general usage after 1850 with the development of colour printing.*

sense Britain lacks a deep history comparable to those of England, Scotland and Wales because much that we associate with one is of no relevance to another. Thus Magna Carta, under which the English barons forced King John (1167–1216) to submit himself to the rule of law in 1215, is a key event in English history but means nothing in Scotland; while the Declaration of Arbroath (1320), which asserted the independence of Scotland, was in no way notable in English history. Moreover, processes common to all parts of the island of Britain – such as conquest by the Romans (who called their province Britannia and attempted to establish a presence even in the north of Scotland), invasions by so-called barbarians (from Germanic Angles and Saxons to Scandinavian Vikings), feudalism, the Protestant Reformation, and the civil wars of the 1640s – played out very differently in the different states of the island, just as the same phenomena did right across Western Europe. Thus, despite retrospective attempts to create a common British

memory of earlier centuries, there was none. In the modern struggle over national identity, many Scots and Welsh see their own identities as more historically grounded than that of Britain. As a result, to begin British history prior to 1707 is a political statement – and one, moreover, that will look increasingly invalid as the groundswell towards separatism increases.

Placing the beginning of British history at 1707, rather than in early medieval forests or even the world of Stonehenge, is much more relevant to our own times. Much that was already in existence and confirmed by the Act of Union and the politics of the surrounding decades seems somehow familiar now. By 1707 the ideas of limited government, representative politics, an accountable monarchy, the rule of law and an absence of religious persecution (although Catholics would not have agreed) were all well established, and they have all been part of Britain's deep history ever since. Indeed, their roots are even older in one or another part of the island.

Thus the common law, with its stress on trial by jury and equality under the law, had long been an important aspect of English distinctiveness, and from the 12th century this was true of both the content of the law and the way it was administered. English common law encouraged a respect for the character and continuity of English political society. The legal tradition was very different in Scotland where there was a basis in Roman law.

As well as having great constitutional and political force, such legal and political practices also reflected and sustained assumptions – notably a belief in fairness and accountability – that could be handed down to immigrants and to new generations. Since 1707 these assumptions have provided a historical basis for a democratic culture in British history, one that is not simply grounded in constitutional provisions of the years before the union, such as the restrictions on royal authority that followed the so-called Glorious Revolution of 1688–89. Modern British democratic culture is not particularly acute in its knowledge of historical facts, but it does reflect a pervasive historicism in the form of values grounded in past events and practices.

The quest for freedom, the defence of liberty, and the respect for both law and individual rights do not provide the entire thrust of British history, yet they do characterize important episodes of which the British are most proud. These episodes are then commonly linked in order to present an account of a benign progress towards liberty; this is referred to as the Whig interpretation of British history, which forms the basis of Britons' representation of their own history.

Moreover, these moral values offer a noteworthy example both to the present and, more generally, across the world. It is the peculiar greatness of British history that those

A national service poster by Septimus Scott, 1917: a call to enlist in the National Service Industrial Army. With so many men in the armed forces, there was a shortage of labour in industry and agriculture. Aside from encouraging men to serve, this shortage led to the recruitment of large numbers of women for war work.

who fought gloriously for national independence, most especially in 1805 against Napoleon and in 1940 against Hitler, were also asserting values more noble and uplifting than those of the nation's enemies.

At the same time there is an uneasiness about aspects of Britain's imperial past, notably the leading role taken by British sailors, traders and plantation owners in the Atlantic slave trade. It is one of the ironies of British history that, having benefited hugely from slavery and the slave trade throughout the 18th century, the country then played the leading role in ending that trade in the 19th century, legislating first against the slave trade (in 1807) and then against slavery itself (in 1833), and finally using the Royal Navy and diplomatic pressure to stamp out both across the world.

This double role indicates the extent to which the national past can resonate with very different themes, and serves as a reminder that what is stressed in a country's history tends to reflect current needs. Thus, while the Conservative administration from 2010 emphasized a patriotic account of British success and achievement, the Labour government of the previous decade had tried to encourage a sense of 'Britishness'.

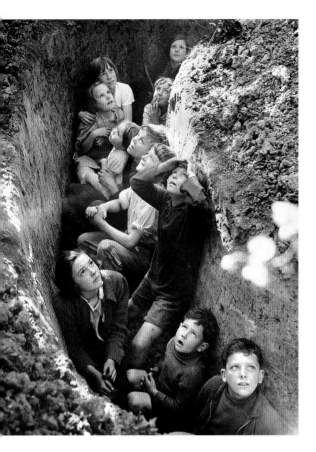

Children shelter from the aerial conflict after the German decision to bomb during the Battle of Britain, 1940. The Blitz mounted by the Luftwaffe continued for nine months; its failure to break down Britain's defences is considered a turning point in the war.

This policy was intended to strengthen national identity in the face of challenging tendencies, notably the rise of radical Islam – but it can also be seen as an attempt by a government heavily dependent on Scottish votes to resist the separation of England and Scotland. The language of Britishness involved an assertion of long-term values, yet it did so very much in relation to the needs of the present day. After the creation in 1997 of a Scottish Parliament and Executive, however, the drift was very much away from a British identity. By the early 2010s, the end of the Union was a real possibility. Just as it was created by act of Parliament, so it may well be dissolved by another.

In recent decades the long tradition of British history that prevailed for a quarter of a millennium from the Act of Union with Scotland has largely collapsed. The empire disappeared, particularly after 1947 when India, which had been the 'jewel in the crown' when Queen Victoria (1819–1901) assumed the title empress of India in 1877, won its independence. Britain's role as a leading maritime nation also disintegrated. Indeed, it has become apparent that British history in large part meant British Empire history, and much of it passed with the loss of empire after 1947. As a result the 'little Britishness' characteristic of the post-war period is of very recent origin and not as deeply rooted as is generally implied.

The Anti-Slavery Society Convention, 1840, *by Benjamin Robert Haydon. Abolitionist tactics involved large public meetings, press agitation and pressure on Parliament. Moral campaigns contributed greatly to the sense that the British government had a role in seeing justice done, at home, across the empire and, eventually, across the world.*

15 August 1947, New Delhi: Lord and Lady Mountbatten shake hands with the public upon arrival at the Indian Constituent Assembly to announce the proclamation of independence. The decision to grant independence to India heralded the speedy process of decolonization across the globe.

Moreover, the cultural and religious continuity of the kingdom was greatly compromised in the 1960s, notably with the decline in the position, popularity and relevance of the established churches. Americanism and globalization also weakened native styles, whether in food or in diction, with all that they meant for distinctiveness and continuity.

All too much of the traditionally British quest for freedom, defence of liberty, and respect for both law and individual rights has been neglected or distorted by governmental and institutional priorities and interests. In particular, a combination of the communitarian solutions pushed by the political left, the inroads of European federalism, and a lack of trust in the individual has transformed the political and legal culture of the country. For example, parliamentary government has been eroded by the rise of European institutions, notably the European Parliament and courts, and by the incorporation of European law.

Indeed, in 1993 historian W. A. Speck published a *Concise History of Britain, 1707–1975*, in which he claimed that his chronology 'spans the whole history of Britain in the precise sense' as membership of what was to become the European Union was, he argued, a partial surrender of British sovereignty. (Britain had joined the European Economic Community in 1973, a decision confirmed two years later by referendum.) Speck's sense of discontinuity carried forward the 1962 remark by Hugh Gaitskell (1906–63), as leader of the Labour Party, that such membership would mean 'the end of Britain as an independent nation'. As a result, the recent past has seen a recasting of the legacy of the more distant past. Whereas some changes, notably the end of empire, have led to little sense of dislocation, this is not the case as far as European integration is concerned.

A failure to appreciate the extent of this recasting represents a key misunderstanding of Britain's past. Foreigners, as well as some Britons, have been sold by the 'heritage industry' an impression of a country full of ancient ceremonial and historic cities, where people take tea with the Queen, or picturesque villages where old colonels commit murder; there is often a failure to appreciate the sweeping changes of recent decades.

But that is not the sole misunderstanding. There is still also a tendency for foreigners to see British and English history as interchangeable, indeed to regard Britain as a greater or another England. Both of these assumptions are far from the case. This misunderstanding is shared by many of the English, who assume that their history is of pre-eminent importance, and fail to see either the importance of the interactions between the parts of the island, or the way in which the English often tended to dominate their smaller neighbours.

Gertrude Shilling in a Royal Ascot 'Common Market' outfit designed by her son, milliner David Shilling. Britain joined the European Economic Community, the precursor of the European Union, in 1973. Membership was controversial then and has remained so into the early 21st century.

There is, of course, no perfect balance. A 'four nations' approach to the history of the British Isles (English, Scottish, Welsh, Irish) is a currently fashionable attempt to counter this Anglocentricity. But in asserting the significance of the Scottish, Welsh and Irish contributions – in the civil wars of the 1640s, for example – it devotes insufficient attention to England itself, which is by far the preponderant nation in terms of population. There is also a common failure to devote sufficient space to the history of the localities and regions of England, which have their own proud traditions and heritage.

The commonly understood account of the British Empire is also an overly critical and somewhat ahistorical one, which reflects the extent to which the overthrow of British rule is important to the foundation accounts of so many of the world's younger states. In particular, critics often forget that Britain was not the sole imperial power in the 19th and early 20th centuries, or that the native peoples conquered by the British were not, for the most part, previously the beneficiaries of democratic self-government. There is also a misleading tendency in many former parts of the empire to blame British rule for many pressures and problems that stem more directly from modernization and globalization. Moreover, it is sometimes forgotten that Britain and its empire combated rival empires, notably that of Nazi Germany, which are correctly seen as genuine tyrannies.

Another source of criticism – but also celebration – of Britain stems from its association with the monarchy. The long reign of Queen Elizabeth II saw the monarchy adjust subtly to changing times, while apparently embodying traditional values and imperial grandeur. The widespread personal respect for the Queen meant that the institution remained surprisingly resilient, even though the old concept of a 'balanced constitution' – in which monarch, aristocracy and commoners shared power within a Parliament established by the rule of law – was often rejected as undesirable for a democratic age.

The standard account of the past misleads by simplifying history and ascribing to the British characteristics that may not be exclusive of them, but are more generally true of the age. The visual strength of film works more powerfully on audiences than does the balancing arguments of scholars. So, more insidiously, does a rather different impression that is often created by television, film and historical novels: that people in the past were like us. This approach is particularly seen in the rendition of novels such as those of Jane Austen (1775–1817) and in dramas based on actual historical events. This approach removes the distance between the present and the past, and encourages a view that people should always have behaved according to today's norms, so that on those occasions in the past when they did not, they can be criticized, or presented as quaint or ridiculous. Britain, of course, is not the only country whose past receives this treatment, but it is particularly pronounced due to the strength and accessibility of Britain's literary tradition.

This loss of distance between present and past leads to a lack of engagement with the past for its own sake, and this absence of specific knowledge captures a key problem with

Modern Britain: young women walking across Westminster Bridge in 2010. Multicultural policies and a fast-growing tolerance of diversity have resulted in a wide range of lifestyles, including the growing popularity of strict Islamic observance.

British history today. Successive governments have wrestled unsuccessfully with the question of which version of history should be learned in British schools and how it should be taught. In partial consequence, those aspects of Britain's past that attract most attention are frequently misconstrued. In truth, Britain, once great, has had a more noble history than is often acknowledged, but it is a history that has been superseded by – and in – a very different age.

The United States

The land that chose to be without history

'History is more or less bunk', automaker Henry Ford famously proclaimed in 1916; 'We want to live in the present, and the only history that is worth a tinker's damn is the history that we make today'. The patriots who vindicated colonial American claims to independence and nationhood expressed the same sentiment, if more eloquently, asserting that this 'new' self-created people owed nothing to the past – except, perhaps, for lessons in tyranny and despotism, the 'long train of abuses and usurpations' that Thomas Jefferson (1743–1826) recited in the Declaration of Independence of 4 July 1776.

If these self-proclaimed Americans had any history, it was not their own but that of Britain, the mother country. As a result, successive generations have looked forward not back, west not east. According to historian Frederick Jackson Turner's *Frontier in American History* (1893), the new nation's free institutions were the spontaneous product of radical individualists, breaking through the crust of custom and returning to first principles as they conquered and cultivated the wilderness. Americans have been renewing themselves ever since, discovering new frontiers across the continent and into space. Even the 'American dilemma' of slavery and its long aftermath can be seen by progressive Americans as an archaic Old World legacy, fundamentally at odds with the genius of American democracy and yet another frontier to be conquered.

Of course, American historylessness is a myth. By denying the claims of the past, Americans have made history central to their self-understanding. Before the French revolutionaries imagined the ancien régime against which they were rebelling, American revolutionaries conjured up images of a corrupt and despotic British metropolis. The Roman analogy elaborated by Edward Gibbon's *History of the Decline and Fall of the Roman Empire* (1776–88) resonated powerfully for republican patriots, who struck neo-classical poses and sometimes even donned togas. If freedom found a home in the New

Pulling Down the Statue of King George III *by Johannes A. Oertel, c. 1859. Grounding the legitimacy of their new republican regime in the sovereignty of the people, these iconoclastic New Yorkers pulled the king off his high horse and thus turned their backs on history.*

World, the Old World provided the necessary counterpoint. Americans kept the past alive as they projected themselves into the future. The frontier marked both a return to the beginning and progress towards the end, the unfolding of what the 19th-century expansionists were to call the country's 'manifest destiny': that America would make its own history, fulfilling God's providential design.

In 1807 Thomas Jefferson underscored the great difference between the two worlds: 'wars and contentions, indeed, fill the pages of history with more matter' in Europe, 'but more blest is that nation whose silent course of happiness furnishes nothing for history to say'. Pursuing happiness, as they had been enjoined by the Declaration of Independence, Americans escaped from history – 'rivers of blood' would continue to flow on the far side of the Atlantic – into a republican millennium of peace and prosperity. Of course, the persistence of slavery and conflicts with imperial neighbours and Native Americans belied that millennial promise. But Jefferson and his fellow Americans could imagine that they were fast approaching something like the 'end of history' that Francis Fukuyama was to celebrate two centuries later, in the 1990s, when democracy triumphed and Communism collapsed.

As Americans have come to view themselves as history's end, 'history' has loomed large in their collective consciousness. The provincial past was depicted as a distant 'foreign country'. Historians are rightly sceptical about the scale and scope of change: the short-term effect of the break with Britain was to demolish prosperous trade links and retard population growth. But independent Americans knew they were different, and as they assumed their place 'among the powers of the earth', they defined that difference in historical terms.

TIMELINE

1497 Explorer John Cabot claims North America for England

1607 The first permanent colony is established at Jamestown, Virginia

1620 The Pilgrim Fathers establish a colony in Massachusetts

1765 The Stamp Act is passed by the British Parliament, seen as despotic by American colonists who are not represented there; the Act is repealed the following year

1775 Armed conflict begins between the American colonists and the British; in 1776 the independence of the former colonies from Britain is declared

1783 The British admit defeat and the independence of the United States is confirmed

1787 The United States Constitution is adopted; in 1789 George Washington becomes the first president

1803 The purchase of Louisiana from the French begins the westward expansion of the United States

1861 The secession of the southern states begins the American Civil War, ending in 1865 with the defeat of the Confederacy

1863 The Emancipation Proclamation abolishes slavery

1890 The Battle of Wounded Knee marks the end of the Indian wars

1917 The United States enters the First World War under Woodrow Wilson

1941 The United States enters the Second World War under Franklin D. Roosevelt

1969 American astronauts land on the moon

2008 Barack Obama is elected the first black president of the United States

A scene of frontier farming from 1886. Soon-to-be-dispossessed Indians look on as pioneers transform the land and game flees the scene. The new nation's 'manifest destiny' was to conquer nature and thereby escape the tyranny of history.

The simple juxtaposition of old and new suggested a straight path forward, breaking out of the cyclical pattern that characterized early-modern conceptions of history. According to the conventional wisdom, free peoples lost their liberty as power coalesced in fewer and fewer hands until despotic regimes toppled from their own dead weight; power was then broadly redistributed and the process resumed. 'Revolution' did not have its modern, progressive connotations, but suggested another turn in the inexorable rise and fall of regimes. Virtuous patriots sought to return to first principles and recover lost liberties, but the logic of history always worked against them, as a rising tide of luxury and corruption subverted the character of formerly free peoples – as in England after 1066, for instance, when liberty-loving Anglo-Saxons had submitted to the Norman yoke. But Americans were now predisposed to think in linear terms, believing that their revolution could simultaneously recover their ancestral freedom – Jefferson wanted

213

A portrait of Thomas Jefferson (1800), the author of the Declaration of Independence, which called on the authority of the people in invoking the 'self-evident', trans-historical principles of equal rights and government by consent. Ordinary Americans would be their own founders.

students at his University of Virginia to study Anglo-Saxon, the language of freedom – and promote the continuing progress of refinement and civility, enabling rustic provincials to match and exceed metropolitan standards.

For radical critics in the British metropolis such as Thomas Paine (1737–1809), the British Empire's astonishing rise to prosperity and power had seemed to jeopardize liberty. For provincials, however, the spectacle of metropolitan corruption and an increasingly despotic colonial administration taught the opposite lesson: liberty and prosperity were inextricably linked and a threat to one was a threat to both. The burgeoning commerce that enriched colonists and enabled them to participate in the 'consumer revolution' did not subvert their liberties. On the contrary, mercantilist trade regulations seemed to impose unnatural restraints on colonists who would have been *more* prosperous had they been able to trade *more* freely. Even as the wealth pouring into the metropolis offered irresistible temptations for the empire's rulers to revel in luxury and abuse power at the expense of the colonies, colonists themselves proved increasingly sensitive to encroachments on their rights that threatened to impoverish

and ultimately to enslave them. Except for those who depended on the favour of metropolitan authority, prosperity did not threaten provincials' virtue. Imperial tax policies portended a massive redistribution of wealth from provinces to metropolis, interfering with what Bishop George Berkeley in the early 18th century had called the 'westward course of empire'.

The rationale for independence, codified in the Declaration of Independence, was predicated on the premise that liberty – the 'inalienable rights' with which a free people were 'endowed by their creator' – and prosperity – the fruits of individual enterprise, or 'pursuit of happiness' – were two sides of the same coin. This new conception of political economy, built on Scottish Enlightenment theories of the progress of civilization – from hunting and gathering, to pastoral, agricultural and commercial stages of development –

enabled American revolutionaries to transcend, or at least deflect, the cyclical logic of early modern history. Significantly, Adam Smith's *Wealth of Nations* (1776) offered a broad, progressive view of historical development that minimized the role of the state in wealth creation and called on policy-makers to expand the ambit of market freedom. Although Smith was primarily concerned with promoting British national wealth, he was impressed by the extraordinarily rapid development of the North American colonies that the limited imperial interference had made possible. Smith's masterpiece became the new gospel for liberal, anti-mercantilist free-traders in the United States, particularly for staple producers seeking expanded access to overseas markets.

Revolutionary Americans did not need Adam Smith to teach them the advantages of free trade. Colonists had already advanced a conception of empire in which provincial governments enjoyed considerable autonomy and provincials enjoyed expanding market opportunities. Americans recognized that their prosperity depended on the

A postcard from c. 1903, depicting the Boston Tea Party. On 16 December 1773 patriots disguised as Indians dumped 342 chests of tea into Boston Harbor. Protesting against Parliament's right to tax and regulate trade, free-traders sought to protect their commercial liberties by destroying the East India Company's monopoly on the sale of tea in the colonies.

An illustration engraved by Paul Revere (1734–1818) and hand-coloured by Paul Walker, depicting the Boston Massacre. British soldiers fired on Boston civilians on 5 March 1770; the death of five 'martyrs' radicalized patriot opposition to imperial taxation and regulation – colonists owed allegiance only to a king who would protect them.

protection that British maritime hegemony afforded them; they also recognized the crucial role of metropolitan markets and credit facilities in sustaining economic growth. Protestations of loyalty and allegiance to George III (1738–1820) before the Declaration testified to this understanding. But a countervailing tendency to question the direction of imperial policy-making and administration gained traction as the crisis escalated. This was reinforced by the radical republican critique of court corruption, social-contract theorizing about the conditions of political legitimacy, and Scottish ideas about social and economic progress. The result was that Americans could project concerns about the degeneracy of the times and the vulnerability of their rights on to the metropolis, imaginatively purging themselves of pernicious foreign influences. American nation-making was predicated on a new, modern, linear way of thinking about history.

The most urgent challenge for Jefferson and his fellows was to establish the legitimacy of their new republican regime in a world of monarchies. The bold solution was to redefine sovereignty in popular terms, first imagining, as Jefferson did in his *Summary View of the Rights of British America* (1774), that kings were 'servants' of the people and then, in the Declaration, peremptorily dismissing the king from service. If the people were sovereign, republican self-government was the only logical and legitimate form of rule. American revolutionaries, unlike their French successors, did not push too hard on this point, for they were seeking recognition – and more substantial forms of assistance – from monarchical powers. But they were nonetheless convinced that they had 'begun the world anew' and that their republican experiment would ultimately become the model for all humankind. There was no need to establish a new revolutionary calendar, beginning with Year I. Americans would instead celebrate 1776, the year of their independence declaration and a pivotal moment in world history.

As revolutionary leaders mobilized popular resistance to British despotism, they insisted that ordinary folk were the true history-makers, emphasizing the artificiality of hierarchy and privilege. In the dark days of the old regime, the masses submitted to kingly rule through ignorance and superstition, but, as Thomas Paine wrote in *Common Sense* (1776), 'no truly natural or religious reason' could justify 'the distinction of men into *kings* and *subjects*'. Recognizing that kings were merely men and that, in the words of the Declaration, 'all men were created equal', enlightened patriots would create governments 'deriving their just powers from the consent of the governed'. The people's recognition of their own rights thus marked the beginning of history, properly understood, or, alternatively, the end of history – the never-ending, blood-soaked cycle of oppression and war – as it was conventionally misunderstood. The image of the United States as an asylum of liberty and a land of opportunity would prove attractive to generations of immigrants.

The American Revolution constituted a fundamental rupture in historical consciousness as well as in what the Declaration of Independence calls 'the course of human events'.

A new cast of characters, the 'people', now crowded the stage. Previously the people – vulgar plebeians, the mob – had been seen as only a lowly part of political society. Now the logic of radical republican ideas transformed their image, making them collectively the source of legitimate authority. Kings and aristocrats were driven into exile and excluded from the otherwise all-inclusive people. It was hardly necessary to specify, as the United States Constitution did (in Article I, Section 9) that 'no title of nobility shall be granted by the United States', for privileged orders and republican equality, 'aristocracy' and 'democracy', were fundamentally opposed. Indeed, that opposition would prove to be central to American national identity.

Americans were very conscious that their revolution – the 'shot heard 'round the world' – would have a profound impact on the histories of peoples everywhere. The revolutionaries' apotheosis of the 'people' was predicated on a universal framework: all peoples, or nations, were created equal, though only self-governing Americans were fully conscious of the implications of this fact and thus prepared to shape their own future. Yet 'all eyes are opened, or opening, to the rights of man', Jefferson proclaimed in 1826. Other peoples would have to 'burst the chains' and 'rivers of blood' would have to flow before darkness gave way to light and the old to the new, but the 'end of history' was now in view. Precocious Americans might be exemplary and therefore 'exceptional', but that sense of national identity was *not* based on geopolitical or ideological isolation or difference. Americans exulted in the world historical significance of their revolution, and their identity as a people only made sense in a world of peoples, all of whom would become free to determine their own destinies. Until that happened, these nations would be victims of history, martyrs in the inexorable march towards liberty. And as nations began to determine their own destiny, they would become more and more alike, finally rising to 'the separate and equal station to which the laws of nature and nature's God entitle them'. Eager to accelerate this process and conscious of their nation's growing power, 20th-century American internationalists would justify – or rationalize – interventions in two world wars and all over the world.

Revolutionary Americans' conception of a republican millennium provided a providential end towards which national histories would converge. In optimistic moments, Americans have congratulated themselves on having arrived at this end point. Yet they have also been periodically reminded that they cannot escape the world and that, until freedom reigns everywhere, their own freedom will remain vulnerable to foreign and domestic threats. Other peoples will experience history's agonies, but revolutionary impulses – and counter-revolutionary reactions – will spill across national boundaries, drawing Americans into the vortex of global conflict. In their private pursuit of happiness, Americans may think with Henry Ford that history is 'bunk', but that forward-looking optimism has always been shadowed by the fear that the repressed will

The beginning and the end: George Washington and his fellow founders sought to create a new order for the ages, but the destruction of the Twin Towers in New York City on 11 September 2001 shattered Americans' complacency and sense of security: they could not escape history after all.

return, as foreigners and 'foreign influences' contaminate the republic or as Americans themselves betray their birthright.

As Americans have imagined themselves a 'chosen people' beyond history, they have been acutely conscious of the dangers of falling back into history, losing sight of their destiny and rejoining the ranks of the damned. The fear has always been that their revolution would be reversed and the republican experiment would fail. Jefferson thus raised the alarm against home-grown aristocrats and monocrats (supporters of monarchy) who might consolidate power in a new American metropolis that would dominate the state republics and destroy civil liberties, making citizens into subjects. In the decades leading up to the Civil War, statesmen called on their countrymen to cherish the Union, the Founding Fathers' greatest legacy. Revolutionary Americans had made themselves a free people by choice, by acts of political will culminating in the ratification of the federal constitution. Those original choices became a 'sacred trust' to rising generations who were taught that the Union's collapse would Europeanize American politics and unleash the 'dogs of war'.

Disunited, Americans would betray themselves and future generations, committing 'treason against the hopes of the world', as Jefferson warned during the bitter struggle over the admission of Missouri in 1820: in seeking to ban slavery in that state northern 'restrictionists' violated the fundamental republican principle of self-government for the

The Civil War peacemakers: Generals William Tecumseh Sherman and Ulysses S. Grant, President Abraham Lincoln and Admiral David Dixon Porter on board the River Queen, *March 1865. For Lincoln and supporters of the Union, the victory over secessionist Confederates vindicated the principles of free government of the Declaration of Independence.*

(white) citizens of the new state. The history Americans had hoped to escape would have its bloody revenge. It was thus with a fateful, even fatalistic sense that patriotic Americans, north and south, turned against each other in the massive slaughter of the Civil War (1861–65). And when Abraham Lincoln (1809–65) sought to justify the carnage at Gettysburg in his address (19 November 1863), he looked back to Jefferson's Declaration ('fourscore and seven years ago'), asking whether 'a new nation, conceived in liberty and dedicated to the proposition that all men are created equal' or 'any nation so conceived and so dedicated can long endure'. Would the reunited states show the way towards a better future for all humankind, or would Americans prove to be no different than other peoples, subject to the vagaries and accidents of history? If free government should 'perish from the earth', the new history Americans imagined – a linear progress across the generations and across the vast spaces of the North American continent – would give way to the cycle of afflictions that marked the histories of other peoples. If Americans themselves could not escape history, there was no hope for humankind.

Americans have always thought of themselves as a new people, as a nation to end nations, a united people drawing strength from their diverse origins and their widely various pursuits of happiness. As they declared their independence, they insisted that through self-determining acts of political will they could make themselves a free people with a glorious future. Paradoxically, however, this sense of providentially sanctioned destiny brings with it an anxious awareness of the possibility of failing and falling back into the history they had escaped. For Americans of all ideological persuasions, these anxieties are manifest in appeals to the popular 'spirit of 1776' or to the original intentions of the Founding Fathers. Fulfilling the hopes of the future depends on fidelity to the republican – they would now say 'democratic' – creed as it was first articulated. The people who would escape history are thus tethered to – and defined by – a revolutionary generation of nation-makers who still 'live' in courts, legislatures and the popular political imagination.

The kind of history that seems so thick on the ground in the Old World and rejected by the revolutionaries – Henry Ford's 'bunk' – may be conspicuously absent in their New World. But a forward-looking conception of history, cherishing the memory of revolutionary founders and glimpsing a republican millennium for all mankind in the distant future, is all the more central to Americans' self-understanding. So, too, is the irrepressible fear of subversion and betrayal by foreign or 'un-American' influences and ideologies. A free people, imagining themselves at the end of history, cannot escape the fear of being sucked back into history's vortex.

Australia

A European nation in an ancient land

A visitor to Australia is likely to come by air and land at the Sydney international airport, hard up against the Pacific Ocean at the very point where eleven vessels dropped anchor in January 1788. The name Botany Bay was conferred by Captain James Cook (1728–79) because of the abundance of new plants collected there twenty years earlier. Cook's enthusiastic description of this fertile and well-watered shelter persuaded the British government to choose Botany Bay as the site for a new settlement.

Botany Bay is now a transport and industrial hub serving an international city that sprawls into the distance. The city's landmarks – the great arched bridge and the concrete shells of the Sydney Opera House – are located to the north on majestic Sydney Harbour. It was here that the founding governor of the colonial venture, Arthur Phillip (1738–1814), transferred the settlement in 1788 after Botany Bay was found to be sandy, swampy and deficient in fresh water. Cook had landed in autumn after the rain had fallen, but Phillip arrived in high summer when the meagre undergrowth revealed the landscape's poverty.

This was the first disappointment that the colonists experienced, but others quickly followed. Their first crops withered in the thin soil; axes lost their edge on the gnarled and twisted trunks of the eucalyptus; stock strayed and died. Hunger strained discipline, for the majority of these settlers were convicts, transported for capital offences and set down in a strange and inhospitable land. Efforts to befriend the original inhabitants failed, and within two years Phillip himself was injured by an Eora tribesman's spear.

Yet the British persevered. Within a decade they had set out their town and put the convicts to productive farmwork. In comparison with the earlier settlements in North America, success came quickly. Moving inland in the early decades of the 19th century, the colonists began producing wool and attracted a stream of free immigrants.

Captain Cook Taking Possession of the Australian Continent. *This historical engraving appeared in 1865, nearly a century after the event it depicts, and puts Cook in a sylvan glade at Botany Bay instead of the island where the ceremony actually took place. It also anticipates the Union flag as devised after 1801.*

Additional colonies were established. With the discovery of gold in the 1850s came half a million more immigrants. The abandonment of convict transportation and the advent of self-government in the same decade allowed for a thrusting settler society with a greater measure of democracy and a higher standard of living than the Old World from which it sprang.

Australia Day, 26 January, marks this success story. It was on 26 January 1788 that Governor Phillip raised the British flag at Sydney Cove and read his declaration of sovereignty. As long understood, this was a story of a sleeping land finally brought to life, a place of novel flora and fauna that existed in undisturbed isolation until it was jolted into motion – a journey that has been repeated ever since to renew the Australian nation.

The evidence for this history of Australia is immediately apparent. At whichever city the newcomer arrives, the colonial origins are immediately apparent – Sydney, Melbourne, Perth and Hobart are all named after British politicians, Adelaide after a queen, Brisbane a governor. Each city has a governor's residence, parliament house and churches, all rendered in a derivative architecture, along with war memorials that commemorate imperial service. But these buildings are now overshadowed by corporate skyscrapers that follow the universal idiom of modernity.

Visitors today are drawn by a different Australia, one that is distinctive and exotic. Many of them make their way into the arid interior, a place of vast space and brilliant skies. They visit places such as Uluru, the great red monolith in the Northern Territory, to seek out a more authentic Australia defined by its longer Aboriginal presence.

Australian citizens have recently been attempting to seek reconciliation with Aboriginal Australia. Discriminatory practices were abandoned from the 1960s, land rights conceded by legislation from the 1970s, prior wrongs recognized in the 1980s and original occupancy recognized by the courts in the 1990s. The prime minister's apology at the beginning of 2008 came after his predecessor had resisted such atonement, but Australians still remain shamed by the patterns of Aboriginal unemployment, poverty,

TIMELINE

60,000 BCE Migration of Aborigines to Australia

13,000 BCE The land bridge between Australia and Tasmania is submerged

1606 CE Dutch navigator Willem Janszoon reaches Western Australia

1770 British navigator James Cook arrives on the east coast

1788 The First Fleet, commanded by Arthur Phillip, establishes a British penal colony at Botany Bay

1803 Matthew Flinders completes the first circumnavigation of the continent

1851 The gold rush begins near Ballarat in Victoria

1901 The Commonwealth of Australia is formed by the federation of six colonies

1915 Australian troops fighting in the First World War suffer defeat by the Turks at Gallipoli

1942–43 Darwin in the Northern Territory is repeatedly bombed by the Japanese

1967 Relaxation of the Immigration Act of 1901 ends with formal abandonment of the White Australia policy

The 'Sea of Hands' in Sydney. This series of installations symbolizing reconciliation with the indigenous population of Australia was first set up in front of Parliament House, Canberra, after John Howard's Liberal–National coalition government introduced changes to native title in 1997. The plastic hands bear signatures from petitions.

morbidity, crime and family breakdown. There has also been a renaissance of Aboriginal culture in art, music, film, literature and sport. A marked increase in the Aboriginal population, from 156,000 in 1976 to 517,000 by 2006, is clear evidence of renewal, and with it has come a heightened awareness of Aboriginal history.

Far from being a new country that began in 1788, Australia is now seen to have a long history. Human occupancy goes back over 50,000 years – to the very limits of reliable measurement – and was marked by continuous adaptation to a strikingly variable environment. The growing recognition of this vastly extended history speaks to current sensibility. It reveals complex forms of organization and ecological practice, hundreds of languages, haunting art forms and spiritual beliefs of great force. By embracing the

Aboriginal rock art dates back many thousands of years. This example shows the barramundi, a northern Australian species of fish, and an ancestral Dreamtime figure. Dreamtime is a complex concept describing Aboriginal spiritual beliefs and creation myths.

Aboriginal past, non-Aboriginal Australians are attaching themselves more firmly to their country.

The history that began in 1788 was a European one. This Australia was a product of British foresight, for British navigators came after the Spanish, Portuguese and Dutch had carved out their territories in the Indian Ocean and dismissed the great southern continent as worthless. The early settlement of Australia was conducted during Britain's extended contest with France for supremacy, and shaped by its ensuing dominance.

Australia took Britain's unwanted criminals – 150,000 of them – and many more enterprising free settlers. It received manufactured goods and investment, and sent back commodities and dividends. The Australian colonies took over British principles of government, law and civil society, reproducing many aspects of its parent society and adapting others. The result was familiar and yet different.

First of all, Australian colonial society was an amalgam of the national components that made up the United Kingdom, with the English, Irish, Scots and Welsh all maintaining elements of their cultures while joining freely in common endeavours; one consequence was an early acceptance of religious equality. Second, the colonies dispensed with institutions such as an established church, a hereditary landed class and military caste that maintained a firm hierarchy; the absence of patronage and deference suggested a new society that had been topped and tailed. Third, the high standard of living and ready opportunities made for fuller participation: there was more leisure, greater literacy and higher rates of church attendance and involvement in voluntary activities. These features were often compared with the United States, but that republic had to win its independence, whereas Australians liked to think of their country as a better version of Britain.

Britain withdrew the imperial garrisons following self-government in the 1850s, but continued to conduct Australia's foreign policy and the Royal Navy remained the guarantor of its security. Forts facing out to sea from the shorelines of the principal cities attested to the unease of a small population – 1.15 million in 1861, 3.77 million in 1901 – occupying a vast continent. The anxiety mounted as other European powers began to challenge Britain and found expression in military commitments to imperial wars, in South Africa and China at the turn of the century, and then in the Middle East and Western Europe during the First World War. The Australian sacrifice on the Turkish Gallipoli peninsula in 1915 thus served as an affirmation of national valour and a down payment on an imperial insurance policy.

There was room for other Europeans, especially after the gold rush of the 1850s brought an influx from the Continent, but not for non-Europeans. Initially the convicts provided cheap labour and subsequent attempts to introduce indentured workers from China or the Pacific islands met with strong resistance. Out of this came the Immigration Restriction Act, which was

Transported convicts were an important feature of the Australian population for eighty years. Among the last shipment to reach Western Australia in 1868 were sixty-two members of the Irish Republican Brotherhood, including Thomas Murragh, who was later rescued by an American whaler.

one of the first measures of the new federal government in 1901. In deference to imperial concern, it used a dictation test rather than explicit racial exclusion, but was known and upheld as the 'White Australia policy'. White Australia was relaxed after the Second World War but not formally abandoned until the late 1960s.

Until the Second World War, Australians liked to boast that they were 98 per cent British. Such eugenicist self-definition was not possible after the war, for Britain could no longer

Dutch immigrants arriving from Rotterdam in 1960. In the decade after the Second World War around 100,000 immigrants made the sea voyage from the Netherlands to Australia and smaller numbers continued to arrive by air from the 1960s onwards.

protect Australia: the fall of its naval base in Singapore to Japanese forces in early 1942 marked the end of imperial defence. Nor could Britain provide the numbers needed to meet Australia's ambitious post-war plans, with an urgent conviction that it must populate or perish. So immigrants were sought from northern Europe, then southern and Eastern Europe, and eventually the Middle East. In two decades, 2 million settled, bringing the population to 12.76 million by 1971.

Meanwhile Australia was drawn into Asia as the European powers withdrew or were driven out. The end of empire and the onset of the Cold War revived fears of invasion among a people who thought of themselves as a European outpost at the bottom of the

Southeast Asian archipelago – and such fears are periodically revived by the arrival of small boats bringing refugees down from the Asian mainland. But the rise of Asia brought a growing demand for Australian commodities – China and Japan are now its two largest trade partners – and increased migration. A quarter of the current population of 23 million was born outside Australia, a larger proportion than any other advanced industrial nation. The transformation from white suprematism to multiculturalism has been swift.

The history that began in 1788 related the taming of a harsh and obdurate environment. It told how visionary explorers opened up the interior for occupation by pastoralists. The wool industry operated on a large scale, employing a small army of shepherds, boundary riders and shearers, and generating a legend of the Australian bushman as practical, suspicious of authority, dismissive of affectation, and always sticking by his mates.

After the wool-growers came the farmers. The government threw open the land for selection on cheap terms; it built and operated the railways that took produce to the cities

Shearing the Rams (1890) is one of the best-known works of Tom Roberts, a leading Australian landscape painter. His sentimental depiction of shearing operations on a large pastoral property near the Murray River conveys the romance associated with the country's largest export industry.

Those who took advantage of government schemes for settlement in the second half of the 19th century faced a formidable challenge in clearing and cultivating the land. The large stumps of eucalyptus trees around this family homestead attest to their arduous labour.

for processing, and constructed the port facilities that allowed it to be shipped to overseas destinations. It created the irrigation works and sponsored the technical improvements that increased yields, and supplied the schools and other facilities that supported rural communities. The family farm generated a complementary legend of the Australian pioneer as an exemplar of agrarian virtue, bringing civilization to the wilderness.

The logic of commodity production was one of continuous improvement that enabled Australian producers to command export markets. The effect of increased productivity was to reduce labour needs and increase the size of the enterprise, a pattern that was repeated in mining and mineral production as well as pastoralism and agriculture. Even so, the vision of development exercised a powerful influence on generations of Australians: primary industries earned the foreign exchange that sustained high living standards and, by generating additional jobs in construction, transport, distribution and services, in turn stimulated urban growth.

The pattern continued into the mining boom during the opening years of the 21st century, but it no longer commands the same acceptance as when Australia rode on the sheep's back. There is now concern about the environmental cost of land-clearing and European farming practices. The longer history of Australia sees an old land mass with a shallow soil that has been leached of nutrients, an unreliable rainfall that makes it susceptible to drought, and vegetation adapted to these circumstances that is highly combustible. This new sensibility prefers forests to farms and rivers to reservoirs, Aboriginal custodianship of the land to development projects. The heavy reliance of the economy on the production of minerals and energy makes a response to greenhouse gas emission all the more difficult.

There is another history of Australia that has more recently been forgotten. Colonial success made for a national sentiment that was realized in the federation of six colonies into the Commonwealth of Australia in 1901. It was done in a uniquely democratic manner: the people elected delegates to federal conventions that drafted the federal compact and put it back to the people for acceptance by popular referendum. Australia was a precocious democracy, the second after New Zealand to enfranchise women and the first to elect a Labour government.

The Commonwealth created distinctive arrangements to meet popular aspirations. The protection of jobs by tariffs on imported goods was tied to the requirement that local industries provide men with wages sufficient to maintain a family in conditions of reasonable comfort. This institutionalization of the male breadwinner came at the expense of female workers and stunted state provision of social welfare; the role of the state was rather to underwrite development and operate the utilities that private industry could not conduct profitably. The basic wage was a legal entitlement and it was assumed that it would allow families to provide for their own needs; hence the description of Australia as a wage-earner's welfare state.

The arrangement lasted until the 1980s, when the terms of trade turned against commodity exports and globalization undermined the protection of local industries. The labour market was deregulated along with the removal of controls on trade and finance and privatization of public enterprises. At this point Australia turned away from its own traditions to embrace a market without borders. Australians looked outwards, joining in the renewed growth of investment, innovation and opportunity, sharing in the global expansion and contraction, and feeling the loss of older certainties. The outcome of this most recent break with the past remains to be determined.

WILHELMINA DONKOH

Ghana

From colony to continental leader

The history of Ghana is inextricably linked to gold. This gold-producing region first attracted the attention of Western Sudanese traders before the 13th century. Later Portuguese traders searched for it as the Eldorado that had supplied North Africa; when they reached the region, they named it the Gold Coast. The region experienced intense European competition, with forts constructed along the coast. Modern Ghana was named after the ancient Western Sudanese Empire, which was also famed for gold and whose people shared cultural similarities (although the empire did not share the same geography as the modern state). It is the combined product of the independent activities of the indigenous peoples, of British colonial rule from the 19th century and of subsequent developments. The people today operate under a dual heritage: 'traditional' and 'Western' or 'modern'.

The first to write about Ghana's past were Western Sudanese Muslims from about the 13th century and European visitors from the 15th century. Some of these writers, particularly the Europeans, implied that the indigenous people contributed little. They branded the local culture barbaric and assumed that, because the indigenous people had written nothing about their past, there was nothing to be recorded. These views have endured in spite of the rich oral traditions, artefacts and archaeological evidence to the contrary. Colonial rule entrenched the Western sense of the superiority of European culture, and many Westerners have misunderstood and misrepresented such indigenous practices as the extended family system.

The peoples of Ghana and their achievements before the Europeans arrived, during the pre-colonial era, and since independence should be regarded as a continuum, and studied and celebrated as the past of the nation. Oral histories, including eyewitness accounts and traditions such as genealogies and folk tales, are as important as written

Gold pendant from the treasury of the ruling Asantehene, Kofi Karikari (r. 1867–74). Apart from being a standard in economic exchanges gold has symbolic value in that it is believed to symbolize generational permanence. Representing permanent wealth, it was often crafted into exquisite artefacts and worn as a sign of social status.

sources, archaeology and ethnography. Examining the views of a wide range of people helps to create a popular history that touches the core issues of the nation's past and rescues the distant past for the majority of Ghanaians from the obscurity to which colonialism subjected it.

Many Ghanaians who are proud of their nation's past look to tradition as a guide for the present and future. The concept of *sankofa* ('go back and retrieve from the past') is the motivational principle behind the establishment of cultural bodies to preserve the national heritage. Generally Ghanaians think of the nation's history as commencing with the movement for self-government after 1945 that led to independence on 6 March 1957. Yet they also unconsciously take into account the distant past when such activities as funerals, naming, marriage, festivals and enstoolment or enskinment (the ceremonial assumption of power) of traditional leaders evolved. Many Ghanaians feel compelled to go back to the past to retrieve the core values underlying some of their historic institutions such as chieftaincy, and cultural practices such as puberty rites. Traditional beliefs and cosmology are widely maintained, even though the majority professes to be Christian and 'modern'. It is not uncommon to find people invoking curses (*duabo*), consulting mediums and traditional priests while at the same time being very active in church.

The indigenous peoples of Ghana evolved their own social, economic and political institutions. They made links with the outside world through the Wangara traders from the Western Sudan, and with Europe and Asia via North Africa, long before the arrival of the Europeans in the 15th century. Yet scholars have still to determine when the region was first inhabited. Much of the history that has been passed on orally has been in the form of 'stool histories' (essentially political histories of traditional states presented in the form of genealogies), or deals with events such as wars or historical matters that enable people to claim offices and property.

TIMELINE

c. **1000** BCE First known habitation of the region of modern Ghana

c. **1000** CE The Ghana Empire emerges, northwest of the region of modern Ghana

1076 Conquest of the Ghana Empire by the Almoravids

1300s Establishment of early Akan and pre-Asante states

1482 Portuguese explorers reach Elmina on the Gold Coast

1600s French, Dutch, English, Danish, German and Swedish traders arrive; the region becomes a major centre of the Atlantic slave trade

1806 The Asante-Fanti War brings the Asante to dominance

1807 Britain abolishes the slave trade

1824 The first Anglo-Asante War breaks out

1874 The Gold Coast becomes a British protectorate

1901 The Asante territories become part of the Gold Coast colony

1957 Ghana becomes the first sub-Saharan country to gain its independence, with Kwame Nkrumah as first prime minister and president

Archaeological evidence indicates that humans have lived in Ghana for over 3,000 years: there is material evidence of ancient human presence, including utensils, implements, dwelling caves and factory sites where stone implements and adornments were produced. Although many Ghanaian peoples tell stories of migration, these all imply an earlier human presence in the region; yet it is almost impossible to determine which modern ethnic groups constitute the descendants of these ancient inhabitants.

Today's Ghanaians number among the peoples of the West African region. They broadly consist of the Guan-speakers, the Akan, the Ga-Dangme, the Ewe and the Mole-Dagbani grouping that includes the Gonja. The diverse ethnic groups speak either Kwa or Gur, also known as the 'Voltaic' sub-group of languages, both of which linguistically belong to the Niger-Congo family. This suggests that all these peoples lived in the same place in the distant past or had close interactions over a long period of time. The groups claim that they either evolved locally or migrated from several locations outside. Most evidence points to the fact that the Guan-speaking peoples were the first settlers. Traditional accounts suggest that the ancestors of most Ghanaians lived in various places both in Ghana and, more widely, in West Africa, with some claiming multiple origins. However, many peoples whose earliest oral traditions suggest local evolution now insist that they migrated from exotic places linked to the Bible and the Koran: Mesopotamia, Ethiopia or Israel.

Funerary terracotta (fired clay) sculptures were used to memorialize important rulers and other royals and constitute an essential aspect of Akan cultural heritage. The preference for fired clay was possibly determined by the durability of the material given the humid climate and the acute problem of infestation by termites.

Several other ethnic groups inhabit the northern savanna belt, known as the Northern Territories during the colonial period. They migrated here from the Western Sudan and became dominant on account of their able leadership. There are also several smaller non-centralized groups. There is a popular assumption that these were aboriginal, but some claim their ancestors migrated from Burkina Faso across the Volta basin. They shared certain cultural practices, such as systems of land ownership, marriage rites and religious beliefs.

In the forest zone to the south of the savanna are the Akan-speaking peoples who constitute the largest ethnic grouping in Ghana. The parent stock of the Akan are the Bono, the earliest group to emerge; the Adanse, who are believed to be the first builders among the groups; and the Twifo, whose language (Twi) is spoken by all the Akan groups. These people gradually spread across the land as a result of population growth, the search for economic resources and the effects of war between the 11th and 13th centuries.

Southeastern Ghana is peopled by the Ga-Dangme and the Ewe. Both developed patrilineal systems. Oral traditions suggest migrations from the east into lands already occupied.

The most powerful polities to emerge in pre-colonial Ghana include the Bono, Adanse Denkyira, Akwamu, Akyem and Asante in the forest zone; the Fantse, Ewe and Ga-Dangme states on the coast; and the Dagbon and Gonja in the north. Most of these achieved prominence through their access to and control over resources, which made it possible to participate in commerce to the north and, from 1471, with the Europeans on the coast. The forest zone was rich in gold, ivory and kola nut, all of which were in great demand; there were also the Lobi goldfields in the north. At the same time there was also considerable demand for slave labour, salt and other exotic commodities within the forest zone.

The first Europeans to arrive were the Portuguese in 1471, followed by the English, Dutch, Danes, Germans, Swedish and French in the 17th century. The gradual process of British colonization from the beginning of the 19th century flowered in 1874 with the creation of the protectorate and was completed in 1902. For the first three hundred years

A Dutch flag flying over Elmina Castle, the first permanent and substantial European fortification constructed in Ghana by the Portuguese in 1482. It was taken over by the Dutch in the 17th century, heralding the intense European competition for dominance of trade in Ghana.

An engraving of The First Day of the Yam Custom. *It shows a durbar, held possibly during the annual Akwasidae festival in Kumase, which coincided with the mission of the English delegation to Kumase in 1817, led by Thomas Edward Bowdich. The picture is replete with symbolic imagery, including the decorations on the canopies.*

of European involvement the indigenous people remained in charge of their own affairs, even while dealing with the agents of the mercantile powers. But colonial rule excluded them from decisive participation in central government, which led to the belief that Ghanaians were incapable of administering themselves. On a more positive note, however, colonial rule endorsed English as the official language, which became a unifying factor underpinning national identity for the newly independent Ghana.

The Europeans introduced crops such as cocoa and coffee, and other foodstuffs. Christianity and other Western influences played an important role in advancing literacy and health, but they tended to mitigate against indigenous cultural practices. The identification, recording and transmission of the processes underlying such institutions as marriage, naming, ethics, beliefs, inheritance systems and languages have provided insights into the people and their past. Most Ghanaians consider their cultures to be rich and varied, while at the same time having shared links that bind the people together. This unity in diversity has been recognized as a fundamental element of the Ghanaian character. Colonial rule has led to membership in the Commonwealth and a shared history with other countries around the world. Ghanaians pride themselves on having been early actors in the nationalist struggle and on the fact that Ghana was the first sub-Saharan country to gain independence from colonial rule after the Second World War, in 1957. The first prime minister and president Kwame Nkrumah (1909–72) was a leader of world stature who took measures that enabled other African countries to liberate themselves and was instrumental in initiating the process of unifying Africa through the Organization of African Unity, the United Nations and the Non-Aligned Movement. This helped to thrust Ghana on to the centre stage of African and world politics. In recent years the role of Kofi Annan (b. 1938) as the first black African secretary-general of the United Nations has generated much pride.

Ghana has become a bastion of peace in a troubled region despite numerous problems, including poverty, inadequate educational and health provision and political instability between 1966 and 1992. Serious efforts have been made to forge a unified nation out of diverse peoples, although Ghanaians continue to be attached to their ethnic groups, an attachment sometimes manipulated by politicians, especially during elections. The modern state is a secular one, although most people have a strong religious attachment, with about 60 per cent professing to be Christian, 20 per cent Muslim and 9 per cent indigenous religious faiths.

One of the most regrettable aspects of the Ghanaian past is the indigenous involvement in the international slave trade. Although various degrees of unfree conditions had prevailed in Ghanaian society, the system had been a means of increasing the population, and it was not pernicious. However, from the mid-17th century the region changed from being a net importer of unfree persons to becoming an exporter of slaves as a response to the intense European demand for labour to work in the New World. The employment of Africans as chattel slaves owned by Europeans has played a significant role in the racial discrimination and stigmatization of the former group. Although it is difficult to give a precise number of slaves shipped out of Ghana, it has been estimated that over a period of two centuries more than 2 million people were sent – out of a region that, by 1960, had a population of just 7 million. The survival of the forts and castles such as Elmina, San Antonio, James Town, Cape Coast and Christiansborg, which served as the

Two Ghanaian women view a giant billboard in Accra showing Queen Elizabeth II and Dr Kwame Nkrumah, the first president of the Republic of Ghana. The Queen was unable to attend the ceremony for Ghana's transition from dominion to republic on 1 July 1960 but visited the country in September 1961.

A football fan with the Ghanaian national colours painted on his face during the 2010 World Cup in South Africa, when Ghana was the only African country to make it to the quarter-finals. Football has developed into a national passion that unites Ghanaians of different ethnic and political backgrounds.

slavers' warehouses and residences, has helped to authenticate a grim aspect of the nation's past and demystify such factors as the slave trade and colonial rule.

Ghanaian contact with Europeans resulted in huge changes in the region's economic, social and political systems. Frequent coups from the 1960s to the 1980s created an environment of instability that delayed development and advancement. The issue of ethnicity has tended to create flashpoints, as some groups, such as the Ewe and those from the north, feel marginalized. Ghanaians who disagree with the agenda of the government point to allegations of constitutional infractions, nepotism and corruption.

In spite of all these challenges and difficulties, the modern nation has been striving to sustain past achievements and to develop values around which it can evolve. If these efforts could be sustained; if the pride in 'Ghanaianness' that prevailed immediately after independence could be retrieved, and the national economic and social wellbeing of the people attended to; if national resources could be exploited effectively and the country be involved prudently in the world community – then the national ideals for Ghana would have been achieved.

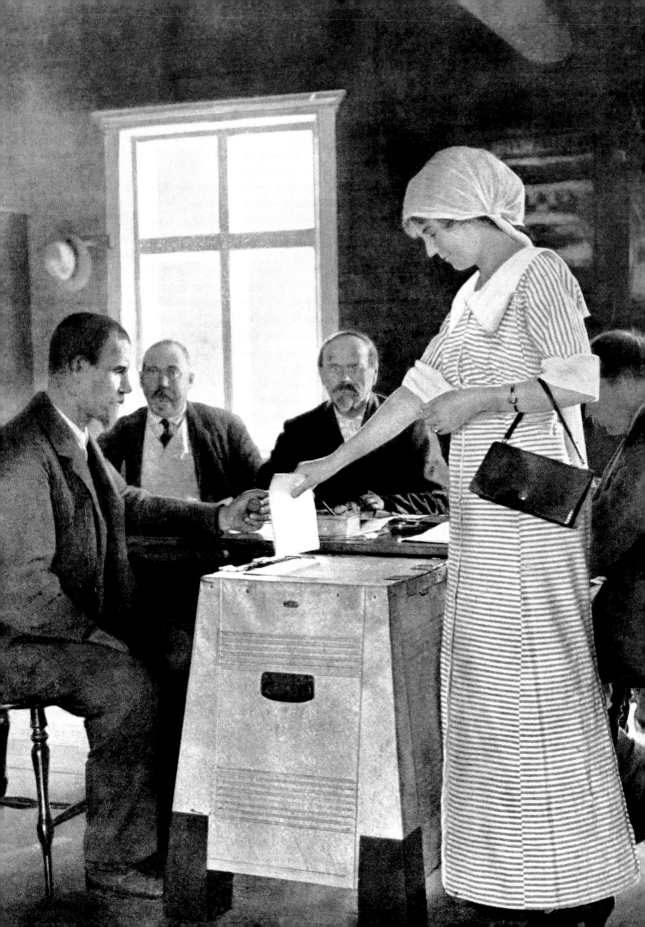

PIRJO MARKKOLA

Finland

Carving an identity from struggle

The history of Finland is often told as a story of survival through wars that foreigners find hard to understand. To many amateur historians the story of Finland, sandwiched between Sweden and Russia – between West and East – seems so complicated that it can only be understood by Finns themselves. Some research historians have been guilty of mythologization, while others have tried to correct misconceptions.

Another version of the country's history is the story of freehold peasant farmers and strong women. The Finns are proud of their farmers, who were never subject to feudalism. The peasant society is also used to explain the country's tradition of strong women, to whom the early achievement of political rights came quite naturally. One tenth of the members of Finland's first parliament of 1907 were women. Finns often claim to have been the first nation in the world in which women could vote and stand for public office, although the pioneers in this respect are found on the other side of the globe. However, the world's first female members of parliament were indeed Finns, ahead of New Zealand and Australia.

The year 2007 saw two important anniversaries: the centenary of parliamentary reform and the 90th anniversary of independence from Russia. The year 1809, when Finland became a Grand Duchy within the Russian Empire, was also remembered in 2008 and 2009. These anniversaries are a way of commemorating the complex story of Finnish history.

Christianity reached this northernmost corner of Europe as a result of the actions of both the Western and Eastern churches. The southern and southwestern region was heavily influenced by Western Europe from the 12th century onwards. This area was defined as part of Sweden in the 14th century, when the so-called Treaty of Nöteborg was signed between Sweden and Novgorod. The Lutheran Reformation arrived in the 1520s.

Finnish men and women of all social classes got the right to vote and to stand as candidates when the unicameral parliamentary system was adopted in 1906. Women actively used their rights from the very first elections in 1907.

Sweden lost its eastern parts to Russia in 1809 and the Grand Duchy of Finland was founded within the Russian Empire. Alexander I, portrayed here, was the first emperor to rule this new administrative unit.

Under Swedish rule a number of institutions, such as the postal system, the Court of Appeal and the University of Turku, were founded; county administration became efficient and new cities brought trade.

The Napoleonic Wars at the beginning of the 19th century turned Finnish history in a new direction. The 600-year connection with Sweden ended and Finland became part of the Russian Empire. Emperor Alexander I (1777–1825) signed the Treaty of Tilsit with Napoleon in 1807, in part to force Sweden to join the Continental System trade blockade against Great Britain. The emperor's subsequent war with Sweden led to an invasion of Finland, which he declared permanently joined to Russia. In late 1808 a decision was made to create a Finnish government, of which the inaugural Porvoo Diet was held in March 1809. Under the terms of the Treaty of Hamina, Sweden handed over its territory east of the Tornio River and the Aland Islands to Russia.

The emperor recognized Finland's Lutheran religion, law and social order, all of which owed much to Swedish influence. A central administration was created for the Grand Duchy under the direct rule of the emperor. Finns gradually developed the notion that in 1809 Finland had become an internally independent state with its own rights, and the turn of the 20th century was marked by a struggle for autonomy. Russian efforts to unify and modernize the state were seen as repressive and accordingly the period became known as the Period of Repression. At the end of Russia's General Strike of 1905, the emperor agreed to parliamentary reform for Finland, giving the Grand Duchy a unicameral parliament. Men and women were given an equal right to vote and stand for election.

TIMELINE

1150s Swedish efforts to conquer Finland begin

1249 The 'Second Swedish Crusade' confirms Swedish domination

1527 Introduction of the Protestant Reformation

1809 Finland becomes a Grand Duchy within the Russian Empire

1907 Parliamentary reform gives the vote to women

1917 Finland proclaims its independence from Russia

1918 Finnish Civil War

1939–40 The Winter War in which Finland is invaded by the Soviet Union

1941–44 The Continuation War between Finland and the Soviet Union

1944–45 The Lapland War between Finland and Nazi Germany

1995 Finland joins the European Union

In December 1917, during the Russian Revolution, the Finnish Parliament declared independence, a status that was recognized by the Russian provisional government by the start of 1918. During the winter and spring of 1918 there was a brief but bloody civil war in Finland between the Red socialists and White bourgeois supporters of the Finnish state. The complex nature of this war is attested by the fact that it has been difficult to find a name that everyone can accept: it has been called a revolution, rebellion, class war, *veljessota* ('war of brothers'), *kansalaissota* ('war of citizens') and a civil war, depending on the viewpoint.

In November 1939 the Winter War broke out between Finland and the Soviet Union, lasting three months. It was closely watched by the international media, and the image of a 'small and brave Finland' subsequently launched the term 'spirit of the Winter War' in reference to the national consensus of that time. After a short peace the so-called Continuation War with the Soviet Union began in June 1941, lasting until the end of summer 1944. The Lapland War followed, during which the Finns, in accordance with the demands of the Soviet Union, forced the Germans, who were using Finland as a route to invading Russia, out of northern Finland. As a result of these wars, Finland lost over 10 per cent of its territory to the Soviet Union; about 12 per cent of the population had to leave their homes in the ceded areas.

After 1945 Finland's relationship with the Soviet Union became a key issue. Trying to establish good Eastern relations during the

Images from Helsinki showing the aftermath of the Civil War in 1918. German troops arrived in April and helped the White Guards to defeat the Reds. Over 9,000 fell in battles, almost 10,000 were executed or murdered and around 14,000 died in concentration camps.

Cold War affected the country's relations with the West. Urho Kekkonen, president from 1956 until the 1980s, emphasized the policy of neutrality and used foreign policy arguments even when dealing with internal matters. Since the collapse of the Soviet Union there has been some debate as to whether Finland's Eastern relations were a case of skilful power politics or unnecessary fawning towards its powerful neighbour. In 1992 the government submitted an application to join the European Community, and Finland became a member of the European Union in 1995. The idea of NATO membership has gained the support of only a few citizens.

All these historical events contain elements that later generations used to define themselves and their past. Since the Finns had no ancient independence and no period of national grandeur, a sense of self-definition has been sought in different ways in different times. Historian Osmo Jussila has identified three central stories that appear, with variations, throughout Finnish history writing. These are Sweden–Finland, Finns' attempts to gain independence and the birth of the state in 1809. Other preoccupations of past historians included Finnish women's early social equality, Finland's role in the Second World War and its wise foreign policy during the Cold War.

Sweden–Finland refers to the period when Finland was part of the Swedish kingdom

Gustav III was King of Sweden from 1771 to 1792 when he was murdered. In Sweden the Gustavian constitution of 1772, which restored absolute monarchy, was changed in 1809, but in Finland it remained in effect in modified form until a new form of government was introduced in 1919.

yet, it is thought, was able to form its own identity with clear borders. This idea won currency only after 1918, and exists in several versions. Some have stressed that Sweden's violent annexation of Finland brought an end to the traditional autonomy of tribal communities, while others have argued that the Swedish administration had control over the Church but not over secular matters. A picture emerged of a time under Swedish rule, during which the Finns were oppressed by the Swedish yet developed their national consciousness. More recent historians have rejected the concept of Sweden–Finland and it does not appear in school textbooks, yet it is not uncommon to hear people talking about the time 'under Swedish rule', and the term Sweden–Finland has not fully disappeared from Finnish discourse.

Attempts to create an independent state of Finland were made from the 18th century, in particular by officers who fell out of favour with Sweden's Gustav III (1746–92) or who were disappointed in him. These men were portrayed as national heroes, but recent scholarship sees them simply as rebellious soldiers, a few of whom actually moved to Russia and fought alongside the Russian troops when they invaded Finland in 1808.

In old interpretations the Porvoo Diet in March 1809 saw the birth of the Finnish state. The idea of a constitution and of the Finnish state dominated the country's image from then until the 1960s. But some utterances of Alexander I have triggered a debate. What did he mean by saying he would raise the Finnish nation to the level of other nations? What was his intention in recognizing the Finnish religion, constitution

The Porvoo Diet was opened by Alexander I of Russia in person. The emperor gave the sovereign pledge and the Estates swore the oath of allegiance, accepting Alexander, Grand Duke of Finland, at Porvoo Cathedral on 29 March 1809.

and privileges – was he referring to the actual constitution or rather the basic legislation? A new study has shown that 19th-century Finnish scholars chose to ignore the change in meaning of these concepts: the terminology of 1809 was given a nationalist twist in the late 19th century when the internal independence of Finland was consciously being created.

After independence was proclaimed in 1917, nationalist historians fed the image of a Finnish state that had already been separate from the Russian state in the 19th century. There was a feeling that the country had always been heading towards independence. Although more recent studies have shattered this concept, the media still portrays 1809 as being part of the story of independence. The desire to find deep roots for Finnish independence is obviously strong.

Deep roots are also sought for the emancipation of Finnish women. The Finns are often pleased to tell foreigners about the poverty of their country and the consequent necessity for hard work. In an agrarian society everyone, men and women alike, had to work. This argument is used to explain the high number of women in the labour force, the high levels reached by women in political and professional organizations, and the high level of female education. The same characteristics are found in all Nordic countries, but in Finland they are transmuted into uniquely Finnish characteristics. A feature often thought to distinguish Finland from other Nordic countries is women's early franchise but, in fact, other Nordic women (other than in Sweden) were also given the right to vote and stand for election by the early years of the First World War.

Nowadays the crucial moments in Finnish history and the essential building blocks of national identity seem to be the wars of the 20th century, to judge from the volume of research and sales of books on the subject. The campaigns of the Second World War, the bloody battlefields of the Civil War, and the political tangles surrounding them all interest both researchers and the public. At the turn of the millennium a project called 'War Victims in Finland 1914–1922' (*sotasurmaprojekti*) tried to map out as accurately as possible the number of people who died, were killed or were executed during the Civil War of 1918. The results are available on the National Archive website. In a conscious act of history-based politics, the aim of the project was to relieve national trauma through the collection of detailed historical data.

A 19th-century European colour print of a female peasant in Finland. While this image idealizes its subject (and fails to depict her in authentic Finnish dress) it also demonstrates the dignity accorded to women in Finland at this time.

One recent example of the politics of the past has been the naming of the 1944 battles as a 'defence victory' (*torjuntavoitto*). This is to highlight the fact that, although Finland lost the war with the Soviet Union, it stopped the major Soviet attack in summer 1944. The term 'defence victory' allows the events of the past to be interpreted according to the demands of the present, while also honouring war veterans.

Another research-based reassessment is being conducted over the relations between Finland and Nazi Germany during the Continuation War. Whereas once historians saw Finland as fighting on its own, more recent historians have questioned this and have shown the central role that Germany, among others, had in the 'defence victory' of summer 1944. Over the last few years a number of studies have been published questioning the concept of a Finnish–Soviet war separate from the wider Nazi–Soviet conflict.

The significance of the wars is stressed even further in internet forums. In spring 2009 there was an eager debate on a forum specializing in historical topics about Estonia

The summer of 1944 became a turning point for Finland: a major Soviet attack was stopped but the end result was a lost war. Over 400,000 Karelians had to leave their homes and about 10 per cent of Finnish territory was ceded to the Soviet Union.

during the Second World War and thereafter. Another debate covered the role that politicians played during the Continuation War and at the war tribunal held after the Second World War. Most of the other popular topics are war-history-related. Yet the war of 1808–9 has ignited less passion, and few discuss the effects of 1809 on Finnish society. The significance of Swedish rule, however, still seems to be a serious question, and writers debate the ways in which both Sweden and Russia have influenced the development of Finnish society.

Study of the history of Swedish rule is not compulsory in Finnish high schools, so 1809 becomes the starting point of Finnish history, at best. This ignorance of earlier periods distorts the Finns' understanding of their history and therefore their image of modern society. It is forgotten that the institutions central to Finnish society – the parliament, legislation, judicial system, educational system, local administrative system and the church – are based on their Swedish heritage. A long-term understanding of how Finnish history has been shaped in a multicultural context could give a sense of proportion, and possibly even reveal elements that would make Finns proud of their distant past.

Nada prefirió mas que la
Libertad de su Patria.

FEDERICO LORENZ

Argentina

Between two centenaries

On 25 May 1910 the Republic of Argentina proudly celebrated the achievements of its first hundred years: a flourishing agro-export economy, the affluence of hundreds of thousands of immigrants, privileged trade links with the British Empire and a flourishing relationship with the cultural world of Europe, especially France. All this was enough to make the ruling elite anticipate Argentina's manifest destiny as a great and dominant nation of the region.

A century earlier, in 1810, a group of lawyers, merchants and military men from Buenos Aires, supported by a popular uprising, had deposed the Spanish viceroy and formed a governing junta. At the time Ferdinand VII, king of Spain (1784–1833), was a prisoner of Napoleon and his land had been invaded. A regency council was governing in his name, but the *porteños* (inhabitants of Buenos Aires) refused to recognize its authority and invoked the principle of returning sovereignty to the people. The members of the junta did not all share the same political position: some were seeking merely to steer the government until the situation in Spain had changed; others, influenced by the French Revolution, wanted independence for Spain's American colonies.

In any case, the junta sought to extend its influence over the rest of the territory of the Viceroyalty of the River Plate (which covered the regions of modern Argentina, Uruguay, Paraguay and Bolivia), whether by accord or by military means. This was a complex process: there were economic and cultural disputes between the port city and the interior, whose economy had suffered from the port being open to legal and illegal trade from overseas. A long period of confrontations and civil wars began. Over the course of the century the centralist state government of Buenos Aires was consolidated as the federal provinces of the interior fell under its control. The country's lands were united and experienced an economic boom based on the export of meat and

A portrait of José de San Martín (1778–1850), Argentina's 'father of the homeland', 1818. He gained saint-like status and is revered as an unquestionable symbol of humble patriotism and sacrifice. Every town in Argentina has a square, school or avenue named after him.

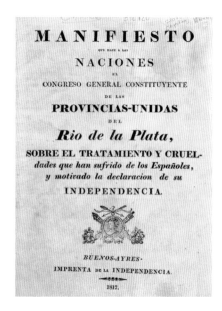

MANIFIESTO
QUE HACE A LAS
NACIONES
EL
CONGRESO GENERAL CONSTITUYENTE
DE LAS
PROVINCIAS-UNIDAS
DEL
Rio de la Plata,
SOBRE EL TRATAMIENTO Y CRUEL-
dades que han sufrido de los Españoles,
y motivado la declaracion de su
INDEPENDENCIA.

BUENOS-AYRES.
IMPRENTA DE LA INDEPENDENCIA.
1817.

Argentina declared independence in 1816, after six years of fighting against Spain. The independence movement began in Buenos Aires but met with resistance in other provinces of the former Viceroyalty of the River Plate.

cereals, and free immigration. The armed forces played a central role in the process.

Although national independence was actually declared in 1816, the founding date of Argentina, as established by triumphant liberal historiography, is 25 May 1810, when the so-called Primera Junta de Gobierno Patrio (the First Governing Junta of the Homeland), was formed. This date has been impressed upon generations of Argentinians through state education and is shared as a symbol by different political factions. This harmonious tale contributes to the concept of an inclusive and conflict-free country, constructed by national heroes, self-sacrificing soldiers and staunch patriots in the French Revolutionary style who gave their lives and resources in the name of the homeland.

The members of the junta of May 1810 were 'revolutionaries' and 'patriots' elevated to the status of role models (although at the time they would not have referred to themselves as such). In the years before the First World War historians and schoolteachers recounted a version of the events of May 1810 in which the foundations of the homeland could be seen. Those who go deep into the land of Argentina today will still find statues of these same men. Some are admired statesmen or lawmakers, but most are soldiers, such as José de San Martín (1778–1850), known as the 'father of the homeland'; after helping Argentina towards independence, he crossed the Andes to inspire a similar movement in Chile and Peru.

TIMELINE

1516 The first Spaniards arrive in Argentina

1580 Buenos Aires is established

1810 Overthrow of the king of Spain by Napoleon; formation of the First Governing Junta of the Homeland in Argentina

1812 José de San Martín leads the Argentine fight for independence

1816 Argentina officially declares independence from Spain

1817 An army led by José de San Martín crosses the Andes to fight for the independence of Chile and Peru

1853 Argentina adopts a republican constitution

1943 Juan Perón comes to power

1947 Juan Perón is elected president and his wife Evita assumes the role of first lady

1955 The army and navy rebel and Juan Perón flees the country

1956 The constitution of 1853 is restored, including labour rights articles from Perón's government

1976 President Isabel Perón is deposed by a military coup led by General Videla

1982 The Malvinas/Falklands War with Britain results in defeat for Argentina

1983 After democratic elections, the military junta loses office; Raúl Alfonsín becomes president

1985 Trial of the Juntas

2010 Argentina celebrates its bicentenary

Fireworks in Buenos Aires, May 2010: in the bicentennial year celebrations were staged across Argentina. More than three million people visited the exhibition and attended rallies in Buenos Aires. The high spirits were taken as a symptom of a new era, as the country moved beyond the traumas of the 1970s and 1980s.

From the perspective of the second centenary, in 2010, the panorama was very different. This patriotic concept of history, which takes the place of a shared sense of the past for the majority of Argentinians, clashes with a deep wound that has yet to find its place in the tale of the country's history. This is not so much the result of Argentina's development as a modern society in the early and mid-20th century, although the unique blend of nationalism, centralization, independence and corporatism of three-times president Juan Perón (1897–1974) left its own troubled legacy. Rather, the portrayal of Argentinian history today is marked by the state terrorism of the years 1976–83, a traumatic time in which the homeland devoured its own children.

On 24 March 1976 a military coup led by Lieutenant General Jorge Rafael Videla (b. 1925) overthrew the constitutional government of Argentina. It is true that the country had been marked by growing political violence since the late 1960s, but the seizure of power by the military signalled a qualitative leap in civil violence. While evoking the homeland, the restoration of order and the traditional values of the nation, the coup led to a system of illegal repression characterized by forced disappearances. Order and moral values were restored on the surface, but in the shadows a parallel state controlled the lives and assets of its citizens, who were stripped of their basic rights. Those considered subversive were abducted and taken to secret detention and extermination centres where they were tortured. Most were murdered, their bodies buried in unmarked graves or thrown into the open sea from planes. They became known as the *desaparecidos* (the 'Disappeared'). To their families and comrades, they were an irreparable loss; to the state that had them killed, they were a mystery for which bureaucracy could supply no answers. They included trade unionists, political activists, students, intellectuals and their families, those who in different ways belonged to revolutionary movements or otherwise opposed

Defeat in the Malvinas/Falklands War contradicted the belief of the armed forces (and many others) that they were invincible. The surrender of the Argentine forces in the islands marked the beginning of the transition to democracy.

the order that the armed forces were seeking to impose. Official figures and estimates number between 14,000 and 30,000 victims.

Then in 1982, in the context of a worsening political situation, Argentina's military dictators entered a conflict with Britain over the Malvinas Islands (known in Britain as the Falklands). Defeat propelled the military from power and the terrorist apparatus of the state now became evident to thousands of citizens who had lived under it without knowing of its existence. The armed forces also lost all respect for their ability to defend the country from external threats.

Those primarily responsible for state terrorism were tried for their crimes in 1985, in the 'Trial of the Juntas', an unprecedented trial of a dictatorial regime by its democratic successors. In this way, the restored democracy under President Raúl Alfonsín (1927–2009) took a historic step to discover what had occurred following the coup of 1976.

There are two possible interpretations of the events of 24 March 1976: the beginning of ignominy, or the beginning of a struggle for memory, truth and justice. Just as the military came to symbolize the worst atrocities, the mothers of the Disappeared, who protested in the Plaza de Mayo with white headscarves, became the emblem of the struggle for civil rights.

To the military, the Disappeared were subversive anti-Argentinian terrorists (whatever their true involvement in revolutionary organizations) who had to be wiped out,

During the dictatorship of the 1970s and 1980s, the main enemies of the military were the human rights organizations, especially the Mothers of May Square (Asociación Madres de Plaza de Mayo) whose children had been abducted. They were depicted as mad by propagandists, but the Malvinas defeat opened the way for their voices to be heard.

and whose slaughter would never be explained. Among their friends and families, in the early years, the Disappeared were spoken of as 'innocents' because they could not be acknowledged as political prisoners. For the rest of society, the status of these individuals as 'innocent victims' allowed people to feel that they were not themselves culpable, and reinforced the belief that only the military junta and terrorist guerrillas were responsible for the violence. Since the 1990s the political commitment of the victims of the dictatorship has become more widely known and sometimes vindicated. As of yet it has not been possible to come to terms with these events, and it will probably take much longer, so raw are the wounds opened by the years of repression.

While in 1910 a history of the nation was written that still feeds passions and rouses patriotic feelings, today the possibility of such a proud and inclusive history is frankly doubtful. The date of the coup, now a national holiday known as the Day of Remembrance, is ambiguous and difficult, because one of the consequences of the military dictatorship was the destruction of the national version of history – complete, all-embracing, indulgent – that Argentinians were accustomed to hearing, sharing and teaching in schools. During the dictatorship the junta described their actions as safeguarding the homeland and its traditional values in the face of the threat of Marxist and unpatriotic subversion.

Dictators Roberto Eduardo Viola and Leopoldo Galtieri attend a military rally in 1981. The military juntas, responsible for state terrorism and the defeat in the Malvinas, destroyed the prestige of the armed forces. The 'glorious history' of Argentinian independence was overlaid with new reports of violence and murder.

In other words, there were respectful and peace-loving 'Argentinians', and there were others who had ceased to be and thus had to be exterminated. Traditionally the armed forces, particularly the army, were the custodians of Argentina's values and it was in their name that power was seized in 1976. Under military rule they abused patriotic symbols, national heroes and historical dates. Therefore after they fell from power there was a growing rejection not only of these symbols but of their study as well. It is also true, however, that in places where less repression was experienced – and where state institutions and the traditional social order are stronger – the traditional patriotic version of history remains just as strong, as if nothing had happened after 24 March 1976.

Culturally this creates a curious duality: the debate over recent history – which is politically sensitive – continues to call on historical tools whose only reference is now a brutal cut-off point: the dictatorship. To some people 'talking about history' means speaking of the wars of independence and national heroes, while talking about the political history of the last quarter of a century is a political act in itself. To those who want to reflect on recent history, this traditional and grandiloquent view of the past is considered to be a tool of the Right, used to vindicate the dictators and an unjust social order that sought to perpetuate itself by means of illegal repression.

In making so many Argentinians 'disappear', did the dictatorship also make the possibility of thinking about national history disappear, while acting in its very name? This question, which cuts through contemporary Argentinian society, is missed by most foreign observers. A glance through the tourist guidebooks reveals an odd mixture of gauchos, Perónism (associated with fascism), General Galtieri and the Falklands, the Disappeared, and the footballer Diego Maradona. There may be some mention of the 'Dirty War' (in fact, the Argentinian oppressors imported this term from the United States, where they trained),

while the images of mothers with white head-scarves or grandmothers seeking their stolen grandchildren are known all over the world. What is missing is any sense of the brutal stress that Argentinian society has suffered since the mid-1970s. This translates, among other things, into the impossibility of a shared national history, the inadequacy of what is taught in schools, and the tremendous difficulties of think-ing and writing about a tale of horror and the men and women forced to face it, all born within the same society as their oppressors.

Every year 24 March 1976 is commemorated, the day on which contrasting interpretations come together. The supporters of the dictatorship speak of a 'war against subversion' and the 'salva-tion of the homeland', and of having been beaten by the Dirty War and destroyed by propaganda. Its opponents talk of 'state terrorism and illegal repression', and of the defeat of a revolution embodied by the Disappeared and the negation of much of its history. More broadly, the Argen-tinian society that emerged from the 1980s liked to view itself as having been reborn in its rejection of all violence and authoritarianism in favour of the values of human rights and a respect for democracy.

A woman protests in Buenos Aires in 1984, demanding that those responsible for kidnapping children be brought to justice. The country's image of the 19th century coexists with the more recent, disturbing history – the national memory has not yet reconciled these different aspects of national history with a modern image.

In parallel, 25 May, the anniversary of the rev-olution, with its stirring tales of the country's origins, carries on as if nothing had happened since then: either since 1810, or since 1976. Argentinian reality is built from parallel histori-cal worlds. An all-inclusive history is not yet possible, for only fragments survive.

Canada

The loose-jointed polity

'A Canadian is someone who knows how to make love in a canoe', popular historian Pierre Berton famously quipped, making reference to the indigenous vehicle that helped to open the North American continent to First Nations (as its aboriginal peoples are known) and recent immigrants alike. How many Canadians have been conceived in a canoe has yet to be determined, but such couplings in the great outdoors perhaps help to account for the cautious style that foreign observers argue is typically Canadian.

For most immigrants to Canada, past and present, it is the sheer space in the world's second largest nation that makes the first impression. So big that few seem able to grasp the whole, Canada is a loose-jointed polity, its provinces often nations unto themselves. Two thirds of Canada's space is encompassed by its three northern territories inhabited by fewer than 110,000 people, half of them Aboriginal. Although four out of five Canadians now live in areas defined as urban, 89 per cent of respondents to a 2004 survey felt that it was the 'overwhelming vastness of the landscape' that defined their country.

Canada is also about weather, both hot and cold, but it is the cold that people remember. 'Until I came to Canada', Argentine-born writer Alberto Manguel observed, 'I never knew that snow was a four-letter word.' Survival in a northern climate is always a challenge. This may be why Canada's modest contributions to international cuisine include the calorie-laden Tim Horton's donut and Quebec's poutine, a concoction of French fries topped with cheese curd and gravy. Making a virtue out of a necessity, Canadians have embraced winter sports, in particular ice hockey, which is something of a national passion.

Space and weather have combined to make Canada a difficult place to inhabit and an even harder place to govern, but the area's vast natural resources have long attracted human attention. In the distant past the ancestors of Canada's First Nations (representing

Inuit from the Belcher Islands in front of the Hudson's Bay Company store at Whale River (now Kuujjuarapik) in Quebec, 1946. At the time the photograph was taken, money made available through the universal family allowance programme was beginning to supplement furs as the medium of exchange.

more than fifty linguistic groups) moved restlessly across the continent in pursuit of fin and fur. When Europeans began arriving 500 years ago, most Natives eagerly traded their resources for guns, knives, pots and blankets that make survival in a cold climate so much easier. Their initial advantage in this exchange evaporated under the assault, not of weapons in most cases, but of disease to which Aboriginal peoples had little immunity. As microbes spread across the continent, sometimes in advance of the human invaders, the indigenous population declined precipitously. Their numbers now advancing dramatically, First Nations have contributed greatly to the development of Canada, so much so that writer John Ralston Saul concludes that 'we are a Métis civilization' (a reference originally to the children of the 'country marriages', advantageous to both sides, of European fur traders and Aboriginal women).

Although most European nations were first drawn to northern North America by the lowly cod and the search for a Northwest Passage, it was the beaver pelt that sustained two colonial empires in much of the area now called Canada. Between 1608 and 1763 France, in alliance with First Nations, pushed up the St Lawrence–Great Lakes system into the western plains and down the Mississippi to Louisiana. By the Treaty of Utrecht (1713), the British whittled away France's eastern seaboard colonies of Newfoundland and Acadia, and confirmed their suzerainty over the vast Hudson's Bay territory known as Rupert's Land. They then scooped up the rest during the Seven Years' War (1756–63), taking the major French strongholds of Louisbourg, Quebec and Montreal in three successive years.

TIMELINE

c. 1000 Norse settlement at l'Anse aux Meadows, Newfoundland

1497 John Cabot reaches Newfoundland

1534–35 Jacques Cartier explores the Gulf of St Lawrence

1605, 1608 French colonies established at Port Royal and Quebec

1670 The English Crown grants Hudson's Bay Company a fur trade charter

1713 The Treaty of Utrecht cedes Newfoundland, Acadia and Hudson's Bay Company territory to the British

1759 Quebec falls to a British attack led by James Wolfe

1775–83 American Revolutionary War

1837–38 Rebellions in Upper and Lower Canada

1848 Britain concedes the principle of responsible government in Nova Scotia and the United Canadas

1867 The confederation of Nova Scotia, New Brunswick, Quebec and Ontario forms the Dominion of Canada

1869–70, 1885 Louis Riel leads resistance against Canadian authority in the northwest

1885 Completion of the Canadian Pacific Railway

1897 The Klondike gold rush begins

1917 Canadian troops fight together at Vimy Ridge in northern France during the First World War

1918 Women are granted the franchise in federal elections

1931 The Statute of Westminster gives Canada complete autonomy from Britain

1969 A policy of bilingualism is adopted by the federal government

1971 Secretary of State for Multiculturalism is established

1982 The new Canadian constitution is ratified

1989 Free Trade Agreement with the United States comes into effect

2001 Canada announces that it will contribute to an international force mobilized by the United States to fight the Taliban in Afghanistan

2003 Canada decides not to join the 'coalition of the willing' in its war against Iraq

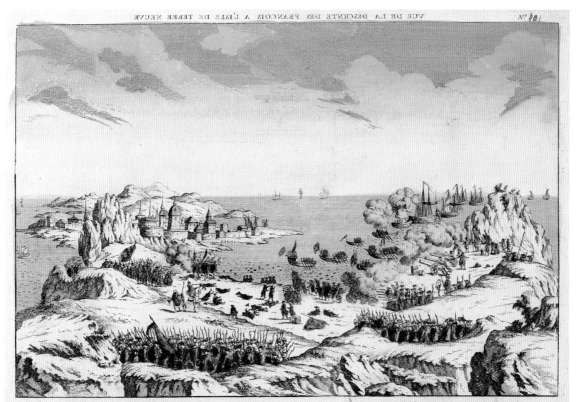

The final battle of the Seven Years' War in North America took place in Newfoundland. This engraving from c. 1792 depicts the French forces occupying St John's in June 1762. Three months later they were defeated at Signal Hill by a hastily assembled British army from Halifax and New York.

The conquest left a significant French population in British territory. French-speaking Canadians now find homes across the country, but especially in their 'nation' of Quebec. In response to growing separatist sentiment in the province, the federal government under Prime Minister Pierre Elliott Trudeau (1919–2000) adopted a policy of bilingualism in 1969 (as did the province of New Brunswick, where many of the descendants of French immigrants to Acadia reside). This initiative failed to prevent the Parti Québecois, committed to independence, from being elected to office and conducting two referenda on Quebec separation (in 1980 and 1995), the latter lost by a minuscule margin.

So prevalent is Quebec in the nation's political discourse that 'the rest of Canada' is now understood by its initials – ROC. Within this designation is a great diversity of

THE EMIGRANTS WELCOME TO CANADA.

An early 19th-century cartoon showing a beleaguered emigrant dressed in flimsy clothing and greeted by a 'Jack Frost' figure in woollen clothes. Advice booklets for prospective immigrants to Upper and Lower Canada provided a glowing image of the country but failed to mention the cold climate that daunted many settlers from Great Britain.

peoples who trace their origins to every nation on earth. Immigrants from England, Scotland, Ireland, New England and Continental Europe began moving to the eastern seaboard colonies in significant numbers following the founding of Halifax in 1749, but it was the arrival of nearly 50,000 Loyalist refugees from the United States following the American Revolutionary War (1775–83) that gave Canada the beginnings of a self-conscious and highly diverse English-speaking population.

In the first half of the 19th century British immigrants, many of them fleeing demons of poverty and oppression, poured into British North America, bringing with them modern capitalism, a squabbling Christianity, a vigorous civil society and the European Enlightenment, complete with its complex conventions relating to class, gender and race. British institutions of governance took root, more or less, in all colonial jurisdictions. After rebellions in Upper and Lower Canada (in 1837–38) and complicated political manoeuvrings everywhere, the eastern colonies achieved 'responsible government', a term used to distinguish it from total independence and from republican variants of democracy in France and the United States. The rebellions and responsible government set in motion what historian Ian McKay describes as 'the project of liberal rule'. Although in Canada, as elsewhere, the tenets of liberalism have been hotly contested and selectively applied, they served as the lodestar for reformers, including many suffragists and labour organizers, and for leaders of most political parties.

Confederation was a major step towards the consolidation of the nation state, undertaken in the context of a civil war in the United States, pressure from financial interests in Great Britain and the rage for industrial development in the Western world. Three 'responsibly governed' eastern colonies – Nova Scotia, New Brunswick and the United Canadas (Quebec and Ontario) – came together in 1867 as the first 'dominion' (the term 'kingdom' might have made the Americans nervous) in the British Empire. The name Canada (originally an aboriginal word for village, which the French attached to the St Lawrence region of New France, and the British retained in Upper and Lower Canada) was applied to the whole. By 1880 Rupert's Land and the Arctic, along with the colonies of British Columbia and Prince Edward Island, had been brought into the fold, so that all of the territory that now makes up Canada was subordinate to a government based in Ottawa, except Newfoundland and Labrador, which remained a separate jurisdiction until 1949.

This audacious attempt at empire-building by fewer than four million people was informed by the model of the United States, blessed by the British government and predicated on a communications network to tie the whole together. In his national policy Canada's first prime minister, Scottish-born Sir John A. Macdonald (1815–91), emphasized agricultural settlement in the west of the country, a transcontinental railway and tariffs high enough to cradle an industrial sector in the St Lawrence–Great Lakes heartland, dominated by the emerging metropolises of Montreal and Toronto. By 1914 three rail lines spanned the continent, and a flood of immigrants from Europe, the United States and elsewhere had settled the 'last best west' and provided the necessary labour for an expanding economy.

Under the leadership of Louis Riel (1844–85), the Métis and First Nation peoples on the prairies twice (in 1869–70 and 1885) mounted unsuccessful resistance to the invading Canadians. The Métis were marginalized in the wake of the 1885 uprising and First Nations, in the developing west and elsewhere, were kept in subordination by the culturally destructive policies that informed the Indian Act of 1876 and Indian residential schools, where Indians were forced to learn Western culture and practices.

The challenge of reaching political maturity as a child of one imperial power and the junior sibling of another is the key to understanding Canada as a nation state. From its founding moment, Canadian leaders were conscious of the role that Great Britain played in providing markets, military protection and, above all, a countervailing force against the 'manifest destiny' of the United States to dominate the entire North American continent. In the 20th century Canadians fought two world wars on Britain's side, helping the embattled 'mother' country to hold on until the prodigal sibling finally decided to join the Allied cause.

Wartime sacrifices, including the lives of more than 100,000 men and women on the battlefields of Europe, helped to move Canada along the road to independence. After the First World War, Canada was a signatory to the Treaty of Versailles in its own right and the 1931 Statute of Westminster confirmed the autonomy of dominions in the British Commonwealth of Nations. The Second World War greatly enhanced Canada's sense of national confidence and productive capacity, both blunted by the Great Depression.

Prime Minister Pierre Elliott Trudeau with Queen Elizabeth II, signing the Constitution Act on 17 April 1982. In his last term in office he left an enduring legacy by moving aggressively to repatriate the Canadian constitution and attaching to it a Charter of Rights and Freedoms.

In 1947 Canada began issuing its own passports and in 1965 finally adopted, though not without noisy controversy, a distinctive flag sporting a red maple leaf.

In a quintessential manifestation of caution, Canadians delayed proclaiming full independence until 1982 when, by the Constitution Act, they were finally able to amend their constitution without resorting to an act of the British Parliament. Nonetheless, the British monarch is still officially the Canadian head of state and Queen Elizabeth's face is found on Canadian currency. 'How', asks *Globe and Mail* columnist Roy MacGregor, 'would you explain to someone that our head of state [Governor General Michaëlle Jean, 2005–10] is from Haiti and had to give up her French citizenship to represent the Queen of England in Canada?'

The answer to this question is found in the transformation of Canada in the three decades following the Second World War. Emerging as a great industrial nation with one of the highest standards of living in the world, Canada also embraced policies worthy of its new-found status. The federal government triumphed over defenders of provincial rights to pass legislation, sometimes described as a second national policy, implementing nationwide universal social programmes, among them the highly popular Medicare. In the 1960s Canada opened its door to 'qualified' immigrants of any hue to provide essential labour in expanding industrial and service sectors and in 1971 officially adopted a programme of multiculturalism. Canada's major cities are now among the most ethnically diverse in the world.

Following the Second World War Canada carefully positioned itself as a 'middle power' internationally, participating in the creation of the United Nations and North Atlantic Treaty Organization, helping to draft the UN Declaration of Human Rights, and emphasizing negotiation and compromise as alternatives to war. Canadian diplomats, among them Nobel Peace Prize-winner Lester Pearson (1897–1972), often played the role of helpful fixers in a room of overinflated egos. In the 1950s 'peacekeeping' became the brand of the Canadian military, but the 'war on terror' after 11 September 2001 exploded what had become an elaborate fiction.

Sceptics had long pointed out that, in most foreign policy initiatives, Canada served as handmaiden to the United States. Indeed, the United States was the elephant in every room. Efforts to define a Canada that was more than a weak echo of its southern neighbour became a major goal of successive governments in the post-war decades. When the Progressive Conservatives under Brian Mulroney (b. 1939) gained power in 1984, they abandoned this seemingly hopeless quest. Protectionism, which was called into question by prevailing neo-liberal orthodoxies, was swept away in January 1989 by the implementation of a comprehensive Free Trade Agreement with the United States, later extended to Mexico. In such a tight embrace with the elephant, formal annexation is beside the point.

Being Canadian, some argue, means never having to say you're sorry; but Canadians have been obliged to apologize for a number of transgressions, among them Indian residential schools, a tax on every Chinese person who entered the country, and the internment of Japanese Canadians during the Second World War. For many Canadians the carbon footprint of the Alberta oil sands, the poverty of Aboriginal peoples, children and recent immigrants in a land of plenty, and the federal government's unwillingness to play a stronger leadership role on the world stage remain sources of regret.

Alberta is home to much of the world's reserves of natural bitumen, commonly known as tar or oil sands. This dense form of petroleum is difficult to process, generating more greenhouse gases than the production of conventional oil. Exploitation of the tar sands counters the Canadian aspiration to be protective of the natural environment.

In 1972 popular CBC talkshow host Peter Gzowski asked his listeners to create a Canadian counterpoint to the aphorism 'as American as apple pie'. The winner of the contest, seventeen-year-old Heather Scott, suggested 'as Canadian as possible under the circumstances'. Nearly four decades later, this still fits. Alternatively, John D. Blackwell and Laurie Stanley-Blackwell argue that 'Canada is one of the great national success stories of modern history, a country where people from all over the world have found opportunity for individuality and community.' This fits, too.

Italy

Catholicism, power, democracy and the failure of the past

Italy is a Catholic country: the Catholic country *par excellence*, the permanent residence of the Pope. Yet when discussing Italian Catholicism, it is important to think of it in anthropological rather than religious terms. By delving deep into the country's Catholic past we can explain the roots of the problems that Italy faces today.

During the 16th century Europe was deeply divided over the political implications of religion. In the Protestant world, power was seen as emanating directly from God. Although this religion was to spawn absolutist ideals as well as constitutional theories, political power was seen as sacred and, even after its theological origins had been forgotten, a sense of respect for its institutions remained. Debates within Protestantism focused on which powers were created by God: those of the prince, the judge, or a sovereign people able to elect its representatives. Over time the sacred aura surrounding political power was internalized as a civic value. Sometimes this led to absolute obedience to authority, but sometimes the right to resist a cruel prince was instituted through democratically elected representatives. According to the Protestant view, all these forms of political power rested on divine intervention. Catholics developed entirely different political theories. For Catholics, God had no role in institutions created by humankind. God made us into social beings who had to create a government for ourselves. But free will meant that we could build whatever government we desired. Humans, though, are sinners and tend to produce imperfect institutions; so the Church was required to correct their actions and lead them to salvation.

This idea took shape with the rebirth of Thomist thought (linked to the writings of Thomas Aquinas) in the 16th century and was refined during the debates at the Council of Trent (1545–63), during which the Catholic Church formulated its response to Protestantism. It became dominant in Catholic political thought, however, through the ideas

The opening of the Council of Trent in December 1545, painted by Niccolo Dorigati (1711), represented the start of the Catholic fightback against the Protestant Reformation. As the home of the papacy Italy has always seen itself, and been seen by others, as an essentially Catholic country despite a strong and ancient tradition of anti-clericalism.

laid out by the Jesuit Francisco Suárez (1548–1617) between 1582 and 1612 and by other theologians through the 16th century. According to them, two forms of authority – the Church and the state – were constantly vying for supremacy, with no clear separation of tasks or hierarchies. Spheres of action and competencies were confused, and rules and principles often contradictory. Man's relationship with government was marked by weak institutions and by a culture of clemency, absolution and legal uncertainty.

Today it could be argued that in Italy religion is no longer particularly important in and of itself. But beneath the surface of an apparently secular society and state, four centuries of cohabitation between church and state have shaped politics and created a sense of justice that is dominated by this dualism. Indeed, Catholic countries around the world share this characteristic of institutions that are weakened by the existence of incompatible systems, with a proliferation of rules and laws. As a result they have rarely been able to create significant levels of consensus.

In Italy both the laws of the state and the moral teachings of religion are feeble. The state is widely seen as extraneous, an institution that everyone has the right (almost a duty) to defraud, and similar attitudes are held towards the Church. Over time these attitudes were internalized and then started to shape social behaviour and political opinions, a problem which Italy has been unable to resolve. A kind of 'Catholic anarchism' emerged, with widespread indifference to and suspicion of public institutions, as well as a contractual idea of religion, which veers between sin and forgiveness, between the power of the pardoner and the weakness of the sinner. This has in turn led to compromise, indulgence, craftiness and errors of judgment.

This incurable illness has had many consequences. Weak institutions have sought to defend themselves by increasing regulation and at times enforcing an authoritarian

TIMELINE

753 BCE The legendary foundation of Rome

27 BCE The foundation of the Roman Empire by Augustus

312 CE Christianity is adopted as the official religion of the Roman Empire

476 Fall of the Western Roman Empire

751 The Papal States are established in central and northern Italy

1200–1500 Independent city states flourish

1848 Popular rising against Austrian rule in northern Italy

1861 The establishment of the Kingdom of Italy

1870 Italian troops take Rome and make it the capital of Italy; dissolution of the Papal States

1922 Benito Mussolini establishes a Fascist dictatorship

1929 The Lateran Treaty between Italy and the Vatican is signed

1943 Italy surrenders to the Allies and declares war on the Germans, who take over Italy with a puppet government; the anti-Fascist resistance movement begins civil war

1945 Liberation; Mussolini is captured and executed

1946 An Italian republic is set up by popular vote

1948 The new constitution comes into force

1984 Catholicism ceases to be the state religion

2001 Silvio Berlusconi becomes President of the Council of Ministers

2011 Mario Monti becomes Prime Minister at the head of an entirely unelected government

transformation of the state as a last resort in the face of insecurity and disorder among the population. Every Catholic country experienced dictatorial forms of government in the 20th century. In Italy the populist success in the 1990s and 2000s of the President of the Council of Ministers, Silvio Berlusconi (b. 1936), can be understood in these terms. Institutional power attacks the institutions themselves – just as individuals do and dream of doing – as well as the tax system, rules controlling financial transactions, the environment and moral etiquette.

It is difficult to imagine any great change in the immediate future. Italy has no founding myths, moments or episodes that can be used for effective nation-building. While some Italians might view as a type of founding myth the mid-19th-century Risorgimento – which saw the kingdom of Piedmont drive out the Austrians from the north and unify the Italian states under its rule – it was in reality a civil war. The key moment was the abolition of the temporal power of the popes through the dissolution in 1870 of the Papal States that had divided the country in two, geographically and in many other ways. Yet for a Catholic country to make its founding myth out of a war against the papacy is unthinkable. At school the Risorgimento is studied not as a civil war, but as one against an external enemy, Austria. History in Italy has not taken shape through the kind of civil conflicts that lie at the heart of other national mythologies, an internal victory of good over evil as in the American Civil War, the French Revolution or the English Civil War.

A poster from the aftermath of the so-called Second War of Independence of 1859. The Risorgimento, in which the Italian states won independence from Austria and eventually united into the Kingdom of Italy, has been claimed as the founding event of the modern state. Despite Garibaldi's decisive liberation of Sicily and Naples, Italians remain uncomfortable with some aspects of this period, especially the defeat of the Papal States.

Even the ultra-nationalistic Fascists, who ruled Italy from 1922 until 1943, were unable to use the Risorgimento as a founding myth; they had to refer back – absurdly – to ancient Rome.

Just as the Risorgimento proved a poor founding myth, so, too, has its more recent alternative: the popular resistance to Fascism after the armistice of September 1943, which culminated in the country's liberation on 25 April 1945. For forty years after the war a shared Catholic–humanist ideal painted Italy as a country where an anti-Fascist majority struggled against the perverse minority, and so the fight between the Fascists and their opponents was not seen as a civil war. More recently, however, historians have shown that a large part of the nation actually backed the regime, so the resistance, too, has become useless as a founding myth.

Neither Italians nor foreigners tend to see Catholicism as playing a key role in the formation of our character. The concept of 'amoral familism' has often been used to describe the strong attachment to the family, the over-protective role of the mother and the near-absence of the father. But these features are the consequence of a perverse tendency to take refuge in familial solidarity, clientelism, and informal and fragmentary institutions in the face of dysfunctional political and religious organizations. In this way an image of Italy has taken shape as a country that is free and anarchic, but also divided and unable to take collective decisions or to complete projects. It is viewed as a nation that combines individual initiative with bureaucratic paralysis, corruption and in-fighting. It is seen as a country that has lost interest in the beauty and culture with which it is filled in its desire to move towards a modernity without culture. This is accompanied by a tendency for Italians simply to get by, without any real link to their past or coherent vision of the future: we live a good life and we let others be. We don't expect things to work but we are interested in how to adapt to their dysfunctional nature.

PER LA XXVII LEGISLATURA RINNOVATRICE DELL'ITALIA
Ecco il giorno, ecco il giorno della prora
. e dell' aratro, il giorno dello sprone
e del vomere. O uomini, ecco l'ora.   D'Annunzio

Electoral poster for Benito Mussolini, the incumbent prime minister and leader of the National Fascist Party in the general election of 1924. Shortly after, he established a full dictatorship and elections were abolished in 1928. The memory of his brutal but vainglorious rule retains an appeal for some even today.

Benito Mussolini (1883–1945), leader of the National Fascist Party, once said that 'It is not difficult to govern Italians, just useless'. Outsiders also view us with irony and surprise, without understanding that this people with so little interest in political and religious rules has been created by a conflict between a weak state and a church that is always ready to forgive – as long as we accept the idea that we are all sinners, ready to be pardoned precisely because of this tragic inevitability.

Today Italy is a demoralized and disenchanted land. From the mid-1990s the disappearance of the Christian Democrats and the Communist Party, the two parties that had managed power and dominated the opposition, transformed all political points of reference. The representative ideal was replaced by the concept of 'governability': a strong political majority reinforced by an electoral system guaranteeing stability within an artificial bipartisan structure. Any sense of popular representation was replaced by the technological management of power – most prominently in 2011, when the elected but discredited government of Silvio Berlusconi was replaced by

The mid-2000s saw a series of general strikes against public service cuts proposed by the Berlusconi government. Mounting debt led to a full-blown financial crisis by 2011, when Berlusconi fell from power, having lost international confidence in his ability to impose financial restraint on the Italians.

Mario Monti, unelected but acceptable to the financial markets. At the same time globalization broke the relationship between the working class and the world of consumption, and the trade unions, important in the post-war democracy, were fatally weakened.

Those forms of association that characterized post-war Italian history have crumbled away. The Communist Party local meetings, where people went to discuss politics or simply to gather information, have disappeared, paying the price for Communist guilt at having supported the Soviet system. This guilt was not tempered by the fact that the left-wing parties played a key role in the creation of a democratic Italy and the drawing up of the constitution. The trade unions have become dominated by pensioners and cannot imagine different forms of organization and struggle capable of defending the new immigrant workers, who are often subject to brutal and invisible forms of exploitation. The bonds within the Catholic community have remained strong, however, linked to deep-rooted parish networks.

This crumbling away of social and political networks led to a deep crisis in the Italian Left. What was once an organized party was transformed into a fragile and divided pressure-group movement. The result was a widespread frustration, a conviction that effective political participation was impossible. This created an atmosphere that was vulnerable to forms of populist demagogy – an atmosphere exploited by Berlusconi, who as a media mogul held a virtual monopoly of the mass media.

It seems to me, therefore, that Catholicism lies at the heart of the Italian problem. This is not a matter of secularism against clericalism, but of how boundaries and powers are defined and divided. It is difficult to see this issue clearly because Catholicism is so pervasive, part of our character: it is intrinsic to us, in the air that we breathe; it is everywhere, but invisible.

It is not surprising, therefore, that foreigners have such a stereotypical view of Italy's past and present, and that their interpretation of our country is often confused. Historians from abroad have generally been most interested in the republican city-state tradition of medieval and Renaissance Italy. Few foreigners find the centuries after the Renaissance very interesting, partly because Italy took a very Catholic path towards the modern age. As a result many people feel that Italy's failure to attain full modernity occurred during those centuries. We are seen as a capitalist country with 'feudal remnants', still linked to familism, a civilized nation still threatened by forms of populism and authoritarianism, a country that has gone through moments of democratic change and which, although able to draw up an advanced constitution, could not use it as a springboard for truly modern civic development.

Italians have a weak sense of national identity. Parish localism or, alternatively, the cosmopolitan Catholic world lie at the roots of a lack of pride in the nation. A strong sense of self-irony, moreover, leads to a preference for narratives focusing on our defects rather than our merits, which are often simply seen in terms of the advantages of one city against another, or in regional terms. In Italy, more than elsewhere, a strong sense of detachment from the past has evolved: it is viewed as principally comprising a series of mistakes rather than successes.

In Italy, therefore, historical revisionism is largely a practice of devaluing the past, rather than justifying or revisiting our history. It is less a matter of the historical relegitimization of Fascism than of dismissing anti-Fascism as having been simply the work of Communists who carried out atrocities during the resistance and after the war. This violence is taken out of context and understood in ways that lead to a bland condemnation of our recent past as a whole, and to a detachment from the memory of past events.

The past carries with it principles and rules that delay the full development of a 'glorious' neo-liberal future with no past, no memory and no definition. For fifteen years Berlusconi refused to participate in the annual 25 April anti-Fascist liberation anniversaries, justifying his position in terms of a national reconciliation that would not accept as a founding document the 1948 constitution born from the resistance, and ignoring the obligations implied by its anti-Fascist values. Berlusconi only agreed to celebrate Liberation Day when Gianfranco Fini, the leader of the ex-neofascist party, began to condemn the dictatorial and racist aspects of Fascism. Even then, Berlusconi tried to distort the meaning of this anniversary into a catch-all celebration of liberty (his new party was called the Party of Liberty, or People of Freedom), rather than specifically a commemoration of liberation from Fascism and Nazism.

So if there is a past about which we can be at all proud, it is a remote one made up largely of art and monuments, nature and landscapes, but even here these traces are undermined by economic interests that have led to speculative building.

Things don't look good. For years Italy has been admired for its non-conformism. Foreigners have a contradictory opinion of a place that they follow from afar, often without real comprehension. They return as tourists, and while holidaying here they eat well and live contentedly, but this is a nation dominated by a corrupt and fragile political class: the Mafia is strong, the environment is damaged, and corruption and disorder are endemic. Italy has only one real national passion, football, and one true collective cultural activity, the Catholic tradition. Although the country remains a joy to visit for its past, this Italy has no possibility of a respectable and respected future, and that past is in any case better appreciated by others than by Italians themselves.

Italy is Europe's most popular tourist destination for its history, culture and heritage. Many visitors tend to believe that Italians are more at ease with their country's past than is the case.

Once the link between democracy and development started to break down, Italian democratic structures underwent a decline. Those systems that counterpoise economic growth and democracy seemed more efficient, at least in economic terms – or rather they did so until rising government debt forced austerity and retrenchment, threatened to force Italy from the Eurozone and led to a hopefully temporary suspension of democracy. Even before the crisis of the early 2010s Italy had already slid towards an authoritarianism disguised as presidentialism. If there is any hope for the future, it must be achieved by the long and difficult return to representative democracy based upon collective participation from below. The situation is depressing – but this the most realistic view of my country at present.

Japan

From isolation to transgression

In his book *Japan, the Ambiguous, and Myself* (1995), the Nobel prize-winning novelist Kenzaburo Oe (b. 1935) categorized Japanese literature according to three models. The first focuses on the 'exceptional' culture of Japan; the second aspires towards 'universality' and produces world literature; the third, which mainly comprises popular literature, 'transgresses' the boundaries of the national mentality. These three literary models – exceptionalism, universalism and transgression – can be applied more widely to the changing face of Japan's identity throughout history.

In 1853 Matthew C. Perry, commander-in-chief of the American East Indies fleet, arrived with a letter from the American president urging the Edo (Tokugawa) shogunate – which had kept Japan virtually closed to outside influences for over two centuries – to open Japan to trade. This year is the starting point for modern Japan. In 1868 the shogunate was overthrown in what was known as the Meiji Restoration, with power centralized under the Meiji emperor in order to promote an urgent policy of modernization. Capi- talist development was pursued, leading to the creation of the railways, telegraphic communication systems and the armed forces.

The formative period of the Meiji era was distinctive due to the perception of Japan as a country arriving late to modernization. It had begun to modernize under huge influence from the West, but Japanese people had a sense that their country lagged behind. The vision of modern Japan in this period was summed up by the commentator and philosopher Yukichi Fukuzawa (1835–1901), who said, 'Personal independence is national independence'. Fukuzawa wanted to energize a people who had been tamed into obedience in a feudal society and to show the way from 'personal independence' to becoming 'an independent nation' and a power in the modern world. This policy was called 'Westernization' and was put into practice to 'enrich and strengthen' the country. However,

A Japanese print from 1870, showing various modes of transport, including a rickshaw, bicycle and hand-drawn carts. The 'opening' of Japan with the arrival of an American fleet in 1853 and the subsequent Meiji Restoration of 1868 saw the wholesale introduction of Western technology into a society that had been effectively isolated for centuries.

The Meiji emperor (r. 1867–1912), photographed here in 1872 in traditional costume. However, he was frequently seen in Western uniform, a choice that was widely copied by his people.

although the Meiji Restoration tried to build a new Japan that was similar to the West, it did so under the traditional symbol of the emperor whose throne had been in existence since ancient times. As a result, three separate naming systems for the years were used simultaneously: 'AD' (taken from the Christian West); the 'Meiji' era; and the 'Imperial reign', which counts the years the emperor has reigned. Further to this, the Gregorian solar calendar was introduced in 1872, but for day-to-day life the lunar calendar, also known as the 'old calendar', was used.

With the introduction in 1889 of the Great Japanese Constitutional System and the Imperial Diet, a formal constitution was established. The constitution centred the state on the power and position of the emperor, while the Japanese people were his 'subjects', with their rights and duties clearly laid out. From the government's point of view, this constitution was intended to promote modernization while setting Japan apart from the West by stressing the continuity of its traditional systems. At the same time, for those opposed to the government, the constitution's definition of 'subject status' also acted as a catalyst for future change and, paradoxically, strongly emphasized the exceptional character of Japan.

Around the turn of the 20th century Japan enjoyed military and political success on the world stage, beginning with its victories in wars against the Chinese Qing (Manchu) dynasty in 1894–95 and tsarist Russia in 1904–5. Taiwan was already colonized; in 1910

TIMELINE

300–710 The Yamato era sees the emergence of powerful states

552 Buddhism is introduced to Japan

c. 600 A centralized state is introduced by Prince Shotoku

794 Kyoto becomes the capital of the Japanese emperor

1477 The end of the Onin War

1542 The first European (Portuguese) traders arrive in Japan

1600 Tokugawa Ieyasu wins power, establishing the Tokugawa shogunate

1639 Europeans are mostly banned and Japan is closed to foreign influence

1853 American Matthew C. Perry arrives in Japan with his 'black ships'

1868 The Meiji Restoration overthrows the Tokugawa shogunate and begins Japan's modernization

1889 The Meiji constitution is promulgated

1894–95 The First Sino-Japanese War

1904–5 The Russo-Japanese War

1910 Japan annexes Korea

1931 Japan invades Manchuria and sets up a puppet regime (Manzhouguo)

1937–45 The Second Sino-Japanese War

1941 The Second World War; Japan attacks the United States and builds an empire in Southeast Asia

1945 The defeat and surrender of Japan and mass bombing of Japanese cities; beginning of the American occupation

1952 Japanese sovereignty is restored

1991 End of the post-war economic boom

2011 Major earthquake and tsunami devastate northeastern Japan

A print, c. 1919, depicting a battle in Ussuri, Siberia. Following victories over China in the 1890s and Russia in 1904–5, Japan futhered its military power by entering the First World War as an ally of Britain, asserting naval superiority over Germany and expanding into China; it was given a permanent seat on the League of Nations Council in 1919.

Japan added Korea to its Great Japanese Empire and moved to invade China. Japan was fast becoming a major military power. It fought with the Allied forces against German interests in East Asia during the First World War and achieved rapid economic growth, sending military materials to its allies in Europe.

In consequence, a sense that modernization had brought real results spread through Japan in the 1920s. A belief in a truly modern Japan took hold, and Western clothing became fashionable among ordinary people. American mass culture infiltrated the country, and the cinema and radio became popular forms of entertainment. There was a new passion for speed and efficiency was the watchword, even within the home where washing machines and other electrical goods were enjoyed.

Folklorist Wajiro Kon (1888–1973) studied the beliefs of people living in the mega-lopolis of Tokyo during the interwar years. He observed that the phrase 'modern age' came to be used widely as the benefits of modernization became more generally appreciated. It was known as the era of 'Japanese modernism'; the realization grew that the Japanese consciousness was amenable to Western forms of modernism, so a partial form of universalist modernity now thrived. Fellow folklorist Kunio Yanagida (1875–1962) described those who had supported the traditional order of Japan as 'common people', and pointed to their impending decline in the face of the rapid modernization of the country's culture.

In 1929, when the Great Depression plunged the world into economic crisis, Japan derived strength from its traditions of authoritarianism. It adopted an aggressive policy of military force and chose fascism as a solution. Since the achievements of modernity had not managed to avert the crisis, the response was now to attempt to transcend the modern period. Due to its Western characteristics, the universalist model was rejected in favour of a return to the exceptionalist Japanese tradition.

This Japanese exceptionalism was now violently enforced and directed towards the mobilization of the population for war. Whereas Mount Fuji and cherry blossom had previously been symbols of Japan itself, they now acquired a specifically military significance as symbols of mobilization and national unity. The emperor, who represented 2,600 years of tradition, was portrayed as a being unlike any other in the world: he was God. Although few seriously believed in his divinity, it was taught rigorously in elementary schools. Japanese exceptionalism was ubiquitous during the war period and it produced a hugely destructive power.

War was all Japan knew from the 1930s onwards. In 1931 the Great Japanese Empire sent troops to Manchuria in northeastern China and by 1937 it was engaged in full-scale war with China. Mythology holds an important place within Japanese culture; despite the fact that warfare requires rational thinking, Japan now turned to irrational forms of motivation to inspire nationalist passion. Meanwhile, within its new colonies Japan adopted a policy of assimilation similar to the French model, rather than one of British-style self-government. Starting with Korea (conquered in 1910) and Taiwan (1895), the Japanese language was taught in these colonies; shrines were built and colonials forced to worship in them. Locals were compelled to take Japanese names and adopt Japanese household customs.

By 1941 the country was at war with the Allied armies of the United States, Britain and France. During the war the Japanese army committed terrible war crimes, such as the massacre of over 100,000 Chinese civilians in Nanjing, the forced labour of Koreans and the use of 'army comfort women' (some Japanese) as sex slaves. There was even an elite group of scientists who researched biological warfare.

However, the effects of the air raids of 1945 on the Japanese population and the use of the atomic bomb by the United States cannot be ignored. Over 150 cities were attacked by

The dropping of the atomic bomb on Hiroshima on 6 August 1945 resulted in 90,000–140,000 deaths by December, with about half occurring immediately after the explosion. Following as it did the devastating bombing of Tokyo and other cities earlier in 1945, the incident left Japan with a sense of exceptional suffering during the war.

air (numbers vary according to sources), resulting in the deaths of over 500,000 people. In Hiroshima and Nagasaki, where the atomic bombs were dropped, 140,000 and 70,000 people respectively lost their lives. Both were indiscriminate attacks aimed at civilians. The effects of radiation continued to increase the death toll in the years that followed, and still affect the children and grandchildren of those who survived the attacks. In Okinawa the war was fought on land and numerous civilians became the victims; some were even persecuted by the Japanese army. As a result of these atrocities, for a long period the Japanese recalled the war from a victim's viewpoint. While pursuing those responsible for the war, they did not answer the accusations of war crimes committed by themselves, and constructed arguments to defend Japan while the question of who bore ultimate responsibility for the war remained ambiguous.

Defeat came in 1945, with a formal announcement by the emperor himself. For the next six years Japan was occupied by the Allied forces but, under the symbolic figurehead of the emperor, and with a constitution re-established in 1947, war was renounced forever and in 1952 Japan regained its sovereignty.

After the catastrophic defeat, political scientist Masao Maruyama (1914–96) spoke of the need to return to modernism. In Maruyama's opinion the introverted, exceptionalist imperial government had twisted the character of Japan during the war, and furthermore had led the country towards devastating defeat. He passionately argued that Japan should again use the modern West as an example in order to put right the distortions of the previous era. As the value of democracy and human rights was asserted, Maruyama led the arguments about the creation of a new modern Japan. Maruyama and his associates are often called 'modern period principalists' but even though they insisted on a universalist model for Japanese modernization, they took the exceptional character of Japan as their starting point. Douglas MacArthur (1880–1964), commander-in-chief of the Allied forces occupying Japan, also recognized this, judging that swift progress towards modernization would be held back by the immaturity of the country's democratic institutions. As a result exceptionalism was the dominant model in the post-war period.

During the late 1950s and 1960s Maruyama and his colleagues were the subject of much criticism, especially from the far Left. The main objections were that they looked to the modern West absolutely, and that their views were not shared by the masses. Asian Marxists, Democrats and historians concerned with the history of the common people criticized Maruyama. The left-wing activist and poet Takaaki Yoshimoto (b. 1924) was a vocal critic, insisting that the social value of a policy was more important than its contribution to national prestige. Yoshimoto emphasized the distinctive culture of the Japanese people, putting him in conflict with Maruyama's Western-influenced views.

The decades following the end of the war saw rapid growth that transformed Japan into a major economic power, despite two periods of slow growth following the oil shocks of 1953 and 1979. The country seemed to be moving towards universalist modernity. However, this development was understood to be based on distinctive 'Japanese-style management' and 'Japanese-style industrial relations': the exceptionalist model was still being stressed. Japan's high volume of exports at this time demonstrated how successfully it was able to use its uniqueness as a selling point. In the 1980s accumulated funds were used to increase export activity, especially for the automobile industry. This created trade friction with the United States and contributed to Japan's 'bubble economy'.

The end of the Cold War and other global changes that came about in 1989 also brought changes to the political and economic systems of Japan. The conservative Liberal Democratic Party, which had enjoyed a long period of rule since its foundation in 1955, went into decline, while their economic methods, which ploughed profits back into renewal of the public infrastructure, ceased to be effective. Neoliberalism has become the dominant approach to the economy in the 21st century.

Following the arrival of a powerful American influence with the occupation in 1945, the second half of the 20th century saw aspects of Japanese cities and landscape become indistinguishable from other big cities in the world as universalism flourished.

Within this pattern of development in Japan's recent history the three models proposed by Kenzaburo Oe can be seen in simplistic terms: the first, the search for a particularist or exceptionalist path to modernity, might be applied to the period up to the Russo-Japanese War of 1904–5; the second, the search for a universalist modernity, to the invasion of China in 1931. The third, transgression of the norms of modernity, has held particular importance since 1973.

However, these chronological divisions are not at all straightforward, as the first two models – exceptionalism and universalism – can be hard to separate into pure forms, and the progression from one to the other took place without obvious changes in outward political expression. Nevertheless, it is clear that during the earlier period the exceptionalist Japanese path to modernity was in the ascendant, while later, during the first half of the 20th century, the universalist model prevailed, until Japan was put on a war footing in the 1930s. The third model, transgression, started to appear from the late 1920s but was initially suppressed and did not achieve full expression for another half century. After 1945 the country saw a repeat of the process.

The rapid economic growth at the end of the 20th century transformed the country into a mass society. The modern phase of transgression is the product of a country that has successfully achieved re-modernization. Although occasionally described as 'post-modern', it is better seen as a 'post-post-war society'. The sociologist Munesuke Mita (b. 1937) has defined the periods of post-war Japanese history as the 'age of ideals' (corresponding to the formative period 1945–52) and the 'age of dreams' (the development period), followed by the 'age of fiction' (the contemporary period, since 1973). Mita sees the contemporary transgression model as completely different to both post-war exceptionalism and universalism. He has highlighted the series of incidents caused by the Aum Shinrikyo cult, culminating in the random release of deadly nerve gas on the Tokyo subway system in 1995, and the random serial killings of young girls by a young man, as acts in which the boundaries between reality and fiction were ambiguous to the perpetrators. Mita argues that Japan itself has entered a situation where the borders between reality and fiction have dissolved, ushering in a new 'age of impossibility'.

In March 1995, members of the religious Aum Shinrikyo cult staged a gas attack on commuters in the Tokyo subway, killing twelve and injuring over 5,000. This perversion of traditional Japanese religion can be seen as an extreme form of a 'transgressive' Japanese culture that has lost touch with reality.

Akihabara, a district in Tokyo, lies at the heart of this idea. Akihabara is home to the technology firms that are emblematic of contemporary Japan. Ever since the post-war development period, Japan has sought advancement through technological capability, starting with the automobile industry in the 1960s, expanding to household electrical goods and computers in the 1900s. These businesses line the streets of Akihabara where, in a trend called *Kosu Pure* ('Costume Play'), youths and waitresses in cafes and restaurants started to dress up as characters from video games and Japanese animation.

What we have seen is the evolution of the concept of 'Japan' itself. The influx of multinational corporations and foreign workers has made the country's borders ambiguous, and the space that 'Japan' comprises is no longer self-evident. The division between exceptionalism and universalism has declined in importance and the question 'What is Japan?' has itself begun to be questioned. A new movement with unconditional faith in 'Japan'

Even though by the end of the 20th century Japan was no longer the sole economic and technological powerhouse of East Asia, it was still a major world centre for new technology and animation. In the Akihabara district of Tokyo new electronic inventions could be explored.

forms one response, insisting on an exceptionalist Japan despite an awareness that the concept is a fiction. Central to this movement is the author Yoshinori Kobayashi (b. 1953), who, through the popular medium of Manga graphic history books, praises the emperor and insists that Japan was right in the Second World War. With the fall in 2009 of the Liberal Democratic Party government, in power continuously for fifty-four years, the signs of change, and perhaps a return to exceptionalism, have been growing.

The Tohoku earthquake of 11 March 2011 was an unprecedented catastrophic event that killed nearly 20,000 people and permanently scarred the history of modern Japan. Japan had experienced other large earthquakes, including the Hanshin earthquake that damaged the city of Kobe in 1995, but the magnitude 9 Tohoku earthquake was one of the most severe ever recorded. It also triggered a tsunami that devastated numerous towns and caused the Fukushima Daiichi nuclear plant disaster, which saw the first victims of a nuclear event on Japanese soil since the bombings of Hiroshima and Nagasaki in 1945. The after-effects of this compound disaster will continue to be felt for decades, with profound impact on Japanese society, in which a new social consciousness and a reassessment of old structures is already emerging in the wake of the catastrophe.

STEFAN BERGER

Germany

The many mutations of a belated nation

When the news of the fall of the Berlin Wall reached the parliament of the Federal Republic of Germany on 9 November 1989, all its members rose to sing the national anthem. One day later the mayor of West Berlin, Walter Momper (b. 1945), seemed to give voice to a widespread sentiment when he said: 'We Germans are today the happiest people in the world.' Less than a year later, on 3 October 1990, Germans celebrated their reunification. The sense of national enthusiasm witnessed between 1989 and 1990 in both parts of Germany was genuine, albeit short-lived. It soon gave way to divisions between East and West, and the tortuous search for an illusory 'normality' as a nation state. Commentators preferred to speak about unification rather than reunification, suggesting that 1990 marked the beginning of something new and not the continuity of something old.

Such a position is indicative of Germany's difficulties with its national history. The country does not possess a single and continuous narrative. While histories of nations around the world have been contested, the degree to which Germans have at different times told very different stories about themselves and held very different views about their national past is striking. The essential plurality of national master narratives was arguably exacerbated by the political events that marked the history of modern Germany: the dissolution in 1806 of the Holy Roman Empire of the German Nation, which had existed under this name since the 15th century; the formation of a loose confederation of largely autonomous states, the German Association (Deutscher Bund), in 1815; the revolution of 1848; the formation of the first modern German nation state in 1871; the creation of the first German republic in 1919; the victory of National Socialism in 1933; the total collapse of the German nation state in 1945; the division of the country in 1949; and the end of the Communist German Democratic Republic in 1989 are all

Young East Germans demolish the Berlin Wall in November 1989, as soldiers standing on top of the wall look on. The fall of the wall was the first step towards the unification of East and West Germany, which was formally concluded in 1990.

important breaks that brought with them significant changes to the way Germans thought of their national history.

National Socialism and in particular the Holocaust form the most important anchor of German historical consciousness today. It arguably took the Germans a long time to accept the historical responsibility for laying much of Europe to waste between 1939 and 1945, and for systematically murdering European Jewry. In the immediate post-war years the national discourse in Germany attempted to salvage a positive national identity by attributing the success of National Socialism to forces and events outside Germany's national history, such as the Versailles Treaty at the end of the First World War or modern mass society. The public discourse about the immediate past was characterized by self-pity for German suffering during the war and concern for German prisoners of war in the Soviet Union. It was only during the 1960s that specifically German sources for the victory of National Socialism and for the Holocaust were more widely acknowledged. A German 'special path' (*Sonderweg*) was now made responsible for Germany's catastrophic history during the first half of the 20th century, with Germany held to blame for two world wars and unprecedented destruction and suffering in Europe. The result was a deep crisis of the national paradigm. The formation of the first nation state in 1871 was now perceived as a historical mistake that brought nothing but instability and misery to Germans and Europeans alike. The lesson was clear: Germans would do best to abandon their search for a unified nation state and instead develop a post-national consciousness, accepting the existence of two separate nation states and the redrawing of German borders after the Second World War.

The most famous attempt to develop a more positive historical consciousness and to remove National Socialism and the Holocaust as the anchor of German identity was made in the mid-1980s. It culminated in the so-called 'historians' controversy'

TIMELINE

9 CE Germanic tribes under Hermann defeat the Romans in the Teutoburg Forest

936 Otto the Great is crowned king of the Germans; he becomes Holy Roman Emperor in 962

1648 The Treaty of Westphalia brings the Thirty Years' War to an end

1806 Dissolution of the Holy Roman Empire

1815 Formation of the German Association, a loose confederation of states

1848 Attempted liberal revolutions across Germany

1871 Proclamation of the German Empire

1918 End of the First World War and abdication of Emperor Wilhelm II

1919 The Treaty of Versailles blames Germany for the war

1933 Hitler becomes Chancellor of Germany

1945 Defeat of Germany; division into occupied zones

1948 Establishment of the Federal Republic of Germany (West Germany)

1949 Establishment of the German Democratic Republic (East Germany)

1956 The Federal Republic is a founder member of the European Economic Community

1989 The Berlin Wall comes down

1990 Reunification of East and West Germany

2005 Angela Merkel becomes the first Chancellor of Germany to come from the German Democratic Republic

This famous painting by Anton von Werner (1843–1915) depicts the foundation of modern Germany at Versailles in 1871 with Bismarck in the centre, a scene that never actually occurred – it is a carefully crafted construction of a particular historical moment.

(*Historikerstreit*) that raged between 1986 and 1987. The change of government in 1982 had seen promises by the Christian Democratic Chancellor Helmut Kohl (b. 1930) to bring about a 'spiritual/moral turn', which would include a more positive self-perception of German national history. Historians close to the government such as Michael Stürmer argued explicitly for a more long-term historical consciousness that would allow Germans to remember not just the catastrophic first half of the 20th century, but also the achievements of Germans over the course of many previous centuries. This was coupled with attempts to diminish German responsibility for the Holocaust by historian Ernst

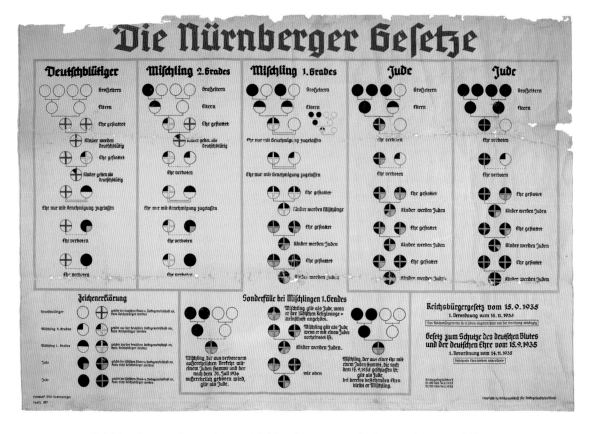

An official chart from 1935 showing the exact definition of a Jew as set out by the Nuremberg Laws, which attempted to define genetically who was a Jew or a half-Jew and marginalized Jews in a variety of ways. The Nuremberg Laws signified an important step in the successive exclusion of Jews from the German body politic.

Nolte, and an unfortunate comparison of 'the destruction of the German east' in 1945 with the Holocaust by historian Andreas Hillgruber. In response, left-liberal historians led by the philosopher Jürgen Habermas spoke of a conservative cabal (which did not exist as such) that aimed to re-nationalize the historical consciousness of Germany. Most commentators would have agreed in 1988 that the result of the debate was an emphatic confirmation of the centrality of National Socialism and the Holocaust in German historical consciousness, and the importance of developing a post-national sense of the past.

Then came 1989–90, and the first half of the 1990s saw a second instalment of the 'historians' controversy'. A group of young neo-nationalist historians, with occasional support from more established conservative figures, aimed at nationalizing the historical consciousness once again. By 1995 it was clear that they would be unsuccessful. Their belittling of National Socialist crimes lost them the support of mainstream conservatives.

Instead, there emerged a new narrative, epitomized by Heinrich August Winkler's hugely successful account of German history entitled *The Long Way West*, first published in German in 2000. It sold around 160,000 copies and has been translated (partially with government support) into English, French and Spanish. It argued that unification of the country in 1990 finally brought to an end all German 'special paths' and allowed the Germans to develop 'normal' Western forms of national identity, including a sense of pride in German achievements. His plea for a 'post-classical national identity' for Germans found widespread support and is reflected in the revival of popular national-ism, perhaps most visible in the flag-waving during the football World Cup of 2006.

It is precisely such acceptance that allowed Germans from the late 1990s onwards to discuss their own suffering in the Second World War. The Allied air raids on German cities, the rape of German women by (mainly) Soviet soldiers and the suffering of mil-lions of Germans who fled the advancing Red Army or who were 'ethnically cleansed' at

The devastation of the northern city of Hanover following bomb attacks in 1944–45. All major German cities sank into heaps of rubble; the bombardment of German civilians was meant to undermine their morale and diminish support for Hitler. More than 600,000 died in the Allied bombing.

the end of the war have all been important topics in public historical debates. However, such contemporary debates avoid a revisionist tone because they always start from the acceptance of German guilt and make it clear that German suffering was ultimately Germany's responsibility. But that it is legitimate to remember German suffering is beyond doubt, and it is reassuring that such remembrance occurs in a wider framework of historical consciousness that acknowledges responsibility not only for German suffering but for the suffering of many people in Europe and in particular the genocide of European Jewry.

If contemporary historical consciousness is still anchored in the memory of National Socialism and if the Holocaust is indeed the 'vanishing point' from which the national narrative is being written, it raises the question: are there any events in history that Germans are proud of today? The answer is yes, and apart from cultural classics created by Goethe (1749–1832) and Beethoven (1770–1827), for example, many of these positive reference points are located in the history of the Federal Republic. It is, above all, the successful rebuilding of the economy, the creation of the welfare state, and the construction of a functioning parliamentary democracy that generate feelings of pride in contemporary Germany. There is also a strong sense that the lessons of 20th-century history point in the direction of the building of a common European home in the form of the European Union.

Where does that leave the citizens of the former German Democratic Republic (GDR)? Celebrations of the achievements of the Federal Republic have gone hand in hand with denunciations of the totalitarian dictatorship of the GDR, which many East Germans have experienced as a devaluation of their own histories. The divided past has therefore fortified the famous 'wall in the heads' of contemporary Germans, and the ongoing divisions between West and East Germans. Only recently have we seen efforts to come to a more balanced historical assessment of the GDR.

Whereas German historical consciousness today is focused on the 20th century, a hundred years ago it reached back deep into the Middle Ages and late antiquity. Today hardly anyone has even heard of the legendary Tuisco, the last adopted son of the biblical Noah, from whom all Germans were allegedly descended. A more historically based figure was Arminius, or Hermann, the leader of a Germanic tribe who annihilated a Roman army under Varus in the Teutoburg Forest in 9 CE. The Germans built a huge memorial to him near Detmold, inaugurated in 1875; anti-Roman (i.e. anti-Catholic) and anti-French in orientation, the monument became a symbol of German national unity and strength. Tourists still visit it today, but it can hardly be described as an important site of national remembrance.

Many of the early images of national history were produced by humanist scholars such as Conrad Celtis and Jakob Wimpfeling in the 15th and 16th centuries. They already

A hand-tinted postcard of the Marienburg Castle, the seat of the German Order of Teutonic Knights during the late Middle Ages. By the early 19th century the ruins had been lovingly restored in what preservationists imagined was the style of the Middle Ages, which made the Marienburg a symbol of German nationalism.

included powerful concepts of foreigners being 'enemies' of the nation. The humanist national discourse was directed, above all, against claims by their Italian and French counterparts of representing superior cultures. By the 18th century a strong anti-Slav bias was added. Medieval history was central to the construction of a national history as a colonial/imperial power in Eastern Europe. The story of the Teutonic Knights, who built a military–clerical state in the Baltic in the later Middle Ages, became emblematic of Germany's civilizing mission, and Marienburg Castle, which was at the epicentre of the order's power, became a strong symbol of Germany's mission in Eastern Europe.

Germany was a latecomer to nation-state formation. The discourse about Germany and the national characteristics of the Germans can be traced back to the humanists and to writings by learned clerics in the Middle Ages, but there was no German nation state. The Holy Roman Empire only added the attribute 'of the German Nation' in the late 15th century, and the extent to which it can be regarded as a proto-nation state is debatable.

Historians in the 19th century such as Heinrich von Treitschke condemned the empire as a monstrosity that stood in the way of German nation-state formation for centuries. This negative view of the empire went back to Samuel von Pufendorf's writings in the 17th century, and coloured the view of the empire until recent decades when it has been recharacterized as a federal nation state with some meaningful central institutions such as the emperor, the Imperial Law Court (Reichskammergericht) and the Imperial Diet (Reichstag), which were successful in guaranteeing stability and peace in Central Europe for centuries. This stability did break down, most spectacularly in the Thirty Years' War of 1618–48, but the empire remained a viable entity able to generate considerable levels of emotional solidarity, which helps to explain why so many lamented its dissolution in 1806.

An image of Germania personified at the time of the 1848 revolutions, with the German flag, sword, double-headed eagle emblem and a symbolic unlocked manacle at her feet.

This would also explain why the first modern German nation state took the name of 'German Empire' when it came into existence in 1871. Although the 19th-century national movement in the German lands had attempted to build a nation state, this could not be brought about by revolution in 1848. It was instead created 'from above', through Prussia's strength in three wars: against Denmark (1864), Austria–Hungary (1866) and France (1870–71). These wars generated enough national feeling to overcome the resistance of the federal German states to a united, albeit still very federal, German nation state. Otto von Bismarck (1815–98), hailed as the 'founder of the Reich', was too much of a pragmatist to have a master plan in waging these wars and bringing the empire into existence, but he did believe that the nation state was a historical necessity, and wanted to make it as Prussian and authoritarian as possible. Yet he had to compromise with the National Liberals in imperial Germany, which gave the empire its peculiar character somewhere between constitutional monarchy and semi-absolutism.

The military was glorified as the key unifying force – after all, German unity had been achieved through three wars. Like the ancient hero Hermann, Germans were portrayed as manly warriors. The victory against France in 1870 on the battlefield near Sedan was celebrated every year on 2 September, so-called Sedan Day. The new emperor, Wilhelm I (1797–1888; r. 1871–88), was compared with the medieval emperor Frederick Barbarossa (1122–90; r. 1155–90). Ever since Barbarossa's failed attempt to unify the empire, legend had it that he awaited the completion of the task sitting at a wooden table in the middle of the Kyffhäuser Mountain with his red beard growing through the table. On account of his own white beard, Wilhelm I was nicknamed 'Barbablanca', and after his death his grandson Wilhelm II (1859–1941; r. 1888–1918) created a cult of his grandfather that was rivalled only by the public cult surrounding the Iron Chancellor and founder of the Second Reich, Bismarck.

Today no German – with the exception perhaps of a small neo-fascist right-wing group, which has no influence over the public discourse on the national past – would think of celebrating Sedan Day or hero-worshipping Bismarck. In 2009 the Germans did remember the 2,000th anniversary of the Teutoburg Forest battle with a major exhibition, but the public debate was far removed from any celebrations of male warriors in the image of Hermann. Quite the contrary: 2009 was declared Varus Year, after the defeated Roman general, and historians busied themselves demonstrating that Varus was not an effeminate and incompetent military leader as 19th-century historians had portrayed him. The rehabilitation of Varus went hand in hand with reminders to the public that Hermann was in no way a representative of the German nation. Today the national narrative is thus deconstructing the nationalist myths of the 19th century rather than building on them. Most ordinary Germans now have little, if any, knowledge of medieval history. The heroes and legends that would have been familiar to every schoolchild in imperial Germany have faded into oblivion.

Foreign observers of German debates on national identity sometimes overestimate the dangers of a recurrence of fascism. In the wake of German reunification the Irish commentator Conor Cruise O'Brien warned of the possible coming of the 'fourth Reich'. Such alarmist perspectives were rare, but worries about the future of a reunified Germany led the British prime minister Margaret Thatcher (b. 1925), not known for her pro-German sentiments, to assemble some of the best-known historians of Germany to discuss the German national character. If we are to trust the report about the meeting, they came up with a remarkable range of national stereotypes and angst-ridden speculations about the future of a unified Germany. In Eastern Europe fears of the revival of German nationalism are, if anything, stronger. After all, East Europeans suffered far more than West Europeans under German dreams of world domination in the 20th century. The crude history politics of the Kaczynski brothers in Poland, with their routine vilification of German politicians as Nazis or under the influence of Nazis, is only the most visible expression of fears which, although perhaps less widespread than they were after the Second World War, have far from disappeared. There is still a lack of recognition of the deep engagement of Germans with the horrific aspects of their national past. The vast majority of them today seem willing to defy the Pied Pipers of extreme nationalism.

There is another myth about contemporary Germany, widely held outside Germany and shared, to some extent, by many Germans: the idea that they are peculiarly lacking in any nationalism, not to say anti-national, and that their enthusiasm for the European Union is the direct result of such anti-nationalism. This perception is sometimes tied to the idea that post-nationalism is yet another German attempt to force their own intellectual predilections on other Europeans, who are perfectly happy with their national identities and histories. More malicious anti-German and anti-European commentators have even argued that the European Union is, in fact, the latest German design to gain dominance over the European Continent. German economic power meant that the 2011–12 debt crisis in some weaker Eurozone countries was experienced as a new form of German domination.

Germans today are not, in fact, troubled by national identity headaches. Most feel proud to be German and their reference points are economic performance, political stability and cultural as well as sporting success. 'Vorsprung durch Technik' ('headstart through technology'), the advertising slogan for Audi cars, is a concept deeply rooted in

Volkswagen became the most popular auto maker in Germany from the 1950s onwards. With roots in National Socialist Germany, when the Nazis promoted cars for 'ordinary people', after 1945 the company managed to shed this association, providing cheap cars for workers and the lower middle classes, the most famous being the Beetle.

Since the 2006 Football World Cup in Germany, the waving of the national flag on sporting occasions has become much more prevalent. It was widely interpreted as Germans developing a 'normal' national identity after all national symbols had become suspect following the National Socialist experience.

19th-century plans to construct economic nationalism, but few Germans today associate pride in economic success with expansionist foreign policies. Their historical consciousness is shallow. Arguably this is also a reaction to the historical consciousness underpinning 19th-century nationalism. When this nationalism turned to hypernationalism and ultimately National Socialism, deep historical consciousness was damaged to such an extent that it seems impossible to resurrect it. But that in itself might be a cause for celebration. A strong unified Germany with a deep and positive historical consciousness did, after all, lead Europe over the brink twice in the last century. A less historically minded Germany, which anchors its historical consciousness in the uniquely negative experience of the Holocaust and of National Socialism, might be better for Europe's health in the 21st century.

Israel
The Zionist experiment

Israel is both an old country and a new one. The modern state was established in the midst of a bloody conflict in 1948 that most Israelis viewed as a zero-sum game in which there could be only one winner. The armies of the invading Arab states could afford to lose a war, but the Israelis believed that they faced annihilation if they did not succeed. United Nations Resolution 181 in November 1947 had offered the partition of British Palestine and a two-state solution. The Zionist Jews accepted this but the Palestinian Arabs did not. The losers in this bitter conflict called the war of 1948 'the Nakhba' ('the Palestinian Catastrophe'), while the victors termed it 'the Israeli War of Independence'. The war precipitated an exodus of up to 760,000 Arabs, some of whom were expelled. The Arab refugees settled mainly in the West Bank and Gaza, as well as in neighbouring Arab countries.

Israel is perceived today as a state of the Jews with a distinct Palestinian Arab minority, and is peppered by a plethora of national and religious communities. Arabs make up almost a fifth of the population; they are mainly Sunni Muslim with a dwindling Christian minority. There are the Arabic-speaking Druse and the non-Arab Muslim Circassians. There is a large Armenian community in Jerusalem, while the headquarters of the Bahai faith is situated in Haifa. Samaritans, whose origins stretch back to the Babylonian conquest of ancient Israel in the 6th century BCE, live in Holon. Tens of thousands of Bedouin dwell in dire conditions in officially 'unrecognized' villages.

Many Israelis speak of 1948 as the re-establishment of a third Jewish Commonwealth, the successor of the ancient Jewish homelands destroyed first by the Babylonians and then again by the Romans at the beginning of the first millennium. The Jewish diaspora is the chronological bridge that spans these events. The Jews never forgot the land of Israel. Indeed, the Judaism that evolved was considered a portable homeland such

An iconic image of Jews in Palestine after the horrors of the first half of the 20th century. Holocaust survivors in striped concentration camp uniforms stand together with a Zionist pioneer below the national flag with the Star of David.

that wherever the Jews wandered, they did not forget the biblical promise of Zion: three times a day they faced in the direction of Jerusalem and prayed for peace.

Persecution down the centuries, beginning with that of the Church Fathers in the early centuries of the Christian era, brought it home to the Jews that they had to seek self-emancipation rather than await liberation by others. They reached this conclusion when they realized that the great hopes raised by the French Revolution and the European Enlightenment during the 18th century remained solely within the realm of theory. The advent of the caring nation state, the secularization of society and the proclamation of the progressive dawn of humanity had not brought the Jews joy. The Dreyfus case, in which a Jewish army officer was unjustly accused of treason in France, revealed the extent to which anti-Semitism pervaded the elite of a 'modern' and republican France at the turn of the 20th century. Nazism then infected enlightened Germany, where Jews had felt similarly secure and at home. The cry 'The Jews are our misfortune!' was heard in a hundred European cities. It ended in Auschwitz and Treblinka. The Allies may have won the war, but the Jews certainly lost it.

During the 19th century most Jews had attempted to adjust to modernity. A minority did not and maintained their religious traditions, unique culture, characteristic garments and common languages such as Yiddish. Thus, at one extreme these ultra-orthodox Jews spiritually rebuilt the ghetto walls to produce a secluded world; at the other, detached Jews sought to assimilate themselves through acculturation and

TIMELINE

70 The destruction of Jerusalem by the Romans; the end of Jewish independence and the enforced dispersion of the Jews

1881 Pogroms in Russia

1882 The first emigration to Palestine

1897 Theodor Herzl founds the World Zionist Organization

1917 The Balfour Declaration by Britain promises a national home for the Jewish people in Palestine

1922 Britain is given a Mandate over Palestine by the League of Nations

1939–45 The Nazi Holocaust results in the extermination of 6 million Jews

1944–47 Military and political struggle by Palestine's Jews to secure independence

1947 The United Nations votes for the creation of both an Israeli state and a Palestinian Arab state

1948 Ben-Gurion proclaims the establishment of Israel as an independent state, followed by immediate invasion by its Arab neighbours

1956 Israel, in collusion with Britain and France, attacks Nasser's Egypt

1967 The Six-Day War unexpectedly results in Israeli control over territory four times its size, including Jerusalem and the West Bank

1973 Israel successfully repels a coalition attack led by Egypt and Syria in the Yom Kippur War

1979 A peace treaty is signed between Israel and Egypt

1982 An Israeli invasion of Lebanon leads to huge protests against the government

1993 Israel's Yitzhak Rabin and the PLO's Yasser Arafat sign the Oslo Accord in the hope of bringing peace to both peoples

2001 The al-Aqsa Intifada begins, accompanied by a wave of suicide bombing

2005 Israel withdraws from Gaza settlements

2006 Israel conducts a thirty-three-day war against the Lebanese Islamist group Hezbollah

2009 Israel initiates Operation Cast Lead against Gaza in response to missiles fired into Israel

conversion to Christianity. Most found a place along this spectrum of accommodation and became loyal citizens of their country. Some 12,000 German Jews died fighting for the Emperor in the First World War.

In Eastern Europe the tsarist authorities had made little attempt to integrate the Jews into the host society. In the late 18th century Catherine the Great (1729–96; r. 1762–96) hemmed them into an area of western Russia known as the Pale of Settlement, where a raft of discriminating laws kept them in check. Between 1881 and 1914 some 2 million Jews emigrated from here to Western Europe and the United States in a search of a better life.

Some who remained became revolutionaries. Many of the early Bolsheviks – Trotsky, Zinoviev, Kamenev, Sverdlov, Radek – were Jews, but in name only. Escaping Jewishness in order to repair the world was common. There were others who did not discard their identity and tried to find a way out of their predicament. Some tried to create local autonomy in their area of Eastern Europe. Many others looked to territorial solutions outside. Such 'Jewish homelands' were located in the four corners of the earth: from Australasia to Latin America, there were projects to build a new 'Israel'. A book by Eliahu Benjamini carries the title *States for the Jews: Uganda, Birobidzhan and 34 Other Plans* (1990). Most of these ideas came to nothing, not least because their adherents perished in the Holocaust. Zionism, though, succeeded because it was essentially a survivalist ideology.

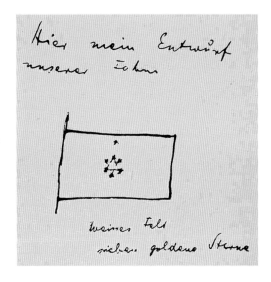

Theodor Herzl's sketch for the Zionist flag, 1890s. The assimilated Herzl was unconnected to the Jewish past and advocated German as the national language in the future Israel; Hebrew would be the domain of the rabbis. His idea for the flag involved eight stars to represent the eight-hour working day.

Many early Zionists in the late 19th century moved away from a religious definition of Jewishness towards a national one. Yet they still retained their affection for the Bible and the Jewish learning of religious texts, which served as a backdrop to their political efforts in the revolutionary sphere. Thus early Zionists such as Theodor Herzl, Moses Hess, Leon Pinsker and Max Nordau believed that Zion should be located in the ancient homeland of Israel.

Zionism was a rebellion against the designated place of the Jew in society, a revolt against oppressors and tyrants. It was also a rebellion against a broad rabbinical authority untouched by modernity, which passively accepted that persecution was the fate of the Jews. The redemption of the Jews would only come, it was argued, with the coming of the true Messiah – and any human intervention in forcing God's hand was disreputable.

Moreover, boundaries had to be built to stop the erosion of traditional Judaism by the lapping waters of rationalism. Hence Shneur Zalman of Lyady, a well-known rabbinic sage, had preferred to endorse the oppression of the tsar in 1812 rather than risk contamination with the free spirit of revolutionary France during the Napoleonic invasion of Russia. Of course, there was a minority of rabbis, such as Zvi Hirsch Kalischer and Yehuda Alkalai, who interpreted Jewish religious texts differently and thereby strongly advocated the settlement of the Holy Land. Their followers became the originators of religious Zionism and opposed anti-Zionist ultra-orthodoxy.

In 1882 the first Zionist immigrants, the Biluim, arrived in Ottoman Palestine from tsarist Russia. Zionists such as the French Baron Edmond de Rothschild began to purchase uninhabited land from local notables and absentee landlords. The pioneers of the early 20th century regarded themselves as part of an international revolutionary movement that would build an exemplary socialist society in Palestine. Indeed, Israel's founders, such as David Ben-Gurion, Yitzhak Ben-Zvi and Yitzhak Tabenkin, were Marxists who arrived in the second wave of immigration in the decade before the First World War. Their socialist desire to change the Jewish world led to the first collective settlements in 1910, of which the kibbutz was but one experiment.

Unlike European imperialists, the Jewish immigrants saw themselves as colonizers not colonialists. They did not come with armies and arms, but with pitchforks and hoes. They wanted to build the country and, in turn, be built by it. The rise of a Hebrew republic in the biblical land of Israel was not simply the transformation of an Ottoman backwater into a modern state. It also symbolized the transformation of the Jews from a marginalized, despised people who had somehow managed to survive on the periphery of history.

The tragedy of this enterprise was that Jewish nationalism arose at approximately the same time as Arab nationalism – and they began to struggle over the same small parcel of land. Although the territory of the Arab world was vastly greater than that of Palestine, the price of Jewish control of its own territory was to live in a perpetual state of siege.

Sixty years after its bloody birth pangs, Israel is recognized as a success even in the Arab world. A quarter of its workforce possesses university degrees – the third highest proportion in the industrialized world. Israel is at the cutting edge of advanced technology. Yet this has meant a break with past values. In embracing globalization and deregulation in the 1980s, Israel turned its back on its socialist heritage. The kibbutz, for example, once universally admired, gradually adopted the practices of privatization in order to survive. Israel is now rated second in the Western world, after the United States, in the size of the gap in income, education and spending between the richest and poorest. A mere 10 per cent of the population owns 70 per cent of private capital. Even so, Israel remains a highly self-critical and, indeed, argumentative country that retains the ideal to improve.

On board the SS Aquitania, *November 1921: Vladimir Jabotinsky (1880–1940), founder of the Jewish Legion and the Revisionist Zionist movement, Nahum Sokolow (1859–1936), writer and president of the World Zionist Organization, Otto Warburg (1859–1938), German Zionist leader and Alexander Goldstein (1884–1949), Russian Zionist leader.*

One common source of identification is the citizens' army, the Israel Defence Forces (IDF). The war of 1948 marked a turning point in Jewish history. No longer would Jews calmly accept their fate: a Jewish fighting force would not allow it. It was Vladimir Jabotinsky, the originator of the Jewish Legion of volunteers for the British army in the First World War, who coined the term 'the Iron Wall' in 1923. Its original use was as a defence, a bulwark against Arab attacks on Jewish settlements. The Haganah (the Jewish settlements' defence organization) was founded in 1920 and then became the nucleus of the IDF. There were also dissident nationalist groups, such as the Irgun and Lehi, which broke away from the Haganah and fought the British in Palestine during the 1940s.

The IDF remains an institution venerated by Israelis. Israeli eighteen-year-olds serve three years in the armed forces – two years if they are women. Post-army reservists are expected to commit one month each year to their unit. This continues until their early forties. Both Druse and Circassians serve in the IDF, but Arabs do not. Such is the

January 2008: paratroopers carry weapons as they prepare to take part in their swearing-in ceremony at the Western Wall compound in Jerusalem, the site for new soldiers to be inducted into the Israel Defence Forces (IDF) after they have completed their basic training.

determination to defend themselves that Israel has the highest military expenditure per head of population of any country in the world.

Many chiefs of staff and senior commanders have used the army as a springboard into politics. Since 1992 three out of the last five Israeli prime ministers – Yitzhak Rabin (1922–95), Ariel Sharon (b. 1928) and Ehud Barak (b. 1942) – emerged from the IDF. Yet the days of pioneering idealism, when Israel was a light unto the nations, were long gone. Corruption and misdemeanours among the political elite no longer surprised Israelis.

In 1993 Yasser Arafat (1929–2004), the leader of the Palestinian nationalists, signed the Oslo Accord with Israel's prime minister Yitzhak Rabin. This was opposed by the Israeli Right and the Jewish settlers on the West Bank, as well as by Palestinian Islamist organizations such as Hamas. The introduction of suicide bombing into Israel by Hamas in 1994 sounded the death knell for the peace process. Thereafter there was political stagnation, interrupted by surges in violence. The advent of Palestinian Islamism precipitated a cosmic move to the right in Israel in the hope that that the 'hard men' would be efficient protectors of the people. The rise to power of previously discredited figures such as Ariel

Sharon, who confronted Hamas with Israel's military might, coupled with the perceived corruption of Yasser Arafat's governing Palestinian National Authority, persuaded many ordinary Palestinians to vote Hamas into power in 2006. Meanwhile, the disputed Jewish settlements in the West Bank continued to expand through a broad interpretation of the 'natural growth' that successive Israeli governments have justified.

According to opinion polls over many years, most Israelis opposed the existence of these settlements in the West Bank – which were first built following Israel's conquest of the territory during the Six-Day War in 1967. It came as a surprise that Prime Minister Sharon's decision to evacuate the settlements in Gaza in 2005 brought no respite from the missiles of Hamas. A growing number of Israelis asked what had been gained from this voluntary withdrawal. Even the peace camp in Israel that had brought about the Oslo Accord was muted. There was therefore no vision of what could be, only a bleak appraisal of what was. Many Israelis battened down the hatches until the religious intensity sweeping the Islamic world blew over.

Israel has changed dramatically since its foundation in 1948 – and some would argue not for the better. In the 1930s and 1940s the European Left fought fascism with the Jews, lived through the Holocaust and witnessed the rise of the state of Israel. In 1947 the leader of the left wing of the Labour Party in Britain, Aneurin Bevan (1897–1960), threatened to resign from the government because of its lack of sympathy for the Zionist cause in Palestine. Non-Jews saw the cause of Israel as akin to that of fighting for Republican Spain in the Spanish Civil War. Several fought and died for Israel in 1948.

The succeeding generation, however, came of political age during the epoch of decolonization. They cut their political teeth in campaigns against the war in Vietnam, apartheid South Africa and minority rule in Rhodesia. But they had not fought fascism, uncovered the existence of the extermination camps, or lived through the bitter war of 1948 in Palestine. The advent of Palestinian nationalism after the Six-Day War in 1967 brought the plight of the Palestinian Arabs to the notice of the international community. The cause of the Palestinians, rather than that of the Jews, fitted in much better with the New Left world view. The settlement drive and the move towards the Right within Israel itself additionally allowed the New Left to characterize Israel as a colonial state, an illegitimate

30 October 2009, Gaza City: a demonstrator holds a mock missile during a rally of thousands of Islamic Jihad supporters to commemorate the killing of their founder Fathi Shaqaqi, probably by the Israeli Mossad, in Malta in 1995.

weed planted by British imperialism during the Mandate. This assertion provoked a sharp reaction from many Israeli Jews, for whom the Holocaust was not merely history.

Some foreign observers simply tired of the unending Israel–Palestine imbroglio and asked whether this troublesome state of Israel should have been created in the first place. After all, Britain took on the responsibility for this region after the First World War under the Mandate of the League of Nations. It had promised, in the Balfour Declaration of 1917, to 'look with favour' on the establishment of a national home for the Jews in Palestine, so long as 'nothing shall be done which may prejudice the civil and religious rights of existing non-Jewish communities in Palestine'. Yet by November 1947 Britain had decided to abstain in the United Nations vote for a two-state solution that legislated for Israeli independence. Britain delayed its formal recognition of Israel and was initially loath to exhibit any form of political sympathy. Israel, for its part, refused to join the Commonwealth.

On the political left, the impasse in the Middle East from the 1990s onwards led to a progressive delegitimization of Israel in Europe. The Israel–Palestine conflict was presented in over-simplistic and unhistorical terms of good versus evil. Of course, all have the right and duty to condemn Israeli policy as they see fit. Yet there were often occasions when the tropes echoed long-buried canards from the past. Images and language conjured up anti-Jewish stereotypes thought to have been banished long ago. Even vociferous Jewish critics of Israeli government policy began to ask whether their comments strengthened the case of those who wished to dismantle the state and leave uncertain the fate of its Jewish inhabitants.

The existence of a 21st-century state with a Jewish majority in the Middle East does not fit Marxist doctrine, post-colonial theory or Islamist belief. It has brought together liberals, social democrats, Trotskyists, Stalinists and Islamists to reaffirm the Comte de Clermont-Tonnerre's contention in the French National Assembly at the beginning of the French Revolution in 1789: 'Everything must be refused to the Jews as a nation; everything must be granted to them as individuals.'

Israel was created from the common purpose of Jews the world over to move history in a new, untested direction. In one sense, an Israeli people is still evolving from the fusion of over a hundred Jewish diaspora communities with their own traditions and histories. There are Jews from Gondar in Ethiopia and from Chennamangalam in southern India, from Tashkent in Central Asia and from Manhattan's Fifth Avenue. There are ultra-orthodox Haredim, who live in their own enclaves; national religious settlers on the West Bank; the Mizrahim, who hail mainly from the Arab world; Reform Jews from the United States; messianic Jews who believe that Jesus is the true Messiah – and the majority of Israelis, who are both culturally traditional and devoutly secular. All this produces an ongoing friction and intense debate. The obligatory service in the IDF serves as a melting pot for Israelis from different backgrounds, but it will take several generations for an equilibrium to be reached.

Shirat Hayam, Gaza, 18 August 2005: most Jewish settlers left peacefully when Israel evacuated their twenty-one Gaza settlements in accordance with Sharon's disengagement plan. However, some settlers, such as those living at Shirat Hayam, founded in 2001 on the Gaza shore, resisted and were forcibly removed by the Israeli police and military.

There are also different appraisals of Zionism – from the Marxist revolutionary who wishes to abolish private enterprise to the ultra-orthodox rebbe who believes Zionism to be evil. Strong emotions are evoked. Is holding on to the West Bank a matter of religion because God gave this land to the Jews? Or is it a question of nationalist expansion according to the original borders of the British Mandate? Or is it simply a matter of security, in that settlements hold up invading armies and territory provides strategic depth?

Much can be said about Israel, but it can never be said to be boring. Israeli Jews, despite everything, see themselves as being on a voyage of discovery and at the forefront of Jewish history. They are a traditionally stiff-necked people involved in a unique, non-conformist and extraordinary project.

FURTHER READING

Argentina

Lewis, Daniel K., *The History of Argentina*, New York and Basingstoke, 2003

Robben, Antonius C. G. M., *Political Violence and Trauma in Argentina*, Philadelphia, 2007

Romero, Luis Alberto and James P. Brennan, *A History of Argentina in the Twentieth Century*, Philadelphia, 2002

Australia

Davison, Graeme, *The Use and Abuse of Australian History*, Sydney, 2000

Hirst, John, *Sense and Nonsense in Australian History*, Melbourne, 2005

Macintyre, Stuart, *A Concise History of Australia*, Cambridge, 2009 (3rd edn)

Brazil

Fausto, Boris, *A Concise History of Brazil*, Cambridge, 1999

Skidmore, Thomas E., *Brazil: Five Centuries of Change*, Oxford, 1999

Canada

Conrad, Margaret and Alvin Finkel, *History of the Canadian Peoples*, 2 vols, Toronto, 2009 (5th edn)

Dickason, Olive P. A., *A Concise History of Canada's First Nations*, Toronto, 2006 (4th edn)

Saul, John Ralston, *A Fair Country: Telling Truths About Canada*, Toronto, 2008

China

Fenby, Jonathan, *Dragon Throne: China's Emperors from the Qin to the Manchu*, London, 2008

Keay, John, *China: A History*, London, 2009

Mitter, Rana, *A Bitter Revolution: China's Struggle with the Modern World*, Oxford, 2005

The Czech Republic

Dowling, Maria, *Czechoslovakia*, London, 2002

Holy, Ladislav, *The Little Czech and the Great Czech Nation: National Identity and the Postcommunist Social Transformation*, Cambridge, 1996

Teich, Mikulas (ed.), *Bohemia in History*, Cambridge and New York, 1998

Egypt

Kepel, Gilles, *Muslim Extremism in Egypt: The Prophet and Pharaoh*, Berkeley, 2003

Petry, Carl F. and M. W. Daly (eds), *The Cambridge History of Egypt*, 2 vols, Cambridge, 1998

Shaw, I. (ed.), *The Oxford History of Ancient Egypt*, Oxford, 2002

Finland

Meinander, Henrik, *A History of Finland: Directions, Structures, Turning-Points*, New York, 2010

Osmo, Jussila, Jukka Nevakivi and Seppo Hentilä, *From Grand Duchy to Modern State: Political History of Finland Since 1809*, tr. David Arter, London, 1999

Singleton, Fred, *A Short History of Finland*, Cambridge, 1998

France

Ladurie, Emmanuel Le Roy, *Histoire de France des régions*, Paris, 2004

Ladurie, Emmanuel Le Roy and Colin Jones, *The Cambridge Illustrated History of France*, Cambridge, 1999

Robb, Graham, *The Discovery of France*, London, 2008

Germany

Clark, Christopher, *Iron Kingdom: The Rise and Downfall of Prussia, 1600–1947*, London, 2006

Evans, Richard J., *Rereading German History: From Unification to Reunification, 1800–1996*, London, 1997

Ghana

Amenumey, D. E. K., *Ghana: A Concise History from Pre-Colonial Times to the 20th Century*, Accra, 2008

Falola, Toyin, *Ghana in Africa and the World: Essays in Honor of Adu Boahen*, Trenton, New Jersey, 2003

Gocking, Roger S., *The History of Ghana*, Westport, Connecticut, and London, 2005

Great Britain

Black, Jeremy, *A History of the British Isles*, Basingstoke and New York, 2003 (2nd edn)

Clark, Jonathan, *A World by Itself: A History of the British Isles*, Portsmouth, 2010

Robbins, K., *Great Britain: Identities, Institutions and the Idea of Britishness*, Harlow, 1998

Greece

Cartledge, Paul, *The Cambridge Illustrated History of Ancient Greece*, Cambridge, 1997

Clogg, Richard, *A Concise History of Greece*, Cambridge, 2002

Hungary

Kontler, László, *A History of Hungary: Millennium in Central Europe*, London, 2002

Molnár, Miklós, *A Concise History of Hungary*, Cambridge, 2001

India

Kosambi, D. D., *An Introduction to the Study of Indian History*, London, 1996 (2nd edn)

Majumdar, R. C., *The Classical Accounts of India*, Calcutta, 1960

Thapar, Romila, *History and Beyond*, New Delhi, 2000

Iran

The Cambridge History of Iran, vols 1–7, Cambridge, 1968–91

Katouzian, Homa, *The Persians: Ancient, Medieval and Modern Iran*, London and New York, 2009

Ireland

Bartlett, Thomas, *Ireland: A History*, Cambridge, 2010

Foster, Roy, *The Oxford History of Ireland*, Oxford, 1992

Israel

Johnson, Paul, *A History of the Jews*, London, 1987

Laqueur, Walter, *The History of Zionism*, London, 2003

Shindler, Colin, *A History of Modern Israel*, Cambridge, 2008

Italy

Duggan, Christopher, *The Force of Destiny: A History of Italy Since 1796*, New York and London, 2008

Foot, John, *Italy's Divided Memory*, London, 2010

Japan

Jansen, Marius, *The Making of Modern Japan*, Cambridge, Massachusetts, 2002

Morton, Scott and Kenneth Olenik, *Japan: Its History and Culture*, New York, 2009

Totman, Conrad, *A History of Japan*, Oxford and Malden, Massachusetts, 2005 (2nd edn)

Mexico

Coe, Michael, *Mexico: From the Olmecs to the Aztecs*, London, 2004

Meyer, Michael C., William L. Sherman and Susan M. Deeds, *The Course of Mexican History*, Oxford, 2002

The Netherlands

Arblaster, Paul, *A History of the Low Countries*, New York, 2006

Blom, J. C. H. and E. Lamberts (eds), *History of the Low Countries*, trans. James C. Kennedy, Oxford, 1999

Schama, Simon, *The Embarrassment of Riches: An Interpretation of Dutch Culture in the Golden Age*, New York, 1987

Poland

Davies, Norman, *Heart of Europe: A Short History of Poland*, Oxford, 1984

Zamoyski, Adam, *Poland: A History*, London, 2009

Russia

Figes, Orlando, *Natasha's Dance: A Cultural History of Russia*, London, 2003

Freeze, Gregory, *Russia: A History*, Oxford, 2009

Hosking, Geoffrey, *Russia and the Russians: From Earliest Times to 2001*, London, 2001

Spain

Carr, Raymond, *Spain: A History*, Oxford, 2001 (rev. edn)

Elliott, J. H., *Imperial Spain 1469–1716*, London, 2002 (rev. edn)

Kamen, Henry, *Spain, 1469–1714: A Society of Conflict*, New York, 2005

Sweden

Aronsson, Peter, Narve Fulsås, Pertti Haapala and Bernard Eric Jensen, 'Nordic national histories', in Stefan Berger and Chris Lorenz (eds), *The Contested Nation: Ethnicity, Class, Religion and Gender in National Histories*, pp. 256–82, Basingstoke and New York, 2008

Trägårdh, Lars (ed.), *State and Civil Society in Northern Europe: The Swedish Model Reconsidered*, Oxford, 2007

Weibull, Jörgen, Paul Britten Austin and Svenska Institutet, *Swedish History in Outline*, Stockholm, 1997

Turkey

Barkey, Karen, *Empire of Difference: The Ottomans in Comparative Perspective*, Cambridge, 2008

Goodwin, Jason, *Lords of the Horizons: A History of the Ottoman Empire*, New York, 2003

The United States

Brogan, Hugh, *The Penguin History of the United States of America*, London, 2001

Foner, Eric, *The Story of American Freedom*, London, 1998

Onuf, Nicholas and Peter Onuf, *Nations, Markets and War: Modern History and the American Civil War*, Charlottesville, Virginia, 2006

Wood, Gordon S., *Empire of Liberty: A History of the Early Republic 1789–1815*, Oxford, 2010

CONTRIBUTOR BIOGRAPHIES

General Editor

Peter Furtado was editor of *History Today* magazine between 1998 and 2008. He edited the *Cassell Atlas of World History* (1998) and *1001 Days that Changed the World* (2007). In 2009 he was awarded an honorary doctorate by Oxford Brookes University for his work in promoting interest in history in Britain.

Contributors

Peter Aronsson SWEDEN

Peter Aronsson is Professor of Cultural Heritage and the Uses of History at Linköping University, Sweden. His interests include local, regional and national interactions in history and historiography, political culture at the lower end of society, historiography and historical culture. He is a member of the Royal Swedish Academy of Letters, History and Antiquities. Currently he is coordinating a large comparative EU-funded project on European national museums.

Elizabeth Baquedano MEXICO

Elizabeth Baquedano is a Mexican-born archaeologist who teaches at Birkbeck College, University of London. She has published several illustrated books on pre-Columbian history and archaeology.

Hussein Bassir EGYPT

Hussein Bassir is an Egyptian archaeologist, novelist and writer based in Cairo. He studied Egyptology in Cairo, Oxford and Baltimore and has participated in many Egyptian and foreign archaeological excavations. He received his PhD from Johns Hopkins University, Baltimore, in 2009 and teaches at Mansoura University and Misr International University. He was the archaeological director of the National Museum of Egyptian Civilization and is currently the director of the International Organizations Administration at the Supreme Council of Antiquities (SCA). His works include articles and books on Arabic literature and cinema, Egyptology and archaeology.

Stefan Berger GERMANY

Stefan Berger is Professor of Social History and Director of the Institute of Social Movements, Ruhr University, Bochum. His research interests include modern European history, especially that of Germany and Britain, comparative labour history, nationalism and national identity studies, and historiography and historical theory. He studied at the University of Cologne and the University of Oxford, and is currently president of the German History Society in the UK and Ireland. He is also chair of the European Science Foundation programme 'Representations of the Past: the Writing of National Histories in Nineteenth and Twentieth Century Europe' and editor of its book series *Writing the Nation*.

Jeremy Black GREAT BRITAIN

Jeremy Black is Professor of History at the University of Exeter. He has written widely on British, European and world history, history and maps, and specializes in 18th-century British political and military history.

Mihir Bose INDIA

Mihir Bose was born in Calcutta and has lived in London for more than forty years. Until 2009 he was the BBC Sports Editor and he now works as a freelance journalist. He has written 23 books on topics including 20th-century Indian history and Indian cricket.

Ciaran Brady IRELAND
Ciaran Brady is Associate Professor of Irish History at Trinity College Dublin. His areas of interest include the Tudors and Stuarts, the teaching of history in Irish schools and historical revisionism.

Margaret Conrad CANADA
Margaret Conrad is a former Professor of Canadian History at the University of New Brunswick. She has written widely on Atlantic Canadian history and women's studies. She is involved in the research project 'Canadians and their Pasts' and in Canada's History Education Network.

Wilhelmina Donkoh GHANA
Wilhelmina J. Donkoh is a Senior Lecturer in African History, specializing in Ashanti history and culture, at the Faculty of Social Sciences at Kwame Nkrumah University of Science and Technology, Kumasi, Ghana. She is the co-author of *The Just King: The Story of Osei Tutu Kwame Asibe Bonsu* (2000). Dr Donkoh has chronicled the importance of traditional governance structures in dealing with modern challenges such as AIDS in Africa.

Willem Frijhoff THE NETHERLANDS
Willem Frijhoff is Emeritus Professor of History at the Free University of Amsterdam. His many books include *1650: Hard-won Unity* (2004), on Holland in the Golden Age, and *Embodied Belief. Ten essays on religious culture in Dutch history* (2002). His main research interests are the cultural and religious history of Europe and North America and the history of education, in particular literacy, schooling and universities in early modern Europe.

Homa Katouzian IRAN
Homa Katouzian is an Iranian-born historian, economist and literary scholar. He moved to Britain to study and is now based at St Antony's College, Oxford. In addition to his book on *Iranian History and Politics, the Dialectic of State and Society* (2003), he has written widely on Iranian history and politics, classical and modern Persian literature and various topics in economics.

Dina Khapaeva RUSSIA
Dina Khapaeva is a researcher at the University of Helsinki. She is the author of *Nightmare: Literature and Life* (2010), a study of nightmare as a mental state, as a literary experiment conducted by Nikolay Gogol and Fyodor Dostoevsky and as a powerful trend in contemporary culture, and *Gothic Society: Morphology of a Nightmare* (2007), a study of the impact of the memory of Stalinism on post-Soviet society. Her research interests include historical memory, Russian and Soviet literature, intellectual history and Soviet history.

László Kontler HUNGARY
László Kontler is Professor of History at the Central European University, Budapest. His interests focus on Hungary and Central Europe and comparative intellectual history. Among the most prominent of his numerous publications is *A History of Hungary: Millennium in Central Europe* (1999).

Emmanuel Le Roy Ladurie FRANCE
Professor Emmanuel Le Roy Ladurie is Emeritus Professor at the Collège de France, Paris, where he has taught for twenty-five years. His research interests focus on the social history of the Languedoc. Among his many publications are the best-selling microhistories *Montaillou* (1975) and *Carnival in Romans* (1980). He is also one of the first serious environmental historians to have emerged during the latter half of the 20th century.

Giovanni Levi ITALY

Giovanni Levi is Emeritus Professor of History at the University of Venice. He is one of the first proponents of microhistory and his book *The Intangible Heritage*, about village life in Piedmont, was published in 1990.

Antonis Liakos GREECE

Antonis Liakos is Professor of History at the University of Athens. He has written on the history of Greece and Italy in the 19th century, social history, historiography and theory of history and nationalism. His most recent publication was *How the Past Turns to History* (2007).

Federico Lorenz ARGENTINA

Federico Lorenz is a historian and history teacher and works for the Ministry of Education. His special interests are the Malvinas (Falklands) War, political violence and the relationship between history, memory and education.

Zhitian Luo CHINA

Zhitian Luo is Distinguished Professor of History at Sichuan University, Chengdu, and Professor of Chinese History at Peking University, Beijing, with a particular interest in the relationship between national history, heritage and memory.

Stuart Macintyre AUSTRALIA

Stuart Macintyre was educated in Melbourne and undertook doctoral studies in history at Cambridge University. Since 1990 he has been the Ernest Scott Professor of History at the University of Melbourne and in 2009 he took up the chair of Australian Studies at Harvard University. He has been president of the Australian Historical Association, is a fellow of the Australian Academy of the Humanities and is currently president of the Academy of the Social Sciences. He has written extensively on Australian labour, political and intellectual history. His publications include *A Concise History of Australia* (1999). He is an editor of a large-scale international project, *The Oxford History of Historical Writing*.

Pirjo Markkola FINLAND

Pirjo Markkola is Professor of Finnish History at the University of Jyväskylä. Her research interests include the history of women's lives, religious faith and social work in Finland since the 17th century.

Luiz Marques BRAZIL

Luiz Marques is Professor of History of Art at the University of Campinas, São Paulo. An expert on Italian Renaissance art, he was previously chief curator of the São Paulo Art Museum. He acts as academic advisor to *História Viva*, the Brazilian popular history magazine.

Ryuichi Narita JAPAN

Ryuichi Narita is Professor of History at the Japan Women's University, Tokyo. He has written widely on Japan in the 20th century, including the effects of war, the role of women and the role of memory in Japanese national consciousness.

Peter Onuf UNITED STATES

Peter Onuf is Thomas Jefferson Memorial Foundation Professor at the University of Virginia. His publications include *Jefferson's Empire: The Language of American Nationhood* (2001) and *The Mind of Thomas Jefferson* (2007).

Iwona Sakowicz POLAND

Dr Iwona Sakowicz teaches history at the University of Gdansk, specializing in Poland during the 19th century.

Pavel Seifter THE CZECH REPUBLIC

Pavel Seifter is a Senior Visiting Fellow at the Centre for the Study of Global Governance, London School of Economics. He was Czech ambassador to Britain from 1997 until his retirement in 2003. A lecturer in Contemporary and Social History in Prague, he was forced to leave his post after the Soviet invasion in 1968. He was involved in the dissident movement and returned to academia as co-founder of the Institute of Contemporary History in Prague, became deputy director of the Institute of International Relations in Prague and from 1993 until the start of his diplomatic mission in London was President Václav Havel's director of foreign policy.

Colin Shindler ISRAEL

Colin Shindler is Emeritus Professor and Pears Senior Research Fellow in Israeli Studies at the School of Oriental and African Studies, University of London, and Chairman of the European Association of Israel Studies. His recent books include *A History of Modern Israel* (2008) and *The Triumph of Military Zionism: Nationalism and the Origins of the Israeli Right* (2010).

Murat Siviloglu TURKEY

Murat Siviloglu, born in Istanbul, is a social and intellectual historian, specializing in the late Ottoman Empire. He is based at Peterhouse College, Cambridge, where he is researching the construction of the public sphere and its effects on the emergence and diffusion of new ideas in the Ottoman Empire during the second half of the 19th century.

Enric Ucelay-Da Cal SPAIN

Enric Ucelay-Da Cal is currently full Professor of Contemporary History at Pompeu Fabra University, Barcelona. He studied at Columbia University, New York, and specializes in the history of Catalonia in the 20th century.

EDITOR'S ACKNOWLEDGMENTS

Among the many people who have given me assistance in preparing this volume, I'd particularly like to thank Jeremy Black, Gloria Cigman, Sheila Corr, Charlotte Crow, Ana Claudia Ferrari, John Foot, Carole Gluck, Anne Gorsuch, Geoffrey Hosking, Jan Jilek, Rana Mitter, Roger Moorhouse, Deborah Morrison, Graham Gendall Norton, Lucy Riall, Norman Stone and Anne Waswo. Also, at Thames & Hudson, Colin Ridler, who has proved most supportive and a good friend, Flora Spiegel, Katharina Hahn; and the picture researcher, Louise Thomas.

The following chapters were translated: Egypt by Matthew Beeston; China by Joseph Lawson; Russia by Paul Podoprigora; The Czech Republic by Derek Paton; Sweden by Birgitta Shutt; Finland by Liisa Peltonen; Italy by Grace Crerar-Bromelow; Japan by Matthew Minagawa, with supplementary material by Melissa Parent.

SOURCES OF ILLUSTRATIONS

Key: **a**-above; **b**-below.

1 Gerard van Schagen, *World Map*, Amsterdam, 1689 **2–3** Austrian Archives/Corbis **4** Gerard van Schagen, *World Map*, Amsterdam, 1689 **8–9** Jiao Weiping/Xinhua Press/Corbis **12–13** Fabrizio Bensch/Reuters/Corbis **17** Chris Ison/Reuters/Corbis **18, 20** Blaine Harrington III/Corbis **21** Musée National du Château et des Trianons, Versailles **22** Hulton Archive/Getty Images **23** Hulton-Deutsch Collection/Corbis **24** Khaled Desouki/AFP/Getty Images **25** Bettmann/Corbis **26, 28** Narinder Nanu/AFP/Getty Images **29** British Library, London **30** National Portrait Gallery, London **32** Royal Geographical Society, London/Bridgeman Art Library **33, 34** National Army Museum, London **35** Bettmann/Corbis **36** Press Information Bureau/Government of India, New Delhi **38, 40** Bodleian Library, Oxford/The Art Archive **41** Roger Wood/Corbis **42** Kazuyoshi Nomachi/Corbis **44** Christine Spengler/Sygma/Corbis **45** Reza Pahlavi **46** Bettmann/Corbis **47** Corbis **48, 50b** Bert Hardy/Picture Post/IPC Magazine/Getty Images **50a** Royal Ontario Museum, Toronto **51** Church of San Vitale, Ravenna **52** National Art Gallery and Alexander Soutzos Museum, Athens **53** Atlantide Phototravel/Corbis **54** George Grantham Bain Collection/Library of Congress, Washington, D.C. **56** Karl Mathis/EPA/Corbis **57** Katerina Mavrona/EPA/Corbis **58, 60** National Palace Museum, Beijing **61** Shanghai Museum **62** China Daily/Reuters/Corbis **64** National Palace Museum, Beijing **67** British Museum, London **68** Library of Congress, Washington, D.C. **69** Jens Buettner/EPA/Corbis **70, 72** Frederick Heppenheimer/Library of Congress, Washington, D.C. **73** John Derrick, *The Image of Irelande*, London, 1581 **75** Rijksmuseum, Amsterdam **76** Eileen Tweedy/The Art Archive **77, 78** Library of Congress, Washington, D.C. **79** Topical Press Agency/Getty Images **81** STR/EPA/Corbis **82, 84** The Art Archive/Alamy **85** iStockphoto.com **86** The Art Archive/Alamy **88** Brooklyn Museum, New York **89** akg-images **90** The Art Archive/Alamy **93** Associated Press Ltd. **95** Photographer's Choice/Getty Images **96, 98** Bibliothèque Municipale, Toulouse/Photo Scala **99** Musée du Louvre, Paris **100** The U.S. National Archives and Records Administration, Maryland **101** Tijl Vercaemer **102** National Gallery, London **103, 104** Library of Congress, Washington, D.C. **107** Jack Downey/Library of Congress, Washington, D.C. **108, 110** RIA Novosti/Alamy **111** Library of the Russian Academy of Sciences, St Petersburg **112** Russian Museum, St Petersburg **113** State Hermitage Museum, St Petersburg **115** INTERFOTO/Alamy **116** Culver Pictures/The Art Archive **118** RIA Novosti/akg-images **119** Oleg Nikishin/Pressphotos/ Getty Images **120, 122** INTERFOTO/Alamy **123** Deutsches Historisches Museum, Berlin **124** University of Glasgow Library **125** Castle of Moravsky Krumlov **126** Sebastian Münster, *Map of Europe as a Queen*, Basel, 1570 **128** Hulton-Deutsch Collection/Corbis **129** akg-images **130** Impact Photos/Alamy **132, 134** Marc Charmet/The Art Archive **135** William Faden, *Map of the Partition of the Kingdom of Poland and the Grand Duchy of Lithuania*, 1799 **136** Private Collection **137** Stanislaw Jankowski **139** Bettmann/Corbis **140** J. Zolnierkiewicz **141** Sygma/Corbis **142, 144** The Art Archive/Alamy **145** Topkapi Sarayi Museum, Istanbul **147** Private Collection **148** City Museum of Ljubljana **150** Underwood & Underwood/Corbis **151** akg-images **152** Hulton-Deutsch Collection/Corbis **153** David Turnley/Corbis **154, 156b** The Art Archive/Alamy **156a** Topkapi Sarayi Museum, Istanbul **157** Library of Congress, Washington, D.C. **159** Topkapi Sarayi Museum, Istanbul **160** George Grantham Bain Collection/Library of Congress, Washington, D.C. **161** Tolga Bozoglu/EPA/Corbis **162, 164** Eduardo Martino/Panos Pictures **165** Library of Congress, Washington, D.C. **166** Amazonaspress/ Reuters/ Corbis **167** Bruno Domingos/Reuters/Corbis

168 S.A. Evaristo/AFP/Getty Images **170, 172** The Art Archive/Alamy **173** World History Archive/Alamy **174** From Bartolomé de las Casas, *A Short Account of the Destruction of the Indies*, 1552 **175** Basilica of Our Lady of Guadalupe, Mexico City **176** Library of Congress, Washington, D.C. **177** Janet Jarman/Corbis **178, 180b** National Gallery, London **180a** Chadbourne Collection of Japanese Prints/Library of Congress, Washington, D.C. **181** Nationaal Archief, The Hague **182** EPA/Corbis **183** Gemäldegalerie Alte Meister der Staatlichen Kunstsammlungen Dresden **184** akg-images **187** Erasmus House, Rotterdam **188, 190** Ulf Huett Nilsson/Johnér Images/Corbis **191** Private Collection **193** Viking Ship Museum, Oslo **194** Frank Chmura/Alamy **196** Vasa Museum, Stockholm **197** Kungliga Biblioteket, Stockholm **198, 200** Art Gallery Collection/Alamy **201, 202** Library of Congress, Washington, D.C. **204** U.S. National Archives and Records Administration, Maryland **205** National Portrait Gallery, London **206** British Library, London **207** Keystone/Getty Images **209** Impact Photos/Alamy **210, 211** Collection of the New York Historical Society/Bridgeman Art Library **213** Library of Congress, Washington, D.C. **214** White House Historical Association, Washington, D.C. **215, 216** Library of Congress, Washington, D.C. **219** Bo Zaunders/Corbis **220** White House Historical Association, Washington, D.C. **222, 224** National Library of Australia, Canberra **225** John Van Hasselt/Sygma/Corbis **226** Pam Gardner/Frank Lane Picture Agency/Corbis **227** Thomas Larcom **228** National Archives of Australia, Canberra **229** National Gallery of Victoria, Melbourne **230** Powerhouse Museum, Sydney **232, 234** Werner Forman/Corbis **235** University of Virginia Art Museum, Charlottesville **236** *Atlas Blaeu van der Hem*, 17th century **237** Bibliothèque des Arts Decoratifs/Bridgeman Art Library **238** Bettmann/Corbis **239** Cameron Spencer/Getty Images **240, 242b** Bettmann Corbis **242a** State Hermitage Museum, St Petersburg **243** Library of Congress, Washington, D.C. **244** Gripsholm Castle, Mariefred **245** National Museum of Finland, Helsinki **246** National Library of Finland, Helsinki **247** INTERFOTO/Alamy **248, 250b** The Art Archive/Alamy **250a** Barros Castro, Ignacio de Pedro, *Manifiesto que hace a las naciones el Congreso General Constituyente de las Provincias-Unidas del Rio de la Plata*, 1817 **251** Leo La Valle/EPA/Corbis **252** Private Collection **253** Eduardo Longoni/Corbis **254** Horacio Villalobos/Corbis **255** Carlos Carrion/Sygma/Corbis **256, 258** Bud Blunz/National Film Board of Canada. Photothèque/PA-161446/Library and Archives Canada **259** Peter Winkworth Collection of Canadiana. Acc. No. R9266-3250/Library and Archives Canada **260** Peter Winkworth Collection of Canadiana. Acc. No. R9266-3510/Library and Archives Canada **262** Government of Canada. Reproduced with the permission of the Minister of Public Works and Government Services Canada (2010). Robert Cooper. PA-141503/Library and Archives Canada **263** Lara Solt/Dallas Morning News/Corbis **264, 266** The Art Archive/Alamy **267** Photo Scala **268** Andrea Jemolo/Photo Scala **269** Claudio Peri/EPA/Corbis **271** Gari Wyn Williams/Alamy **272, 274b** Chadbourne Collection of Japanese Prints/Library of Congress, Washington, D.C. **274a** Uchida Kuichi **275** Library of Congress, Washington, D.C. **277** Bernard Hoffman/Time Life Pictures/Getty Images **279** Keystone Getty Images **280** Tokyo Shimbun/Sygma/Corbis **281** Everett Kennedy Brown/EPA/Corbis **282, 284** David Brauchli/Reuters/Corbis **285** Bismarck Museum, Friedrichsruh **286** United States Holocaust Memorial Museum, Washington, D.C. **287** U.S. Air Force **289** Library of Congress, Washington, D.C. **290** Städel Museum, Frankfurt **292** Private Collection **293** Thorsten Eckert/Alamy **294, 296** Zoltan Kluger/Getty Images **297** Theodor Herzl, *Sketch design for the Zionist flag*, 1890s **299** George Grantham Bain Collection/Library of Congress, Washington, D.C. **300** Kevin Lamarque/Reuters/Corbis **301** Mohammed Saber/EPA/Corbis **303** Jim Hollander/EPA/Corbis

INDEX